Study Guide

for

Hess and Orthmann's

Criminal Investigation

Ninth Edition

DELMAR
CENGAGE Learning

Australia • Brazil • Japan • Korea • Mexico • Singapore • Spain • United Kingdom • United States

Study Guide for Hess and Orthmann's Criminal Investigation, 9th Edition

Vice President, Career and Professional Editorial: Dave Garza

Director of Learning Solutions: Sandy Clark

Senior Acquisitions Editor: Shelley Esposito

Managing Editor: Larry Main

Product Manager: Anne Orgren

Editorial Assistant: Danielle Klahr

Vice President, Career and Professional Marketing: Jennifer McAvey

Marketing Director: Deborah S. Yarnell

Senior Marketing Manager: Erin Coffin

Marketing Coordinator: Shanna Gibbs

Production Director: Wendy Troeger

Production Manager: Mark Bernard

Senior Content Project Manager: Betty Dickson

Senior Art Director: Joy Kocsis

For product information and technology assistance, contact us at **Cengage Learning Customer & Sales Support, 1-800-354-9706**
For permission to use material from this text or product, submit all requests online at **www.cengage.com/permissions.**
Further permissions questions can be e-mailed to **permissionrequest@cengage.com**

Library of Congress Control Number: 2008934273

ISBN-13: 978-1-4354-6996-9

ISBN-10: 1-4354-6996-8

Delmar
5 Maxwell Drive
Clifton Park, NY 12065-2919
USA

Cengage Learning is a leading provider of customized learning solutions with office locations around the globe, including Singapore, the United Kingdom, Australia, Mexico, Brazil, and Japan. Locate your local office at: **international.cengage.com/region**

Cengage Learning products are represented in Canada by Nelson Education, Ltd.

To learn more about Delmar, visit **www.cengage.com/delmar**

Purchase any of our products at your local college store or at our preferred online store **www.ichapters.com**

Notice to the Reader
Publisher does not warrant or guarantee any of the products described herein or perform any independent analysis in connection with any of the product information contained herein. Publisher does not assume, and expressly disclaims, any obligation to obtain and include information other than that provided to it by the manufacturer. The reader is expressly warned to consider and adopt all safety precautions that might be indicated by the activities described herein and to avoid all potential hazards. By following the instructions contained herein, the reader willingly assumes all risks in connection with such instructions. The publisher makes no representations or warranties of any kind, including but not limited to, the warranties of fitness for particular purpose or merchantability, nor are any such representations implied with respect to the material set forth herein, and the publisher takes no responsibility with respect to such material. The publisher shall not be liable for any special, consequential, or exemplary damages resulting, in whole or part, from the readers' use of, or reliance upon, this material.

Printed in Canada
1 2 3 4 5 6 7 13 12 11 10 09

Contents

Chapter 1   Criminal Investigation: An Overview   1

Chapter 2   Documenting the Crime Scene: Note Taking, Photographing, and Sketching   13

Chapter 3   Writing Effective Reports   33

Chapter 4   Searches   49

Chapter 5   Forensics/Physical Evidence   71

Chapter 6   Obtaining Information and intelligence   91

Chapter 7   Identifying and Arresting Suspects   107

Chapter 8   Death Investigations   123

Chapter 9   Assault, Domestic Violence, Stalking and Elder Abuse   143

Chapter 10   Sex Offenses   161

Chapter 11   Crimes Against Children   177

Chapter 12   Robbery   199

Chapter 13   Burglary   217

Chapter 14   Larceny/Theft, Fraud, and White-Collar Crime   231

Chapter 15   Motor Vehicle Theft   253

Chapter 16   Arson, Bombs and Explosives   269

Chapter 17   Computer Crime   287

Chapter 18   A Dual Threat: Drug-Related Crime and Organized Crime   311

Chapter 19   Criminal Activities of Gangs and Other Dangerous Groups   337

Chapter 20   Terrorism and Homeland Security   357

Chapter 21   Preparing for and Presenting Cases in Court   375

CRIMINAL INVESTIGATION

An Overview

OUTLINE

- Criminal Investigation Definitions
- Goals of Criminal Investigations
- Basic Functions
- Characteristics of an Effective Investigator
- An Overview of the Investigative Process
- The Preliminary Investigation: Basic Considerations
- Crime Scene Investigators
- The Follow-Up Investigation
- Computer-Aided Investigation
- Problem-Oriented Policing
- Investigative Productivity
- The Investigative Function: The Responsibility of All Police Personnel
- Interrelationships with Others—Community Policing
- Major-Case Task Forces
- Law Enforcement Resources
- Avoiding Civil Liability

Chapter 1
Criminal Investigation: An Overview

By the end of this chapter you should know how to define the terms and understand the application of the concepts below. Test your understanding of the chapter by verifying that you know this information. If you do not know it, review the chapter.

Can you define these words?

civil liability	data mining	intuition
community policing	deductive reasoning	investigate
crime	elements of the crime	leads
crime mapping	exculpatory evidence	Locard's principle of exchange
criminal intent	fact	
criminal investigation	felony	misdemeanor
criminal statute	forensic science	modus operandi (MO)
criminalist	hot spots	opinion
criminalistics	inductive reasoning	ordinance
culturally adroit	inference	*res gestae* statements

Do you know?

- What criminal investigation is?
- What the major goals of criminal investigation are?
- What basic functions investigators perform?
- What characteristics are important in investigations?
- Who usually arrives at a crime scene first?
- What should be done initially?
- What to do if a suspect is still at a crime scene? Has recently fled the scene?
- How the crime scene and evidence are protected and for how long?
- What responsibilities are included in the preliminary investigation?
- What the meaning and importance of *res gestae* statements are?
- How to determine whether a crime has been committed?
- Who is responsible for solving crimes?
- With whom investigators must relate?
- How to avoid civil lawsuits?

Chapter Outline

I.   Criminal Investigation Definitions

   A.   Terms defined

II. Goals of Criminal Investigations

   A.   Determine whether a crime has been committed.

   B.   Legally obtain information and evidence to identify the responsible person.

   C.   Arrest the suspect.

   D.   Recover the stolen property.

   E.   Present the best possible case to the prosecutor.

III. Basic Functions

   A.   Provide emergency assistance.

   B.   Secure the crime scene.

   C.   Photograph, videotape, and sketch.

   D.   Take notes and write reports.

   E.   Search for, obtain, and process physical evidence.

   F.   Obtain information from witnesses and suspects.

   G.   Identify suspects.

   H.   Conduct raids, surveillances, stakeouts, and undercover assignments.

   I.   Testify in court.

IV. Characteristics of an Effective Investigator

   A.   Knowledgeable

   B.   Creative

   C.   Patient

   D.   Persistent

V.   An Overview of the Investigative Process

   A.   Stages

      1.   Reporting of a crime

      2.   Initial Investigation

      3.   Case Screening

      4.   Follow-up Investigation

      5.   Case Preparation

      6.   Prosecution

VI. The Preliminary Investigation: Basic Considerations

A. Initial response
    1. First response is usually a patrol officer.
    2. Preplanning routes to high crime areas is critical to rapid response.
B. Point of arrival
    1. Officers need to take charge.
C. Set priorities at the scene.
    1. Handle emergencies.
    2. Secure the scene.
    3. Investigate.
D. Handle emergency situations.
E. Protect the crime scene.
F. Conduct the preliminary investigation.
    1. Question victims, witnesses, and suspects.
    2. Conduct a neighborhood canvass.
    3. Measure, photograph, videotape, and sketch the scene.
    4. Search for evidence.
    5. Identify, collect, examine, and process physical evidence.
    6. Record all statements and observations in notes.

VII. Crime Scene Investigators

A. A crime scene investigator is a specialist in the organized scientific collection and processing of evidence.
B. Crime scene investigators collect, handle, and process all physical evidence.

VIII. The Follow-Up Investigation

A. The follow-up phase builds on what was learned during the preliminary investigation.
B. Coordination between patrol officers and investigators is critical.

IX. Computer-Aided Investigation

A. Computers help analyze information, and information is a critical tool of investigators.
B. Computers allow access to databases and other sources of identification and analysis.
    1. Crime mapping
    2. Geographic information systems (GIS)
    3. Data mining

X. Problem-Oriented Policing

XI.   Investigative Productivity
    A.   It is possible to screen cases for how easily they can be solved and assign only cases that have a higher probability of being solved.
    B.   This approach can lead to a better understanding of investigative workload.

XII.   The Investigative Function: The Responsibility of All Police Personnel

XIII.   Interrelationships with Others—Community Policing
    A.   Community policing
    B.   Uniformed patrol
    C.   Dispatchers
    D.   Prosecutor's staff
    E.   Defense counsel
    F.   Physicians, coroners, and medical examiners
    G.   Forensic crime laboratories
    H.   Citizens
    I.   Witnesses
    J.   Victims
    K.   Media

XIV.   Major-Case Task Forces

XV.   Law Enforcement Resources

XVI.   Avoiding Civil Liability
    A.   Civil liability refers to a person's degree of risk of being sued.
    B.   Section 1983
    C.   Leaving out exculpatory evidence
    D.   False affidavits

XVII.   Summary

Chapter Questions

1. What year was DNA discovered?
   a. 1973
   b. 1986
   c. 1868
   d. 1915

2. Effective investigators
   a. obtain and retain information.
   b. apply technical knowledge.
   c. remain open-minded, objective, and logical.
   d. are culturally adroit.
   e. are all of these.

3. Locard's principle of exchange is
   a. a forensic theory that similar items have similar material.
   b. a theory that items that come close to each other may transfer important evidence at times.
   c. a forensic theory which holds that objects that come in contact with each other always transfer material, however minute, to each other.
   d. the idea that the laboratory can exchange minute evidence when placed on the same counter.

4. A field test allows investigators to
   a. evaluate stains and suspicious items at the scene.
   b. prepare evidence for court.
   c. determine if an item was left there by the suspected offender.
   d. determine if a substance is something that the investigator believes it to be.

5. A command center is needed when
   a. a command officer arrives on the scene of a crime.
   b. the media is present.
   c. the investigation is a complex investigation and when enough resources are on the scene to require coordination.
   d. there is a large crowd of observers.

6. If investigators must complete a follow-up investigation, it means that
   a. the initial investigation was poorly handled.
   b. the officers were not able to complete the investigation for personal reasons and additional work is needed.
   c. the initial investigation lacked the needed expertise.
   d. none of these.

7. Computers can assist investigators to
   a. efficiently access existing information.
   b. record new information.

    c.   analyze information for patterns.

    d.   manipulate digital representations to enhance the images.

    e.   all of these.

8. Crime mapping focuses on
   a.   hot spots where crime occurs.
   b.   developing leads through the use of city maps and districts.
   c.   use of pins and other markings to identify areas for high risk to citizens.
   d.   none of these.

9. Data mining can be used to
   a.   find new patterns or trends or to confirm suspected patterns or trends.
   b.   discover new data.
   c.   add to the data base.
   d.   none of these.

10. Problem-oriented policing makes use of
    a.   crime mapping.
    b.   data mining.
    c.   crime analysis.
    d.   all of these.

11. Because there is a wide range of variables in individual crimes, it is impossible to establish fixed rules for conducting an investigation.   True or False

12. Shoplifting is automatically a felony in every state.   True or False

13. Investigators follow a logical sequence when conducting an investigation that includes obtaining all physical evidence, interviewing witnesses, interrogating suspects, developing leads, and recording details.   True or False

14. A *fact* is an action, an event, or a circumstance. In contrast, an *inference* is a process of reasoning by which a fact may be deduced.   True or False

15. According to the text, most cases are lost (not solved) due to failures of the investigators or officers in the first hour of an investigation.   True or False

16. The use of a siren to speed the response to the scene by patrol officers or investigators is sometimes of value, but the siren may cause the offender to flee the scene.   True or False

17. Prior to their investigation, investigators need to determine if a crime has actually occurred.   True or False

18. The media has a right to enter parts of a crime scene.   True or False

19. Law enforcement agencies are suffering from the CSI effect.   True or False

20. A forensic specialist is someone whose specialty is the organized scientific collection and processing of evidence.   True or False

21. Criminal investigation is a reconstructive process that uses _____, a logical process in which a conclusion follows from specific facts.

22. The abbreviation "MO" stands for _____ _____.

23. List one of the five goals of criminal investigation: _____ _____.

24. A _____ is an act of violation against penal law and an offense against the state.

25. A criminal _____ is a legislative act relating to a crime and its punishment.

26. An _____ is an act of the legislative body of a municipality or county relating to all the rules governing the municipality or county, including misdemeanors.

27. The prosecution has to prove the _____ of a crime.

28. _____ statements are spontaneous statements made at the time of a crime concerning and closely related to actions involved in the crime.

29. _____ are avenues bearing clues or potential sources of information relevant to solving the crime.

30. A _____ is an action, an event, a circumstance, or an actual thing done.

31. Clarify the role of a criminal investigation.

32. What are the major goals of criminal investigation?

33. What basic functions do investigators perform?

34. What characteristics are important to an effective investigator?

35. What do you do if a suspect is still at a crime scene?

Case Study

36. Detective Joe Richardson was assigned a case by his sergeant. Joe works thefts and forgeries, and has a caseload of over 150 cases. The case he is assigned is similar to a series of cases that he has been assigned in the last few days. Last week he started to receive a series of cases where someone was passing bad checks at small stores in the north end of town. The license number on all the checks was the same and the handwriting seemed to be the same.

    What initial steps should Detective Richardson take to start the investigation of this case? List the first two things that you would do as the investigator.

Answer Key

1. c	11. True
2. e	12. False
3. c	13. True
4. d	14. True
5. c	15. True
6. b	16. True
7. e	17. True
8. a	18. False
9. a	19. True
10. d	20. True

21. deductive reasoning

22. method of operation or modus operandi

23. The answer may be any of the following: determine whether a crime has been committed, legally obtain information and evidence to identify the responsible person, arrest the suspect, recover stolen property, or present the best possible case to the prosecutor.

24. crime

25. statute

26. ordinance

27. elements

28. *Res gestae*

29. Leads

30. fact

31. It is the process of discovering, collecting, preparing, identifying and presenting evidence to determine what happened and who is responsible.

32. • Determine whether a crime has been committed.
    • Legally obtain information and evidence to identify the responsible person.
    • Arrest the suspect.
    • Recover stolen property.
    • Present the best case to the prosecutor.

33. • They provide emergency assistance.
    • They secure the crime scene.
    • They do photography, videotaping, and sketching.
    • They take notes and write reports.
    • They search for, obtain, and process physical evidence.
    • They identify suspects.
    • They conduct raids, surveillances, stakeouts, and undercover assignments.
    • They testify in court.

34. Effective investigators obtain and retain information, apply technical knowledge, and remain open-minded, objective, and logical. They are also culturally adroit, that is, skilled, in interacting across gender, ethnic, generational, social and political group lines. They are emotionally well-balanced, detached, inquisitive, discerning, self-disciplined, and persevering. They are physically fit and have good vision and hearing.

35. Any suspect at the scene should be detained, questioned, and then released or arrested, depending on circumstances.

Case Study Answer

36. Detective Richardson's initial steps should be to
    • read the full case report and determine if additional evidence or information is needed and
    • review information about other cases.

Two things you would want to do as an investigator are to
    • review what data or other information is available and
    • meet with the crime analyst of the department to see what patterns exist.

There are many possible first steps an investigator could take, but any first step should include activities that allow for the analysis of the available information.

DOCUMENTING THE CRIME SCENE

Note Taking, Photographing, and Sketching

OUTLINE

- Field Notes: The Basics
- Characteristics of Effective Notes
- Filing Notes
- Investigative Photography: An Overview
- Basic Photographic Equipment
- Training in and Using Investigative Photography
- Types of Investigative Photography
- Identifying, Filing and Maintaining Security of Evidence
- Admissibility of Photographs in Court
- Crime Scene Sketches: An Overview
- The Rough Sketch
- Steps in Sketching the Crime Scene
- File the Sketch
- The Finished Scale Drawing
- Computer-Assisted Drawing
- Admissibility of Sketches and Drawings in Court

Chapter 2
Documenting the Crime Scene:
Note Taking, Photographing, and Sketching

By the end of this chapter, you should know how to define the terms and understand the application of the concepts below. Test your understanding of the chapter by verifying that you know this information. If you do not know it, review the chapter.

Can you define these words?

backing	marker	relevant photograph
baseline method	material photograph	resolution
compass-point method	megapixel	rogues' gallery
competent photograph	microphotography	rough sketch
cross-projection sketch	mug shots	scale
finished scale drawing	overlapping	sketch
forensic photogrammetry	Pictometry®	trap photography
immersive imaging	pixel	triangulation
laser-beam photography	PPI	ultraviolet-light photography
legend	rectangular-coordinate method	
macrophotography		

Do you know?

- Why notes are important in an investigation?
- When to take notes?
- What to record in investigative notes?
- How to record the notes?
- What the characteristics of effective notes are?
- Where to file notes if they are retained?
- What purposes are served by crime scene photography?
- What the advantages and disadvantages of using photography and videography are?
- What the minimum photographic equipment for an investigator is?
- What to photograph at a crime scene and in what sequence?
- What errors in technique to avoid?
- What types of photography are used in criminal investigations?
- What basic rules of evidence photographs must adhere to?
- What purposes are served by the crime scene sketch?
- What should be sketched?
- What materials are needed to make a rough sketch?
- What steps to take in making a rough sketch?
- How plotting methods are used in sketches?
- When a sketch or a scale drawing is admissible in court?

Chapter Outline

I.   Field Notes: The Basics

   A.   When to take notes

   B.   What to record: As you take notes, ask yourself specific questions such as these:

      1. When: did the incident happen? was it discovered? was it reported? did the police arrive on the scene? were suspects arrested? will the case be heard in court?

      2. Where: did the incident happen? was evidence found? stored? do victims, witnesses, and suspects live? do suspects frequent most often? were suspects arrested?

      3. Who: are suspects? accomplices? Complete descriptions would include gender, race, coloring, age, height, weight, hair (color, style, condition), eyes (color, size, glasses), nose (size, shape), ears (close to head or protruding), distinctive features (birthmarks, tattoos, scars, beard), clothing, voice (high or low, accent), and other distinctive characteristics such as walk.

      4. Who: were the victims? associates? was talked to? were witnesses? saw or heard something of importance? discovered the crime? reported the incident? made the complaint? investigated the incident? worked on the case? marked and received evidence? was notified? had a motive?

      5. What: type of crime was committed? was the amount of damage or value of the property involved? happened (narrative of the actions of suspects, victims, and witnesses; combines information included under "How")? evidence was found? preventive measures had been taken (safes, locks, alarms, etc.)? knowledge, skill, or strength was needed to commit the crime? was said? did the police officers do? further information is needed? further action is needed?

      6. How: was the crime discovered? does this crime relate to other crimes? did the crime occur? was evidence found? was information obtained?

      7. Why: was the crime committed (was there intent? consent? motive?)? was certain property stolen? was a particular time selected?

      8. Information establishing a suspect's innocence is as important as establishing a suspect's guilt.

      9. Include all evidence, including inculpatory and exculpatory.

    10. Record everything you observe in the overall scene: all services rendered, including first aid, description of the injured, location of wounds, who transported the victim and how.

    11. Record complete and accurate information regarding all photographs taken at the scene.

12. As the search is conducted, record the location and description of evidence and its preservation.

13. Record information to identify the type of crime and what was said and by whom. Include the name, address, and phone number of every person present at the scene and all witnesses.

14. Take notes on everything you do in an official investigative capacity. Record all facts, regardless of where they may lead. Information establishing a suspect's innocence is as important as that establishing guilt.

15. When evidentiary conflicts exist, the general rule is that all of the evidence, both inculpatory and exculpatory should be reported to the prosecutor for evaluation.

C. Where to record notes

1. Opinions vary about whether it is better to use a loose-leaf notebook or separate spiral-bound notebooks for each case.

2. If you use a loose-leaf notebook, you can easily add paper for each case you are working on as the need arises, and you can keep it well organized.

3. Most investigators favor the loose-leaf notebook because of its flexibility in arranging notes for reports and for testifying in court.

4. However, use of a loose-leaf notebook opens the opportunity of challenge from the defense attorney that the officer has fabricated the notes, adding or deleting relevant pages.

5. This can be countered by numbering each page, followed by the date and case number, or by using a separate spiral notebook for each case.

6. Disadvantages of the latter approach are that the spiral notebook is often only partially used and therefore expensive and may be bulky for storage.

7. If other notes are kept in the same notebook, they also will be subject to the scrutiny of the defense.

8. A final disadvantage is that if you need a blank sheet of paper for some reason, you should not take it from a spiral notebook because most of these notebooks indicate on the cover how many pages they contain.

D. How to take notes

1. Note taking is an acquired skill. Time does not permit a verbatim transcript.

2. Learn to select key facts and record them in abbreviated form.

3. Write brief, legible, abbreviated notes that others can understand.

4. Do not include words such as *a*, *and*, and *the* in your notes. Omit all other unnecessary words.

5. If you make an error, cross it out, make the correction, and initial it. Do *not* erase. Whether intentional or accidental, erasures raise credibility questions.

6. Whenever possible, use standard abbreviations such as *mph, DWI, Ave.*

7. Do *not,* however, devise your own shorthand.

8. Using a tape recorder

    a. Advantage of recording exactly what was stated with no danger of misinterpreting, slanting, or misquoting

    b. Disadvantages of tape recording:

        (1) The most serious is that they can malfunction and fail to record valuable information.

        (2) Weak batteries or background noise can also distort the information recorded.

        (3) In addition, transcribing tapes is time consuming, expensive, and subject to error.

        (4) The tapes themselves, not the transcription, are the original evidence and thus must be retained and filed.

II.   Characteristics of Effective Notes

   A. Effective notes describe the scene and the events well enough to enable a prosecutor, judge, or jury to visualize them.

   B. Effective notes are complete, accurate, specific, factual, clear, well organized, and legible.

   C. The basic purpose of notes is to record the *facts* of a case, accurately and objectively.

III.   Filing Notes

   A. Decisions to keep or destroy notes are critical.

      1. If department policy is to keep the notes, place them in a location and under a filing system that makes them available months or even years later.

      2. As long as the system is logical, the notes will be retrievable.

      3. If they are retrievable, in any way, they are "discoverable."

   B. Admissibility of notes in court

      1. The use of notes in court is probably their most important legal application.

      2. They can help discredit a suspect's or a defense witness's testimony; support evidence already given by a prosecution witness, strengthening that testimony; and defend against false allegations by the suspect or defense witnesses.

3. They must be legally retrievable and "discoverable" by both the prosecution and the defense.

IV. Investigative Photography: An Overview

    A. Advantages and disadvantages of photographs

        1. The basic purpose of crime scene photography is to record the scene permanently.

        2. They can be taken immediately, accurately represent the crime scene and evidence, create interest, and increase attention to testimony.

        3. They accurately represent the crime scene in court.

        4. The effect of pictures on a jury cannot be overestimated.

        5. Photographs are highly effective visual aids that corroborate the facts presented.

    B. Disadvantages of photographs

        1. They are not selective, do not show actual distances, and may be distorted and damaged by mechanical errors in shooting or processing.

    C. Advantages and disadvantages of video

        1. A videocassette or DVD, played before a jury, can bring a crime scene to life and offers some distinct advantages over photographs, such as showing distance and being cost-effective.

        2. A slow pan of a crime scene is more likely than a series of photographs to capture all evidence, including that in the periphery of view, which might seem rather inconsequential at the time.

        3. Many agencies fail to provide adequate training to those tasked with videotaping a crime scene.

        4. The negative consequences of poor video is that it can damage a case.

        5. Untrained crime scene videographers may shoot without planning ahead, not shooting enough, shooting too much (resulting in a boring presentation), poor focusing, overusing the zoom feature, making jerky camera movements, including unintentional audio, and failing to use a tripod or proper lighting.

        6. Keep in mind that every comment, utterance, or even conversations off-camera may be recorded on the audio portion.

V. Basic Photographic Equipment

    A. A photographer must have a good camera bag or case.

    B. A high-quality, sturdy tripod is essential equipment.

    C. The type of camera and features appropriate for a department depends greatly on who is going to use it.

D. At a minimum, have available and be skilled in operating a 35-mm single-lens reflex (SLR) camera (film or digital), a Polaroid-type instant-print camera, a press camera, a fingerprint camera, and video record/ playback equipment.

VI. Training in and Using Investigative Photography

A. 35-mm SLR (single lens reflex) film cameras

B. Digital cameras
1. These provide instant feedback and access to photos, the ability to keep imaging services in-house, and lower ongoing costs.
2. One advantage of digital cameras is eliminating the time and expense involved in processing photographic film, while ensuring strict confidentiality.
3. Another advantage is that most digital cameras record technical information about each photograph, such as the date and time and specific camera settings, in a text file associated with the image.
4. Digital cameras suitable for law enforcement are usually either point-and-shoot cameras (which have a fixed lens) or single lens reflex (SLR) cameras (which have interchangeable lenses).

C. Press cameras provide excellent photographs of a general scene as well as of smaller areas or small pieces of evidence.

D. Fingerprint cameras are specially constructed to take pictures of fingerprints without distortion.
1. An investigator photographing latent prints at a crime scene must know that the FBI's Integrated Automated Fingerprint Identification System (AFIS) requires a latent print to be photographed with a minimum resolution of 1,000 PPI.

E. Video cameras are used to record alleged bribery, payoffs, and narcotics buys (surveillance).

F. Computer software
1. A major advance is the ability of computer software to stitch together digital photos of 180 degrees or more to create one 360-degree photo—a panoramic view of a crime scene that is interactive, allowing viewers, including jury members, to walk through it as though they were there.
2. This type of 360-degree photographic view is called immersive imaging.
3. Crime Scene Virtual Tour (CSVT) software lets jurors virtually step into a crime scene.
4. The software allows the scene to be viewed from any angle with zoom, pan, tilt, and rotate features.

G. What to photograph or videotape

1. Photograph the crime scene as soon as possible and photograph the most fragile areas of the crime scene first.

2. First photograph the general area, then specific areas, and finally specific objects of evidence.

3. Take exterior shots first because they are the most subject to alteration by weather and security violations.

4. This progression of shots or video will reconstruct the commission of a crime:

    a. Take *long-range* shots of the locality, points of ingress and egress, normal entry to the property and buildings, exterior of the buildings and grounds, and street signs or other identifiable structures that will establish location.

    b. Take *medium-range* shots of the immediate crime scene and the location of objects of evidence within the area or room.

    c. Take *close-range* shots of specific evidence such as hairs, fibers, footprints, and bloodstains. The entire surface of some objects may be photographed to show all the evidence; for example, a table surface may contain bloodstains, fingerprints, hairs, and fibers.

    d. Zoom lenses allow close shots without disturbing the crime scene, and close-ups are possible with macro lenses.

    e. Such close-range shots usually should include a marker, or scale.

    f. Photogrammetry can be used at most crime scenes.

        (1) It is the technique of extrapolating three-dimensional (3-D) measurements from two-dimensional photographs.

H. Photographing injuries.

1. Start with overall photographs and then take closer, more detailed pictures.

2. The close-up photos should nearly fill the frame.

3. One photo should be taken without a marker and a second taken with a marker.

4. Control the surroundings, as cluttered, busy backgrounds in photos are distracting.

I. Errors to avoid.

1. To obtain effective photographs and videos, be familiar with your equipment and check it before you use it.

2. Take photographs and/or videos before anything is disturbed.

3. If something has been moved, do not put it back. It is legally impossible to return an object to its original position.

4. To minimize distortion or misrepresentation, maintain proper perspective, and attempt to show the objects in a crime scene in their relative size and position.

     5. Take pictures from eye level, the height from which people normally observe objects.

  J. Photo logs and checklists.

     1. Checklists are a critical aspect of the law enforcement function, especially when it comes to crime scene photography.

     2. These can include the following:

       a. Are the batteries in the camera, is the film loaded, is the camera on, is the flash cable connected to the flash and to the camera, and is the lens cap removed?

       b. Settings such as film speed, shooting mode, white balance, shutter speed, lens focal length, and aperture should also be included.

       c. Similar items should be checked for digital SLR cameras.

VII. Types of Investigative Photography

  A. Surveillance photography

     1. With a well-thought-out plan, surveillance tapes can increase the efficacy of a law enforcement agency.

     2. Surveillance photography is also called trap photography.

     3. Many agencies are switching to digital formats rather than videotapes.

     4. Video analysis is the "new DNA of law enforcement."

     5. Soon forensic video evidence will have the Regional Forensic Video Analysis Labs—a national database of criminals caught on tape.

     6. Enhanced surveillance capability can be provided by using robots.

     7. Small video cameras have also been attached to radio-controlled model airplanes.

  B. Aerial photography

     1. Geographical Information Systems (GIS)

     2. Pictometry: computer technology that integrates various aerial shots of a land-based artifact taken straight down (orthogonal) and from numerous angles (oblique). The software also features extreme zooming capabilities, allowing investigators to rotate and zoom in on a particular structure.

  C. Night photography

  D. Laboratory photography

     1. Microphotography takes pictures through a microscope and can help identify minute particles of evidence such as hairs or fibers.

     2. In contrast, macrophotography enlarges a subject. For example, a fingerprint or a tool mark can be greatly enlarged to show the details of ridges or striations.

     3. Laser-beam photography

          a.   Reveals evidence indiscernible to the naked eye.

          b.   For example, it can reveal the outline of a footprint in a carpet, even though the fibers have returned to normal position.

    4. Ultraviolet-light photography

          a.   Uses the low end of the color spectrum, which is invisible to human sight, to make visible impressions of bruises and injuries long after their actual occurrence.

          b.   Bite marks, injuries caused by beatings, cigarette burns, neck strangulation marks, and other impressions left from intentional injuries can be reproduced and used as evidence in criminal cases by scanning the presumed area of injury with a fluorescent or blue light.

E. Mug shots

    1. The pictures of people in police custody are kept in department files for identification and are known as *mug shots.*

    2. Gathered in files and displayed in groups, they are called a *rogues' gallery.*

F. Lineup photographs

    1. Officers can select 6 to 12 other "hits" to be used for presentation with the suspect's photo.

    2. Videotapes or photographs of people included in lineups may be taken to establish the fairness of the lineup.

VIII. Identifying, Filing and Maintaining Security of Evidence

A. Identifying

    1. In the field notes, the photographs taken should be dated and numbered sequentially.

    2. Include the case number, type of offense, and subject of the picture.

    3. Record the photographer's name, location and direction of the camera, lens type, approximate distance in feet to the subject, film and shutter speed, lighting, weather conditions, and a brief description of the scene in the picture.

    4. Backing: On the back of the photo, write your initials, the date the photo was taken, what the photo depicts, and the direction of north.

B. Filing

    1. File the picture and negatives for easy reference.

    2. Pictures in the case file are available to others.

    3. Use a filing system just for photographs.

    4. Always cross-reference by case number.

C. Maintaining security

    1. Record the chain of custody of the film and photographs in the field notes or in a special file.

2. Mark and identify the film as it is removed from the camera.

3. Each time the film changes possession, record the name of the person accepting it.

4. If a commercial firm develops the film, take it to the company in person or send it by registered mail with a return.

IX. Admissibility of Photographs in Court

    A. Photographs must be

        1. Material

            a. Related to a specific case and subject

            b. Material evidence is relevant and forms a substantive part of the case presented or has a legitimate and effective influence on the decision of the case.

        2. Relevant

            a. This helps explain testimony and is relevant to the case.

        3. Competent

            a. The photograph accurately represents what it purports to represent, is properly identified, and is properly placed in the chain of evidence and secured until court presentation.

    B. Authenticating digital images

        1. Image authentication is providing proof that the image introduced into evidence is the same image taken at the crime scene.

        2. This can be done through testimony of the photographer, other persons present when the photo was taken, and/or the use of authentication software.

        3. Several software programs have been developed that "watermark" or authenticate the original image, either at the point of capture (within the camera) or as it is downloaded from the camera to a computer.

        4. A new technology for authentication is the Lexar LockTight system.

X. Crime Scene Sketches: An Overview

    A. Crime scene sketches should

        1. Accurately portray the physical facts.

        2. Relate to the sequence of events at the scene.

        3. Establish the precise location and relationship of objects and evidence at the scene.

        4. Help create a mental picture of the scene for those not present.

        5. Be a permanent record of the scene.

        6. Be usually admissible in court.

    B. A crime scene sketch assists in

        1. Interviewing and interrogating people.

2. Preparing the investigative report.

3. Presenting the case in court.

XI. The Rough Sketch

A. This is the first pencil-drawn outline of a scene and the location of objects and evidence within this outline.

1. It is not usually drawn to scale, although distances are measured and entered in the appropriate locations.

2. Sketch all serious crime and crash scenes after photographs are taken and before anything is moved. Sketch the entire scene, the objects, and the evidence.

B. Sketching materials

1. Materials for the rough sketch include clipboard, paper, pencil, long steel measuring tape, carpenter-type ruler, straightedge, clipboard, eraser, compass, protractor, and thumbtacks.

2. Plain white or graph paper is best.

3. Today's contemporary crime scene specialist is likely to be equipped with a GPS instrument (Global Positioning System) for extreme accuracy.

XII. Steps in Sketching the Crime Scene

A. Step One: Once photographs have been taken and other priority steps in the preliminary investigation performed, you can begin sketching the crime scene.

1. Observe and plan.

2. Decide where to start.

B. Step Two: Measure and outline the area.

1. Always measure from fixed objects.

2. Always position north at the top of the paper.

3. Determine the scale: Use the largest, simplest scale possible.

C. Step Three: Plot objects and evidence.

1. Plotting methods

2. Rectangular-coordinate method

a. Uses two adjacent walls as fixed points from which distances are measured at right angles

b. Locates objects by measuring from one wall at right angles and then from the adjacent wall at right angles

c. This method is restricted to square or rectangular areas.

3. Baseline method

a. Establishes a straight line from one fixed point to another, from which measurements are taken at right angles

        b.   Take measurements along either side of the baseline to a point at right angles to the object to be located.

    4. Triangulation method

        a.   Uses straight-line measures from two fixed objects to the evidence to create a triangle with the evidence in the angle formed by the two straight lines

        b.   Commonly used outdoors but can be used indoors also

    5. Compass-point method

        a.   Uses a protractor to measure the angle formed by two lines

    6. Cross-projection method

        a.   Presents the floor and walls as though they were one surface

  D. Step Four: Take notes and record details.

  E. Step Five: Identify the scene.

    1. Prepare the legend.

  F. Step Six: Reassess the sketch.

XIII.   File the Sketch

XIV.   The Finished Scale Drawing

XV.   Computer-Assisted Drawing

  A. Forensic software programs, such as Crime Zone, are easy to use and can create diagrams with great precision and attention to detail, giving the drawing greater credibility in court.

  B. Software graphics have been used to diagram the trajectory of bullets, to document the scene of a carjacking, and to help a jury visualize the locations of witnesses, victims, and suspects at the scene of a shooting.

  C. Speed and portability are two other features investigators look for when selecting a CAD program.

XVI.   Admissibility of Sketches and Drawings in Court

  A. An admissible sketch is drawn or personally witnessed by an investigator and accurately portrays a crime scene.

  B. A scale drawing also is admissible if the investigating officer drew it or approved it after it was drawn and if it accurately represents the rough sketch.

  C. The rough sketch must remain available as evidence.

  D. Well-prepared sketches and drawings help judges, juries, witnesses, and other people to visualize crime scenes.

XVII. Summary

Chapter Questions

1. What information should you record when taking notes at a crime scene?
   a. known facts
   b. everything you see and hear
   c. only what you are told
   d. only those things that are out of the ordinary

2. Record all information that helps to answer the questions of
   a. Who? What? Which? When? How? and Why?
   b. Who? What? Where? When? How? and Why?
   c. Which? When? Why? Where? and How many?
   d. Who did it? and Why?

3. What is referred to as the "new DNA for law enforcement"?
   a. retinal scans
   b. fingerprints
   c. digital video analysis
   d. gunshot residue scanning

4. Which of the following is *not* a disadvantage of photographs?
   a. They are not selective.
   b. They do not show actual distances.
   c. They may be distorted and damaged by mechanical errors in shooting or processing.
   d. They are not admissible into court.

5. When taking photographs/videotape, the investigator should
   a. focus on the primary points of concern or interest.
   b. take only those shots wanted by the prosecutor.
   c. examine the scene from all sides and take only the sides of the crime scene that show the best view.
   d. take sufficient photographs and/or videotape to reconstruct the entire scene.

6. Which of the following is *not* a plotting method useful in locating objects and evidence?
   a. rectangular-coordinate
   b. baseline
   c. triangulation
   d. matrix
   e. compass-point

7. A crime scene sketch does all but one of the following. Which does a crime scene sketch *not* do?
   a. accurately portrays the physical facts
   b. relates to the sequence of events at the scene

    c.   establishes the precise location and relationship of objects and evidence at the scene

    d.   is always considered a true and accurate depiction and cannot be challenged

8. Which of the following is an *incorrect* statement?
    a.   Resolution refers to the fineness of image detail either captured with a camera, displayed on a monitor, or printed on paper.
    b.   High resolution produces a sharp image.
    c.   A low resolution image is a blurrier image.
    d.   Pixels are the largest unit of a digital image, generally a dot within the image.

9. Which is true regarding including the location of evidence in a sketch?
    a.   Opinions differ on whether to include the location of evidence in a sketch.
    b.   If evidence is placed within the sketch, some courts have withheld introduction of the sketch until the evidence has been approved.
    c.   If the evidence is placed only in the finished scale drawing, the sketch can be introduced and used by witnesses to corroborate their testimony.
    d.   All the above are correct.

10. Which term is used on a crime scene sketch, and contains the case number, type of crime, name of the victim or complainant, location, date, time, investigator, anyone assisting, scale of the sketch, direction of north, and name of the person making the sketch?
    a.   logo
    b.   legend
    c.   nexus
    d.   matrix

11. Note taking is unique to the police profession.   True or False

12. If you make an error in your notes, you should erase and correct it.   True or False

13. Notes are not admissible in court.   True or False

14. Videos have many advantages, including immediate viewability, accurate representation of the crime scene and evidence, ability to show distance, and sound capability.   True or False

15. One of the disadvantages of digital photographs over film is that copies of photos may look slightly different than the original.   True or False

16. Digital cameras should not be used for crime scene photography.   True or False

17. To be admissible in court, photographs must be material, relevant, competent, accurate, free of distortion, and noninflammatory.   True or False

18. An investigator's sketch of a crime scene can be more descriptive than hundreds of words and is often an extremely important investigative aid.   True or False

19. Because of the existence of computer programs such as Photoshop, investigators are not allowed to use digital cameras.   True or False

20. A cross-projection sketch presents the floor and walls as though they were one surface.   True or False

21. _____ shots can be used in photographic lineups to help identify suspects.

22. _____ is commonly used in outdoor scenes but can also be used indoors. This process of locating evidence or other items uses straight-line measures from two fixed objects.

23. Take photographs and video the entire crime scene before anything is disturbed, and avoid inaccuracies and _____.

24. Rules of evidence dictate that photographs be material, relevant, competent, accurate, free of distortion, and non-_____.

25. The disadvantages of videos center around the mistaken belief that no _____ in videotaping is necessary, which leads to poor video quality and a diminishing of the video's value in documenting the crime scene.

26. _____ notes are legally admissible in court and may be used to testify from or to refresh your memory.

27. A(n) _____ *sketch* is drawn or personally witnessed by an investigator and accurately portrays a crime scene.

28. Surveillance photography is often called _____ photography because the photos prove that an incident occurred and can help identify suspects and weapons.

29. A _____ photograph relates to a specific case and subject.

30. Fingerprint cameras are specially constructed to take pictures of fingerprints without distortion. They provide their own light through four bulbs, one in each corner. Removing a bulb from any corner provides slanted lighting to show fingerprint _____detail.

31. When should the investigator start taking notes?

32. How would you learn to take investigative notes?

33. Why would an investigator use a tape recorder during an interview?

34. What type of items would one photograph in a laboratory?

35. What is a video imaging system?

Case Study

36. As an investigator, you respond to a sexual assault. The victim was assaulted in her home; she escaped from the suspect and fled out the front door. It had rained, and the ground was wet and muddy in some areas. The suspect chased the victim around the area and then carried her back into the house. Later, the victim escaped out a bathroom window and ran to a neighbor's house. The officers responded and found the man driving away from the scene. You are in charge of the sketch of the crime scenes. Describe the scene as well as which sketch approaches would be most appropriate for it.

_____

_____

_____

_____

_____

_____

_____

_____

_____

_____

_____

_____

_____

Answer Key

1. a
2. b
3. c
4. d
5. d
6. d
7. d
8. d
9. d
10. b

11. False
12. False
13. False
14. True
15. False
16. False
17. True
18. True
19. False
20. True

21. Mug
22. Triangulation
23. distortions
24. inflammatory
25. training
26. Original
27. admissible
28. trap
29. material
30. ridge

31. Investigators should start taking notes as soon as possible after they arrive at the scene.

32. Practice, use abbreviations for words, do not use *and, the,* and so on. Learn to select key facts and record them.

33. To record the actual words said, and to make certain that the investigator is able to concentrate on the interview and not on taking notes.

34. Sometimes objects are photographed in a laboratory with special equipment that is too large, delicate, or expensive to use in the field. An example would be infrared film, microphotography, or laser-beam photography.

35. A video imaging system allows officers to sort a database using specific characteristics—race, sex, hair color, height, age, distinguishing marks—in faces—any feature that can be visually described.

Case Study Answer

36. You will need to use a sketch approach that allows both inside and outside sketches. You do not need to use the same system for both, but you have a scene inside a house as well as two outside scenes. You might use the outdoor baseline method or the compass-point method for the outside scenes and the rectangular-coordination method or the triangulation method for the inside scene.

WRITING EFFECTIVE REPORTS

OUTLINE

- The Importance of Reports
- Uses of Reports
- The Audience
- Common Problems with Many Police Reports
- The Well-Written Report: From Start to Finish
- Taping and Dictating Reports
- Computerized Report Writing
- Evaluating Your Report
- Citizen Online Report Writing
- The Final Report
- A Final Note on the Importance of Well-Written Reports

Chapter 3
Writing Effective Reports

By the end of this chapter, you should know how to define the terms and understand the application of the concepts below. Test your understanding of the chapter by verifying that you know this information. If you do not know it, review the chapter.

Can you define these words?

active voice	content	narrative
chronological order	denotative	objective
concise	first person	past tense
conclusionary language	form	proofread
connotative	mechanics	slanting

Do you know?

• How reports are used?	• What the characteristics of effective investigative reports are?
• Who reads your reports?	• How to differentiate between facts, inferences and opinions?
• Why reports are important to an investigation?	• Why your reports should be well written?
• What common problems occur in many police reports?	
• Which is more important: content or form?	

Chapter Outline

I.   The Importance of Reports

    A.   An estimated 20 percent of an officer's time is spent writing reports.

    B.   Reports are used, not just filed.

    C.   Your reputation as an officer or investigator often rests on your report writing skills.

    D.   Poor police reporting can jeopardize effective criminal prosecution.

II.   Uses of Reports

    A.   Reports are permanent records of all important facts in a case.

    B.   Reports are initially used to continue the investigation of the offense. They may also be used for other purposes, such as to

        1.   Examine the past.

        2.   Keep other officers informed.

        3.   Continue investigations.

        4.   Prepare court cases.

        5.   Provide the courts with relevant facts.

        6.   Coordinate law enforcement activities.

        7.   Plan for future law enforcement services.

        8.   Evaluate individual officer and department performance.

        9.   Refresh a witness's memory about what he or she said occurred.

      10.   Refresh the investigating officer's memory during the trial.

      11.   Compile statistics on crime in a given jurisdiction.

      12.   Provide information to insurance investigators.

      13.   Aid in assessing police performance and investigating possible abusive police practices, such as racial profiling.

III. The Audience

    A.   Other officers

    B.   Supervisors

    C.   Attorneys and judges

    D.   Jurors

    E.   City officials

    F.   Insurance adjusters and investigators

    G.   Citizens

    H.   Reporters

IV.   Common Problems with Many Police Reports

    A.   Writing to impress rather than express

    B.   Confusing or unclear sentences

C. Conclusions, assumptions, and opinions presented as facts

D. Extreme wordiness and overuse of police jargon and abbreviations

E. Missing or incomplete information

F. Misspelled words and grammatical/mechanical errors

G. Referring the reader to "the information above," rather than restating the information for them

V. The Well-Written Report: From Start to Finish

A. Organizing information

1. Chronological order

2. Structuring the narrative

a. The opening paragraph of a police report states the time, date, and type of incident, and how you became involved.

b. The next paragraph contains what you were told by the victim or witness. For each person you talked to, use a separate paragraph.

c. Next, record what you did based on the information you received.

d. The final paragraph states the disposition of the case.

e. A brief look at law enforcement report forms

(1) Law enforcement report forms vary greatly in format.

(2) Some report forms contain boxes or separate category sections, e.g., property loss section, for placement of descriptive information, addresses, and phone numbers of those involved. It is unnecessary to repeat this information in the narrative *unless it is needed for clarity* because it tends to interrupt the flow of words and clutter the narrative.

(3) In contrast, narrative reports that do *not* use the box-style format include descriptive information, addresses, and phone numbers within the body of the narrative.

B. Characteristics of effective reports: content and form

1. Content

a. What is said

b. The elements of the crime

c. Descriptions of suspects, victims, etc.

d. Evidence collected

e. Actions of victim, witnesses, and suspects

f. Observations: weather, road conditions, smells, sounds, oddities, etc.

2. Form

a. Word choice

b. Sentence and paragraph length

      c.   Spelling

      d.   Punctuation

      e.   Grammar

      f.   Mechanics

C. "The ability of investigators to explain both verbally and in writing how inferences (e.g., clues, evidence, etc.) lead them to draw logical and reasonable conclusions (e.g., probable cause, facts, etc.) remains a critical skill in investigative work." (Jetmore, 2007, p.22)

D. Factual

E. Fact, inference, or opinion

    1. Fact: A statement that can be proven

      a.   *Example:* The man has a bulge in his black leather jacket pocket.

    2. Inference: A conclusion based on reasoning. Also referred to as "conclusionary language."

      a.   *Examples:* The man is probably carrying a gun.

      b.   "They *denied* any involvement in the crime."

      c.   "She *confessed* to seven more arsons."

      d.   "He *admitted* breaking into the warehouse."

      e.   "He *consented* to a search of the trunk."

      f.   "She *waived* her rights per Miranda."

    3. Opinion: A personal belief

      a.   *Example:* Black leather jackets are cool.

F. Accurate

    1. To be accurate, you must be specific and correct.

    2. Verify all spellings, phone numbers, addresses, emails, etc.

    3. Ensure accuracy of measurements, location of evidence, skid marks, bullet holes, etc.

    4. You don't need to say "PC for the stop," because only reasonable suspicion is needed, not probable cause.

G. Objective

    1. Keep reports objective and factual.

      a.   Denotative, objective words, have little emotional effect, for example, *cried* vs. *wept.*

      b.   Connotative words evoke empathy or sympathy.

      c.   Avoid derogatory or biased terms.

      d.   Avoid "slanting" your reports—remain objective.

      e.   Include both inculpatory as well as exculpatory statements.

H. Complete

    1. What officers write in their reports stays with them forever.

       2. If it isn't written, it didn't happen.

I.   Concise
    1. You can reduce wordiness in two basic ways:
       a.   Leave out unnecessary information.
       b.   Use as few words as possible to record the necessary facts.

J.   Clear
    1. Use specific, concrete facts and details.
    2. Keep descriptive words and phrases as close as possible to the words they describe.
    3. Use diagrams and sketches when a description is complex.
    4. Do not use uncommon abbreviations.
    5. Use short sentences, well organized into short paragraphs

K.   Grammatically and mechanically correct
    1. Check the mechanics—spelling, capitalization, and punctuation.
    2. Spelling is perhaps the most important part of writing.
    3. A good rule is, "If you can't spell it, don't use it."

L.   Written in Standard English
    1. Note differences between spoken English and the written word.

M.   Paragraphs
    1. Discuss only one subject in each paragraph.
    2. Start a new paragraph when changing speakers, time, or ideas, or, from observations or descriptions to statements.

N.   Past tense
    1. Write in the past tense, and with the first-person active voice.

O.   First person

P.   Active voice

Q.   Audience focused
    1. Remember who your audience is.
    2. Write for the people who will read the report and need to use the reports.
    3. Avoid "Cop Speak," or police jargon.
    4. Articulate any use of force in everyday language
       a.   Note objectively reasonableness test under *Graham v. Connor.*
       b.   Was the officer's actions reasonable under the circumstances as viewed by the "objectiveness" of a jury?

R.   Legible and on time
    1. A key factor in legibility is speed.
    2. Most officers need to slow down their writing speed.

VI.   Taping and Dictating Reports

A.   In effect, tape-recording or dictating reports shifts the bulk of writing/ transcribing time to the records division.

B.   Even with taping or dictating, however, officers must still take final responsibility for what is contained in the report.

C.   Technology innovations:

    1.   Departments are making use of technology to complete reports in a timely manner.

    2.   Example: the Intuitive Pen

VII.   Computerized Report Writing

A.   Computer-assisted report entry system (CARE) is used.

B.   Computer hardware/software is now in many police vehicles for immediate reporting.

C.   Software selection may be tailored for specific departmental needs and linked to state and national databases for inquiries.

VIII.   Evaluating Your Report

A.   Proofread before submitting.

B.   Ask a colleague to proofread because it is difficult to proofread your own writing.

C.   Evaluating your report: A checklist. (See Table 3.4 in the core text.)

IX.   Citizen online report writing

A.   Some departments are allowing citizens to write and submit reports using online systems.

B.   These are often used for minor thefts, lost property, vandalism, and graffiti and will vary by agency.

C.   This prevents busy or understaffed departments from having to create "no-response" policies for low-priority calls.

D.   Staff resources can also be better allocated as online reports gradually replace telephone reports and the workload for desk officers becomes manageable compared with a never-ending stream of citizens visiting police station lobbies to report crimes.

E.   The monetary savings are quite substantial when considering the volume of reports that are taken online rather than having officers take reports and write them.

F.   Depending on the vendor an agency chooses, online reporting systems can also facilitate crime tips, special form submissions, and volunteer applications and can even serve as a 3-1-1 system, so that citizens can conveniently report abandoned vehicles, barking dogs, or even streetlight outage.

X.   The Final Report

    A.   The culmination of the preceding steps is the final, or prosecution, report, containing all essential information for bringing a case to trial.

XI.   A Final Note on the Importance of Well-Written Reports

    A.   A report written well the first time means less time spent rewriting it. A well-written report also keeps everyone involved in the case current and clear about the facts, which can lead to higher prosecution rates, more plea bargains, fewer trials, and an easing of caseloads on the court system.

    B.   A well-written report can also save an investigator from spending an inordinate amount of time on the witness stand, attempting to explain any omissions, errors, or points of confusion found in poorly written reports.

    C.   All these benefits ultimately save the department time and expense.

    D.   Every police report must jump over the substantial hurdle of the *exclusionary rule*—which states that illegally obtained evidence can't be used against a defendant in a criminal trial—by explaining in detail how and under what conditions a person's preexisting individual rights were provided during the investigative process.

    E.   The investigative report may be the one pivotal piece of documentation that makes a difference in the prosecution of a murderer or a serial rapist.

    F.   Well-written reports can reduce legal liability for both the officer and the department by clearly documenting the actions taken throughout the investigation.

XII.   Summary

Chapter Questions

1. Which is not one of the primary purposes of a report?
   a. to examine the past
   b. to continue investigations
   c. to inform the media of events
   d. to evaluate officer performances

2. Some of the common problems with police reports include which of these:
   a. confusing or unclear sentences.
   b. conclusions, assumptions, and opinions in the report.
   c. missing or incomplete information.
   d. misspelled words.
   e. all of these.

3. In writing a report, the officer should
   a. plan in advance.
   b. start writing without planning.
   c. start at the end of the story and work back to the beginning.
   d. none of these.

4. Officers should write reports in
   a. past tense.
   b. first person.
   c. active voice.
   d. all of these.

5. "The man could not walk a straight line" is an example of
   a. a fact.
   b. a conclusionary statement.
   c. an observation.
   d. an allegory.

6. A primary concern of the investigator is
   a. to prove the guilt of the suspect through the gathering and recording of information and evidence.
   b. to provide the facts and information needed to show that a crime occurred.
   c. to gather information that will convince the court or the jury of the guilt of the suspect.
   d. to build a case that will enhance sentencing.

7. Clarity in reports can be increased by using
   a. sketches.
   b. diagrams.
   c. either a or b.
   d. neither a nor b.

8. Being concise means
   a. leaving out details.
   b. limiting yourself to one paragraph.
   c. eliminating wordiness.
   d. using only nouns.

9. Which is not included in a final report?
   a. laboratory reports
   b. the complaint
   c. summary of negative evidence
   d. All of these are included in the final report.

10. The computer-assisted report entry (CARE) system
    a. has reduced the time officers spend writing reports.
    b. has improved the quality, accuracy, and timeliness of police reports.
    c. automatically aggregates UCR information.
    d. all of these.

11. Reports are permanent written records of important facts of a case to be used in the future.   True or False

12. Reporters do read police reports.   True or False

13. Report writing is not a talent.   True or False

14. An inference is not really true or false; it is sound or unsound (believable or not believable).   True or False

15. Officers should review their reports to make certain that they are well organized.   True or False

16. An effective report is subjective.   True or False

17. Never use diagrams and sketches when a description is complex.   True or False

18. A reader-friendly report would begin, "On the above date at the above time, I responded to the above address to investigate a burglary in progress."   True or False

19. Although computerized report writing has greatly increased officers' efficiency, it cannot correct sloppy data entry.   True or False

20. Use the first person to refer to yourself.   True or False

21. _____ language may also lead to inaccuracies in your report.

22. A technology called the_____ Pen recognizes handwriting, taking what an officer has written and converting it into an electronic form.

23. In the _____ voice the subject of the sentence performs the actions—for example, "I wrote the report."

24. "*This officer* responded to the call" uses the _____ person.

25. Another way to write a reader-friendly report is to avoid police lingo and other bureaucratic language and use plain English rather than "_____ Speak."

26. Being able to refer to those trained techniques in reporting a use of force makes it easier to show the officer's use of force was objectively _____ under the circumstances, a requirement under *Graham v. Connor.*

27. A key factor in legibility is _____ and most officers need to slow down when writing.

28. One of the most important tasks in writing your reports is to _____ it to look for mistakes in spelling, punctuation, and capitalization.

29. A new trend allows citizens to file crime reports _____ , which has the potential of easing reporting delays for those jurisdictions suffering from staffing shortages or unmanageable caseloads.

30. Every police report must jump over the substantial hurdle of the _____ rule—which states that illegally obtained evidence can't be used against a defendant in a criminal trial.

31. Describe the use of police reports.

32. What order is ususally best for a report and how should the report be structured?

33. What are the most important reasons that officers must write clear reports?

34. What did Robinson say about excessive-force lawsuits and good reports?

35. What tense should you write a crime or arrest report in and why?

Case Study

36. An individual calls the police department to ask that an officer respond to his business because someone has started selling important business secrets to his competitors. How should you respond to his call?

_____

_____

_____

_____

_____

_____

_____

_____

_____

_____

_____

_____

_____

_____

_____

_____

Answer Key

1. c	11. True
2. e	12. True
3. a	13. True
4. d	14. True
5. b	15. True
6. b	16. False
7. c	17. False
8. c	18. False
9. d	19. True
10. d	20. True

21. Conclusionary

22. intuitive

23. active

24. third

25. cop

26. reasonable

27. speed

28. proofread

29. online

30. exclusionary

31. Reports are used to examine the past, to keep other police officers informed, to keep records of a continuing investigations, to prepare court cases, to provide relevant facts to courts and prosecutors, to coordinate law enforcement activities, to plan for future law enforcement services, to evaluate officer and department performance, to refresh the memory of witnesses and officers, to compile crime statistics, and to provide information to insurance investigators.

32. Chronological order is usually best for a report. The opening paragraph of a police report states the time, date, and type of incident and how the officer became involved. The next paragraph contains what the officer was told by the victim or witness(es). Next, the officer records what he or she did based on the information received. The final paragraph states the disposition of the case.

33. The reports are used for prosecuting a case, by other members of the department, by juries, and for other purposes.

34. Robinson concludes, "If officers learn to articulate their use of force in specific, everyday language, the reasonableness will become more apparent. A good report can make an excessive-force lawsuit less likely to be filed in the first place, and if it does go to court, less likely to be successful."

35. Write in the past tense throughout the report. Past-tense writing uses verbs that show that events have already occurred. Your report contains what *was* true at the time you took your notes. Use of present tense can cause tremendous problems later.

Case Study Answer

36. This is a critical case, and the investigation of the case will be complex and involved. In this situation, depending on department policy, you should first respond to the location to obtain an overview of the case. If it seems complex enough, contact an investigation supervisor and discuss the case with the supervisor. Even starting this case is probably beyond the skills or available time of a patrol officer. Investigators should be involved in this type of case from the beginning. However, if investigators are temporarily unavailable because of their workload, you may be called upon to start the investigation. If that happens, you should get clear direction from the investigation supervisor and follow the supervisor's instructions. This case may be primarily criminal, primarily civil, or contain both criminal and civil elements. The supervisor will be able to discuss the case with you and help you determine the most important elements of the case. This is an example of a case that will need to be carefully handled, using complete and detailed reports to offer information to the investigators.

SEARCHES

OUTLINE

- Legal Searches and the Fourth Amendment
- Basic Limitation on Searches
- The Exclusionary Rule
- Justification for Reasonable Searches
- The Crime Scene Search
- Search Patterns
- Other Types of Investigatory Searches
- Use of Dogs in a Search
- Warrant Checklist
- A Reminder

Chapter 4
Searches

By the end of this chapter, you should know how to define the terms and understand the application of the following concepts. Test your understanding of the chapter by verifying that you know this information. If you do not know it, review the chapter.

Can You Define?

anticipatory warrant *Buie* sweep *Carroll* decision *Chimel* decision circle search curtilage "elephant-in-a-matchbox" doctrine exclusionary rule exigent circumstances frisk	"fruit-of-the-poisonous-tree" doctrine good-faith doctrine immediate control inevitable-discovery doctrine lane-search pattern no-knock warrant patdown particularity requirement plain feel/touch evidence	plain-view evidence probable cause protective sweep strip-search pattern *Terry* stop totality-of-the-circumstances test true scene uncontaminated scene zone

Do you know?

- Which constitutional amendment restricts investigative searches?
- What is required for an effective search?
- What basic restriction is placed on all searches?
- What the exclusionary rule is and how it affects investigators?
- What the preconditions and limitations of a legal search are?
- When a warrantless search is justified?

- What precedents are established by the *Carroll, Chambers, Chimel, Mapp, Terry* and *Weeks* decisions?
- What a successful crime scene search accomplishes?
- What is included in organizing a crime scene search?
- What physical evidence is?
- What search patterns are used in exterior searches? interior searches?
- How to search a vehicle, a suspect and a dead body?
- How dogs can be used in searches?

Chapter Outline

I.   Legal Searches and the Fourth Amendment

    A.   Investigators need an understanding of the Fourth Amendment to the U.S. Constitution.

        1.   The Fourth Amendment is all about privacy. The critical distinction to be made at this point is that the only "privacy" that counts is the privacy that society is willing to accept as reasonable as interpreted by the courts.

        2.   The determination of reasonableness depends on the balance between the public interest and the individual's right to be left alone from arbitrary interferences from law enforcement.

        3.   Legally, to search is to go over or look through a house or other building, a person, or a vehicle to find contraband or illicit or stolen property, or some evidence of guilt to be used in prosecuting a criminal action or offense.

        4.   In *United States v. Jacobsen* (1984), the Supreme Court defined a search as "a governmental infringement of a legitimate expectation of privacy."

        5.   Rutledge (2008, p.28) explains, "In situations where it would be unreasonable for a person to expect privacy, there is no 'search' to justify, so no warrant is needed."

II.   Basic Limitations on Searches

    A.   The most important limitation on any search is that the scope must be narrow.

    B.   General searches are unconstitutional.

    C.   The Fourth Amendment forbids unreasonable searches and seizures, not any searches.

III.   The Exclusionary Rule

    A.   *Weeks v. United States* (1914) made the rule applicable at the federal level; *Mapp v. Ohio* (1961) made it applicable to all courts.

    B.   "Fruit-of-the-poisonous-tree" doctrine

        1.   Established that evidence obtained as a result of an earlier illegality must be excluded from trial.

    C.   The inevitable discovery doctrine

        1.   *Nix v. Williams* (1984) states that if illegally obtained evidence would in all likelihood eventually have been discovered legally, it may be used.

    D.   Good-faith doctrine: *United States v. Leon* (1984)

IV.   Justification for Reasonable Searches

A. The basic restriction is the exclusionary rule under *Mapp v. Ohio* (1961).

   1. The seizure of the evidence is constitutional if the following conditions are met:

      a. A search warrant has been issued.

      b. Consent is given.

      c. The officer stops a suspicious person and believes the person may be armed.

      d. The search is incidental to a lawful arrest.

      e. An emergency exists.

B. Searches with a warrant

   1. To obtain a valid search warrant, officers must appear before a judge, establish that there is probable cause to believe that the location contains evidence of a crime and specifically describe the evidence.

   2. Probable cause is more than reasonable suspicion. Here are explanations of probable cause:

      a. "Probable cause is a commonsense, non-technical conception that deals with the factual and practical considerations of everyday life on which reasonable and prudent men, not legal technicians, act" (Scarry, 2007b, p.59).

      b. Jetmore (2007b, p.28) explains probable cause as "less than proof, but more than suspicion that a crime is being, has been or will be committed. Thus, probable cause requires a higher standard than reasonable suspicion, but less than the proof beyond a reasonable doubt required for a conviction in court."

      c. These can include flight, furtive movements, hiding, an attempt to destroy evidence, resistance to officers, evasive answers, unreasonable explanations, contraband or weapons in plain view, a criminal record, police training and experience, unusual or suspicious behavior, and information from citizens.

   3. Using informants

      a. The Supreme Court has established requirements for using informants in establishing probable cause.

      b. *Note:* there are two separate tests established in *Aguilar v. Texas* (1964):

         (1) Is the informant reliable/credible?

         (2) Is the information believable?

      c. This two-pronged approach was upheld in *Spinelli v. United States* (1969).

      d. However, the Supreme Court most recently changed the two-pronged test to a totality-of-the-circumstances test, *Illinois v. Gates* (1983), which most states have adopted.

e. Note that federal courts are still guided by the two-pronged *Aguilar-Spinelli* test, and several states also adhere to this more stringent requirement for establishing probable cause.

4. Other requirements:

    a. In addition to establishing probable cause for a search, the warrant must contain:

        (1) The reasons for requesting it (probable cause)

        (2) The names of the people presenting affidavits (officers)

        (3) What specifically is being sought (evidence, weapons, drugs)

        (4) The signature of the judge issuing it

    b. The warrant must be based on facts and sworn to by the officer requesting the warrant (affidavit).

    c. An address and description of the location must be given—for example, "100 S. Main Street, the ABC Liquor Store," or "1234 Forest Drive, a private home."

    d. Warrants can be issued for the following:

        (1) Stolen or embezzled property.

        (2) Property designed or intended for use in committing a crime.

        (3) Property that indicates a crime has been committed or that a particular person has committed a crime.

    e. In *Groh v. Ramirez* (2004), the Supreme Court sent a message to law enforcement on the importance of paying attention to detail.

        (1) The section that was to contain a list of *items* to be seized instead described the place to be searched.

        (2) As a result, the warrant was invalid, and evidence was lost.

        (3) In addition, the officer was sued for an alleged Fourth Amendment violation.

5. The knock-and-announce rule: Officers are required to knock and announce their identity.

    a. In *Wilson v. Arkansas* (1995), the Court made this centuries-old rule a constitutional mandate.

    b. Officers may obtain a no-knock warrant if the evidence may be easily destroyed, explosives are present, or other dangers exist.

    c. Unnecessary damage to the structure may make the entry unreasonable.

    d. Case law:

        (1) In a unanimous ruling in *United States v. Banks* (2003), the Supreme Court upheld the forced entry into a suspected drug dealer's apartment 15 to 20 seconds after police knocked and announced themselves.

(2) In 2006, the Supreme Court ruled in *Hudson v. Michigan* that the Constitution does not require the government to forfeit evidence gathered through illegal "no knock" searches while executing a search warrant. In this case *(Hudson),* the police only waited approximately 3 to 5 seconds before making their entry. In effect, the court upheld the evidence (gun and drugs) despite the officers' "error" in not waiting longer. In the 5-to-4 vote, writing for the Court's five-member conservative majority, Justice Alito said police blunders should not result in a "get-out-of-jail-free card" for defendants.

(3) Officers must still balance the knock, announce, and wait requirements against both officer safety and evidence destruction issues, and the entry must still be reasonable.

    e. Particularity requirement

    (1) *Stanford v. Texas* (1965)

    (2) During a search conducted with a warrant, items not specified in the warrant *may be seized* if they are similar to the items described, if they are related to the particular crime described, or if they are contraband.

6. Anticipatory search warrants

    a. The Court noted that, in a sense, all search warrants are anticipatory (*United States v. Grubbs,* 2006).

    b. These warrants are "based upon an affidavit showing probable cause that at some future time (but not presently) certain evidence of crime will be located at a specified place."

C. Search with consent

1. Search is okay if "based on the voluntary consent of a third party—generally an occupant—who shares 'common authority' over the premises or effects sought to be inspected."

2. Searching without a warrant is allowed if consent is given by a person with the authority to do so.

3. The consent must not be in response to an officer's claim of lawful authority and may not be in response to an officer's command or threat.

4. Silence is *not* consent. A genuine affirmative reply must also be given.

5. When possible, it's a good practice to ask for consent.

6. The consent must be voluntary and limited to the area for which it is granted.

7. Denial of consent by one resident

    a. In *Georgia v. Randolph* (2006), the Supreme Court changed the rules governing some consent searches of private premises.

        b.   Result: "If any party who is present and has authority to object to the search does object to the search, the police may not conduct the search on the authority of that party who gave consent."

    8. General rules on third-party consent:

        a.   "Property owners cannot validly consent to police entry or search while a tenant or guest has lawful right of possession of the premises,"

        b.   "When the suspect is not present or makes no objection, a co-occupant can give valid consent, but"

        c.   "If one co-occupant is present and objects, another cannot give valid consent as to evidence incriminating the objector." (Rutledge, 2006d, p.72)

D. Patdown or frisk during a stop

    1. The *Terry* decision (*Terry v. Ohio,* 1968) established that a patdown or frisk is warranted if officers believe that the person they have stopped to question might be armed and dangerous. (*Note:* Officers must articulate that danger.)

        a.   The "search" in a frisk is sometimes referred to as a safety search.

        b.   Officers may ask the stopped individual for his or her name.

        c.   In *Hiibel v. Sixth Judicial District Court of Nevada, Humboldt County* (2004), the Court ruled that state statutes requiring individuals to identify themselves as part of an investigative stop are constitutional and do not violate the Fourth or Fifth Amendments.

        d.   Officers do not need to advise individuals *of their right not to cooperate with police* on a bus that has been stopped. (*United States v. Drayton,* 2002)

        e.   The Court has also ruled (*Illinois v. McArthur,* 2001) that officers may detain residents outside their homes until a search warrant can be obtained if necessary.

E. Search following an arrest (search incidental to arrest)

    1. Every lawful arrest is accompanied by a search of the arrested person.

    2. The *Chimel v. California* (1969) decision ruled that officers may search the area around the arrested individual for protective purposes.

    3. The police can search within a person's *immediate control*, which encompasses the area within the person's reach.

    4. *Maryland v. Buie* (1990) expanded the area of a premises search following a lawful arrest to ensure officers' safety.

5. The Supreme Court added authority for the police to search areas immediately adjoining the place of arrest.

    a. Called a "protective sweep," or *Buie* sweep, this is justified when reasonable suspicion exists that another person might be present who poses a danger to the arresting officers.

    b. The search must be confined to areas where a person might be hiding.

F. Search in an emergency situation (exigent circumstances)

    1. In situations where police officers believe that there is probable cause but have no time to secure a warrant (for example, if shots are being fired or a person is screaming), the search must be conducted immediately.

    2. The circumstances must include the following:

        a. There must be reason to believe a real emergency exists requiring immediate action to protect or preserve life or to prevent serious injury.

        b. Any entry or search must not be motivated primarily by a wish to find evidence.

        c. There must be a connection between the emergency and the area entered or searched.

    3. In *Mincey v. Arizona* (1978), the Supreme Court stated that the Fourth Amendment does not require police officers to delay a search in the course of an investigation if to do so would gravely endanger their lives or the lives of others.

    4. In *Brigham City, Utah v. Stuart* (2006), the Supreme Court ruled that law enforcement officers could enter a house without a warrant to render emergency assistance to an injured occupant or to protect an occupant from imminent injury.

    5. Once the danger has been eliminated, however, any further search should be conducted only after obtaining a search warrant.

G. Warrantless searches of vehicles

    1. The *Carroll* decision (*Carroll v. United States,* 1925) established that automobiles may be searched without a warrant if

        a. There is probable cause for the search.

        b. The vehicle would be gone before a search warrant could be obtained.

    2. The judge in *Carroll* found that warrantless searches are often justified because of a vehicle's mobility, that is, because the vehicle can be easily moved.

    3. Pretext stops

        a. The so-called *pretext* stop is overridden by an officer's probable cause to believe the motorist is, or is about to be, engaged in criminal activity.

    b.   Probable cause trumps pretext.

4. Searches of passengers in a stopped vehicle

    a.   All passengers in private vehicles are detained at a stop.

    b.   Passengers may be ordered out and kept from leaving.

    c.   Passengers may be arrested for joint possession of contraband.

    d.   Passengers' property and the vehicle may be searched incident to their arrest.

    e.   "Passenger property exception" ruling, *Wyoming v. Houghton* (1999):

        (1) An officer may search an automobile passenger's belongings simply because the officer suspects the driver has done something wrong.

        (2) However, in *Brendlin v. California* (2007), the Supreme Court reaffirmed what officers already knew—that they must have at least a *reasonable suspicion* of criminal activity to stop a vehicle.

5. Searches of vehicles incident and contemporaneous with lawful arrests

    a.   *New York v. Belton* (1981) established that the vehicle of a person who has been arrested can be searched without a warrant.

    b.   In *Thornton v. United States* (2004), the Supreme Court ruled that police can search the passenger compartment of a vehicle incident to arrest when the arrestee was approached after recently occupying that vehicle.

6. Vehicle searches at roadblocks and checkpoints

    a.   In *United States v. Martinez-Fuerte* (1976), the Supreme Court ruled that (immigration) checkpoints at the country's borders were constitutional because they served a national interest and that this interest outweighed the checkpoint's minimal intrusion on driver privacy.

    b.   The *functional equivalent doctrine* establishes that routine border searches are constitutional at places other than actual borders where travelers frequently enter or leave the country, including international airports.

    c.   In *Brown v. Texas* (1979), the Supreme Court created a *balancing test* (an evaluation of interests and factors) to determine the constitutionality of roadblocks, using three factors:

        (1) The gravity of the public concerns served by establishing the roadblock

        (2) The degree to which the roadblock is likely to succeed in serving the public interest

      (3) The severity with which the roadblock interferes with individual liberty

   d. *Michigan v. Sitz* (1990) established that *sobriety checkpoints* to combat drunken driving were reasonable under the *Brown* balancing test if they met certain guidelines.

   e. However, the Court ruled in *City of Indianapolis v. Edmond* (2000) that checkpoints for *drugs* are unconstitutional.

   f. In *Illinois v. Lidster* (2004), the Court upheld the constitutionality of *informational checkpoints.*

   g. In *United States v. Flores-Montano* (2004), the Court ruled that privacy interests do not apply to vehicles crossing the border.

  7. Inventory searches

   a. *Chambers v. Maroney* (1970) established that a vehicle may be taken to headquarters to be searched.

   b. Officers have the right to inventory vehicles if it is necessary to

      (1) Protect the owner's property.

      (2) Protect the police from disputes and claims that property was stolen or damaged.

      (3) Protect the police and public from danger.

      (4) Determine the owner's identity.

V. The Crime Scene Search

 A. A successful crime scene search involves locating, identifying, and preserving all evidence present.

 B. The goals of a search include

  1. Establishing that a crime was committed and what the specific crime was.

  2. Establishing when the crime was committed.

  3. Identifying who committed the crime.

  4. Explaining how the crime was committed.

  5. Suggesting why the crime was committed.

 C. Organizing the crime scene search involves

  1. Organizing a search includes dividing duties, selecting a search pattern, assigning personnel and equipment, and giving instructions.

  2. Determining whether the scene was immediately secured, and if the scene is considered to be a true, or uncontaminated, scene.

 D. Physical evidence

  1. Physical evidence ranges in size from very large objects to minute substance traces.

  2. Knowing what to search for is indispensable to an effective crime scene search.

3. *Physical evidence* is anything material and relevant to the crime being investigated.

4. The "elephant-in-a-matchbox" doctrine requires that searchers consider the probable size and shape of evidence they seek because, for example, large objects cannot be concealed in tiny areas.

VI. Search Patterns

    A. All search patterns have a common denominator: They are designed to systematically locate any evidence at a crime scene or at any other area where evidence might be found.

    B. Exterior search patterns

        1. Lane-search pattern—partitions the area into lanes, using stakes and string.

        2. Strip-search pattern—if only one officer is available for the search, the pattern can be divided into lanes.

        3. Grid-search pattern—uses a modified grid.

        4. Circle-search pattern—begins at the center of an area to be searched and spreads out in ever-widening concentric circles.

        5. Zone- or sector-search pattern—an area is divided into equal squares on a map of the same area.

    C. Interior search patterns

        1. Most searches are interior searches.

        2. Interior searches go from the general to the specific.

        3. Process:

            a. Start at an entry point.

            b. Search the floor first.

            c. Then search the walls.

            d. Then search the ceiling.

    D. General guidelines

        1. In general, the precise pattern used is immaterial as long as the search is systematic.

    E. Plain-sense evidence

        1. The most common type of plain-sense evidence is that seen by an officer.

        2. Plain-view evidence.

            a. Anywhere officers have a right to be, they have a right to see—through the use of their unaided senses.

            b. Unconcealed evidence seen by an officer engaged in a lawful activity is admissible in court.

            c. An officer cannot use the plain-view doctrine to justify the seizure of an object that the warrant in use does not mention.

d. An officer may also seize evidence indicated by a sense other than sight.

e. Officers may seize any contraband they discover during a legal search.

f. Containers can be opened where their outward appearance reveals criminal contents, for example, a kit of burglar tools or a gun case.

   (1) By their nature, they do not support a reasonable expectation of privacy because their contents can be inferred from their appearance.

3. Plain feel/touch

a. The "plain-feel/touch" exception is an extension of the plain-view exception. If a police officer lawfully pats down a suspect's outer clothing and feels an object that he *immediately* identifies as contraband, a warrantless seizure is justified (*Minnesota v. Dickerson*, 1993).

4. Plain smell

a. Evidence may also be seized if an officer relies on a sense other than sight or touch.

5. Plain hearing

a. Officers or undercover agents can position themselves in accessible locations where they can overhear criminal conversation without any extraordinary listening devices (such as wiretaps or parabolic microphones).

b. Anything overheard can be used as evidence.

VII. Other Types of Investigatory Searches

A. In addition to crime scene searches, officers may search buildings, trash or garbage cans, vehicles, suspects, and dead bodies as they investigate criminal offenses.

B. Building searches.

1. "Building search and the entry into non-secured areas is one of the most intricate skills that are not routinely taught to police officers." (Oldham, 2006, p.73)

2. Clear the fatal funnel (zone outside and inside the doorway) quickly.

3. When executing a warrant to search a building, officers should first familiarize themselves with the location and the past record of the person living there.

4. Do not treat the execution of a search warrant as routine. Plan for the worst-case scenario.

5. Have a plan before entering the building.

6. Keep light and weapons away from your body.

7. Officers may, for their own safety, detain occupants of the premises while a proper search is conducted.

8. Officers may also require residents to remain outside of their homes.

9. Officers should be aware of the ruling in *Kyllo v. United States* (2001), which held that thermal scanning of a private residence from outside the residence is a search.

C. Trash or garbage can searches.

1. In *California v. Greenwood* (1988), the Supreme Court ruled that containers left on public property are open to search by police without a warrant.

   a. The most important factor in determining the legality of a warrantless trash inspection is the physical location of the retrieved trash. Police cannot trespass to gain access to the trash location.

   b. Officers need to know if the trash is within the curtilage of the person's property, which is that part of the property that is not open to the public and that is reserved for the property owner.

D. Vehicle searches.

1. Remove occupants from the car or other vehicle.

2. Search the area around the vehicle.

3. Search the interior.

4. Take precautions to prevent contamination of evidence.

E. Suspect searches.

1. If the suspect has not been arrested, confine your search to a patdown or frisk for weapons.

2. If the suspect has been arrested, make a complete body search for weapons and evidence.

3. Under the Fourth Amendment, officers are permitted to handcuff, detain, and question occupants when executing high-risk search warrants.

   a. Before conducting any search, ask the suspect if he has anything on him that could get the officer into trouble, asking specifically about needles and blades.

   b. When possible, search a suspect while a cover officer observes. If arresting the suspect, first handcuff and then search.

   c. Every search should be done wearing protective gloves.

4. Thorough search

   a. If you arrest a suspect, conduct a complete body search for both weapons and evidence.

   b. Strip searches may be conducted only after an arrest and when the prisoner is in a secure facility.

(1) Such searches should be conducted by individuals of the same gender as the suspect and in private and should follow written guidelines.

(2) Cavity searches go beyond the normal strip search and must follow very strict departmental guidelines. Such searches should be conducted by medical personnel.

   5. Inhibitors to a thorough search:

      a. The presence of bodily fluids is one factor that may interfere with a complete search.

      b. Officers must also be alert to suspects who may spit on or bite them.

      c. Another inhibitor to thorough searches is a fear of needles.

      d. Weather can also compromise the thoroughness of a search.

F. Dead body searches

   1. Searching a dead body should be done only after the coroner or medical examiner has arrived or given permission.

   2. Do *not* turn the body over to search for identification or other wounds or evidence. This causes major problems in documenting the body's original position

G. Underwater searches

   1. Conditions beyond the control of the investigator may dictate what type of search is conducted.

   2. Metal detectors are a necessity in underwater searches.

VIII. Use of Dogs in a Search

A. A dog can be an invaluable resource to a patrol officer.

B. Dogs "are good for bomb, chemical and drug detection; tracking both suspects and lost persons; and finding real and counterfeit money, land mines, people hiding, weapons, buried bodies or fire igniters/accelerants in arson cases." (Falk, 2006, p.48)

C. Canines are a great force multiplier and a psychological advantage.

IX. Warrant Checklist

A. No search warrant required:

   1. No search (plain sense, open fields, abandoned property, private-party delivery, controlled delivery, exposed characteristics)

   2. Independent justification (consent, probation or parole, incident to arrest, officer safety, booking search, inventory)

   3. Exigent circumstances (rescue, protection of property, imminent destruction of evidence, fresh pursuit, escape prevention, public safety)

   4. Fleeing target (car, van, truck, RV, bus, boat, aircraft, etc.) with PC and lawful access

B. The courts have also identified several "special needs" exceptions.

    1. These do not fit into other categories such as school searches, searches of highly regulated businesses (such as firearms dealers, pawn shops, and junkyards), employment and educational drug screening, and the immediate search for "evanescent" evidence (such as blood-alcohol content)

X. A Reminder

A. Jetmore (2007b, p.26) stresses, "Ability to skillfully document in writing facts and circumstances that lead to logical inferences and reasonable conclusions remains a professional requirement in criminal investigation. Excellent investigative work is negated and the guilty may walk free if the legal framework on which it was based can't be adequately explained."

B. The Fourth Amendment requires that officers' actions be *reasonable:* clearly outlining every detail known to you at the time in your report so that the reasonability of your actions will be clear.

XI. Summary

Chapter Questions

1. To conduct an effective search
   a. the officer must know the legal requirements for searching.
   b. the officer must know the items being searched for.
   c. the officer must know the elements of the crime being investigated and be organized, systematic, and thorough.
   d. all of these.

2. All searches must be conducted under the authority of a warrant unless
   a. the court is too distant.
   b. a supervisor authorizes the officer to search without a warrant.
   c. there are exigent circumstances.
   d. none of these.

3. A search can be justified and therefore considered legal if any of the following conditions are met:
   a. A search warrant has been issued.
   b. Consent is given.
   c. An officer stops a suspicious person and believes the person to be armed.
   d. The search is incidental to a lawful arrest, or an emergency exists.
   e. all of these.

4. The goal of any search during an investigation, at the crime scene or elsewhere, is to discover evidence that helps to
   a. establish that a crime was committed.
   b. establish when the crime was committed.
   c. identify who committed the crime.
   d. explain how and why the crime was committed.
   e. all of these.

5. Organizing a search includes
   a. dividing duties.
   b. assigning a search pattern.
   c. giving instructions.
   d. all of these.

6. A lane search, in which the area is partitioned into lanes,
   a. may involve any number of police personnel.
   b. is intended to only be used with one officer.
   c. works well inside.
   d. all of these.

7. Which amendment to the U.S. Constitution forbids unreasonable searches and seizures?
   a. the First Amendment
   b. the Third Amendment

c. the Fourth Amendment
d. the Fourteenth Amendment

8. To obtain either arrest warrant or search warrants, the key issue officers must present to a judge, while under oath or affirmation, is that there is sufficient
a. reasonable doubt.
b. reasonable suspicion.
c. probable cause.
d. unequivocal proof.

9. The U.S. Supreme Court has established requirements for using informants in the establishment of probable cause. Although a two-pronged test was initially adopted, it was later abandoned in favor of a *totality of the circumstances test*. Which court case was responsible for this more practical concept?
a. *Illinois v. Gates*
b. *Terry v. Ohio*
c. *Mapp v. Ohio*
d. *Miranda v. Arizona*

10. In *United States v. Ramirez*, the court said that if officers attempting to serve a search warrant are not admitted by occupants following a knock-notice announcement, forcible entry may be made, but they also said that
a. unnecessary damage to the structure may make the entry unreasonable and negate the search.
b. officers must give residents a voucher for any damage done.
c. any damage would be considered "cruel and unusual punishment" under the Eighth Amendment.
d. officers would be personally liable and subject to punitive civil damages.

11. A search warrant can be issued for and officers may seize the following: stolen or embezzled property, property designed or intended for use in committing a crime, property that indicates a crime has been committed or a particular person has committed a crime.   True or False

12. A search, with consent of the property owner or the suspect, must be clearly voluntary.   True or False

13. A voluntary search must be limited to the area where the officer is standing.   True or False

14. Every lawful arrest does not allow the officer to search the person arrested.   True or False

15. In *Wyoming v. Houghton*, the court ruled that an officer may search the belongings of an automobile passenger simply because the officer suspects the driver has done something wrong.   True or False

16. In a few, rare instances, evidence may not exist at the crime
    scene.   True or False

17. All search patterns are designed to systematically locate any
    evidence at a crime scene or any other areas where evidence
    might be found.   True or False

18. Interior searches move from the general to the specific,
    usually in a circular pattern, covering all the surfaces of a
    search area.   True or False

19. Plain-view evidence is admissible in court, no matter what
    the circumstances.   True or False

20. Officers may not seize contraband they discover during a
    legal search.   True or False

21. The Fourth Amendment to the U.S. Constitution forbids
    _____ searches and seizures.

22. The Supreme Court has ruled that probable cause should be based on a
    _____.

23. A search conducted with a warrant must be limited to the specific area and
    the specific items named in the warrant, in accordance with the _____
    requirement.

24. The landmark decision in *Terry v. Ohio* established police officers' right
    to patdown or frisk a person they have stopped to question if they have
    _____ _____ that the
    person might be armed and dangerous.

25. In a situation where the police officer believes that probable cause exists, but
    there is no time to obtain a search warrant the officer may search. Examples
    include _____ and _____.

26. The *Carroll* decision establishes that automobiles may be searched without
    a warrant if (1) _____,
    and (2) _____.

27. The most important limitation on any search is that the _____
    must be narrow. General searches are unconstitutional.

28. The exclusionary rule establishes that courts may not accept evidence
    obtained by _____ search and seizure, regardless of its
    relevance to a case.

29. The "fruit-of-the-poisonous-tree" doctrine established that _____
    obtained as a result of an earlier illegality must be excluded from trial.

30. A search warrant can be issued to search for and seize the following: _____ _____, property designed or intended for use in committing a crime, or property that indicates a crime has been committed or a particular person has committed a crime.

31. Define "curtilage."

32. Describe the "fruit-of-the-poisonous-tree" doctrine.

33. The courts have upheld the right of an officer to inventory a vehicle for what reasons?

34. Probable cause is needed to obtain a valid search warrant. Describe probable cause in detail.

35. Describe the limitations on officers concerning a search incidental to an arrest found in the decision of *Chimel v. California* (1969).

Case Study

36. You have been assigned to coordinate an outside search. The area includes approximately 1 acre. You have two officers plus yourself to complete this search. What search approach would you use and why?

_____

_____

_____

_____

_____

_____

_____

_____

_____

_____

_____

_____

Answer Key

1.	d	11.	True
2.	c	12.	True
3.	e	13.	False
4.	e	14.	False
5.	d	15.	True
6.	a	16.	True
7.	c	17.	True
8.	c	18.	True
9.	a	19.	True
10.	a	20.	False

21. unreasonable

22. totality-of-the-circumstances test

23. particularity

24. reasonable suspicion

25. shots being fired and a person screaming

26. there is probably cause for the search; and the vehicle would be gone before a search warrant could be obtained.

27. scope

28. unreasonable

29. evidence

30. stolen or embezzled property

31. *Curtilage* is that portion of a residence that is not open to the public. It is reserved for private owner or family use and an expectation of privacy exists for it.

32. Evidence obtained as a result of an illegal search must be excluded from trial.

33. To protect the owner's property, to protect the police from disputes and claims that the property was stolen or damaged, to protect the police and public from danger, to determine the owner's identity.

34. Probable cause is more than reasonable suspicion. To obtain sufficient probable cause to search requires a combination of facts that make it likely that the items sought are where the police believe them to be. It is what would lead a person of reasonable caution to believe that something connected with a crime is on the premises or person to be searched.

35. This decision established that a search incidental to an arrest must be made simultaneously with the arrest and must be confined to the area within the suspect's immediate control. Simply stated, the police can only search areas encompassing the area within the suspect's reach. A search of the kitchen area would not be upheld if the subject was arrested in the bedroom of his home.

Case Study Answer

36. The purpose of a search is to locate, identify, and preserve all evidence. The process or system used is less important. However, based on the size of the area to be searched and the number of officers available, a lane search would probably be the most appropriate, the reason being that this approach allows you to search the area most effectively with the number of officers present. The area is large, so your decision will also depend on the nature of the evidence you are searching for in this case.

FORENSICS/PHYSICAL EVIDENCE

OUTLINE

- Definitions
- Investigative Equipment
- Crime Scene Integrity and Contamination of Evidence
- Processing Evidence: Maintaining the Chain of Custody from Discovery to Disposal
- Frequently Examined Evidence
- Evidence Handling and Infectious Disease

Chapter 5
Forensics/Physical Evidence

By the end of this chapter, you should know how to define the terms and understand the application of the following concepts. Test your understanding of the chapter by verifying that you know this information. If you do not know it, review the chapter.

Can You Define?

associative evidence	cross-contamination	physical evidence
automated fingerprint identification system (AFIS)	*Daubert* standard	plastic fingerprints
	direct evidence	*prima facie* evidence
ballistics	DNA	probative evidence
best evidence	DNA profiling	proxy data
biometrics	elimination prints	psycholinguistics
bore	evidence	relevant evidence
caliber	forensic anthropology	rifling
cast	forensic science	spectrographic analysis
chain of custody	genetic fingerprint	standard of comparison
chain of evidence	indirect evidence	striations
circumstantial evidence	individual characteristics	tool mark
class characteristics	inkless fingerprint	trace evidence
competent evidence	integrity of evidence	ultraviolet (UV) light
contamination	lands	visible fingerprints
corpus delicti	latent fingerprints	voiceprint
corpus delicti evidence	material evidence	X-ray diffraction

Do you know?

- What is involved in processing physical evidence?
- How to determine what is evidence?
- What the common errors in collecting evidence are?
- How to identify evidence?
- What to record in your notes?
- How to package evidence?
- How to convey evidence to a department or a laboratory?

- How and where evidence is stored?
- How to ensure admissibility of physical evidence in court?
- How physical evidence is finally disposed of?
- What types of evidence are most commonly found in criminal investigations and how to collect, identify and package each?
- Where fingerprints can be found and how they should be preserved?

(continued)

(continued)

• What can and cannot be determined from fingerprints, DNA, bloodstains and hairs? • What DNA profiling is? • How identifying blood and hair are useful? • Where shoe and tire impressions can be found and how they should be preserved? • How to preserve tools that might have been used in the crime, as well as the marks they made?	• How to mark and care for weapons used in crimes? • How to preserve such things as glass fragments, soil samples, safe insulation material, rope, tapes, liquids and documents? • What evidence UV light can help discover? • What evidence to collect in hit-and-run cases? • What can be determined from human skeletal remains?

Chapter Outline

I. Definitions

    A. Forensic science is "the application of scientific processes to solve legal problems most notably within the context of the criminal justice system." (Fantino, 2007, p.26)

        1. Criminal activity always removes something from the crime scene and leaves behind incriminating evidence.

        2. Remnants of this transfer are called proxy data.

    B. Types of evidence

        1. Best evidence, in the legal sense, is the original evidence.

        2. Physical evidence is anything real—i.e., which has substance—that helps to establish the facts of a case.

        3. Direct evidence establishes proof of a fact without any other evidence.

        4. Indirect evidence merely *tends* to incriminate a person—for instance, a suspect's footprints found near the crime scene.

        5. Indirect evidence is also called circumstantial evidence.

        6. Extremely small items, such as hair or fibers, are a subset of direct evidence called trace evidence.

        7. Evidence established by law is called *prima facie* evidence.

        8. Associative evidence links a suspect with a crime. Associative evidence includes fingerprints, footprints, bloodstains, hairs, and fibers.

        9. Corpus delicti evidence establishes that a crime has been committed.

        10. Probative evidence is vital to the investigation or prosecution of a case, tending to prove or actually proving guilt or innocence.

11. Material evidence forms a substantive part of the case or has a legitimate and effective influence on the decision of the case.

12. Relevant evidence applies to the matter in question.

13. Competent evidence has been properly collected, identified, filed, and continuously secured.

II. Investigative Equipment

A. Equipment needed for each type of investigation will vary, however investigators and officers need specialized equipment to properly process the various crime scenes. Examples would include cameras, chalk, containers, fingerprint kit, labels, magnifiers, measuring tape, notebooks, paper, pens, and other equipment listed in the text.

B. More expensive and elaborate equipment is also needed, such as more elaborate cameras and laptop computers.

C. Selecting equipment

1. Work with other organizations to identify what is needed. It is helpful to contact other law enforcement agencies to determine what equipment they use and what they suggest for purchase.

2. Select what you want to have for your organization. Investigators know best what is needed and what is needed by the organization.

D. Equipment containers

1. Equipment may be stored in one or more containers. The equipment needs to be carefully cared for so that it will work when needed, and the purchase of specialized containers will help.

2. The containers need to look professional. It is important that investigators make use of professional containers and equipment to create a consistent image.

E. Transporting equipment

1. There are many possible ways to transport equipment to a crime scene from the use of a police car to a specially equipped vehicle.

2. A mobile crime lab is generally a specially equipped van that contains the type of equipment needed to process most crime scenes.

F. Training in equipment use

1. Most failures when equipment is used are because of lack of training given to those using it, rather than to any problem with the equipment.

2. Crime scene investigators need to examine the scene carefully before entering it.

III. Crime Scene Integrity and Contamination of Evidence

A. The value of evidence is directly affected by what happens to it immediately following the crime.

B. Cordon off the crime scene.

C. Maintain evidence integrity.

　　1. Integrity of evidence refers to the requirement that any item introduced in court must be in the same condition as when it was found at the crime scene.

　　2. This is documented by the chain of evidence, also called the chain of custody: documentation of what has happened to the evidence from the time it was discovered until it is needed in court, including every person who has had custody.

　　3. Recalling Locard's principle of exchange, the very act of collecting evidence, no matter how carefully done, will result in a postcrime transfer of material—contamination.

　　4. The value of evidence may be lost because of improper collection, handling, or identification.

IV. Processing Evidence: Maintaining the Chain of Custody from Discovery to Disposal

A. Discovering or recognizing evidence

　　1. To determine what is evidence, first consider the apparent crime. Then look for any objects unrelated or foreign to the scene, unusual in location or number, or damaged or broken or whose relation to other objects suggests a pattern that fit the crime.

　　2. Sometimes it is difficult to recognize items as evidence. Investigators need to consider the type and nature of crime and carefully examine what items are in the area of the crime scene.

　　　　a. Plain-view evidence can be seized legally.

　　　　b. Recall also that the Brady Rule requires law enforcement to gather all evidence that helps establish guilt *or* innocence.

　　3. A standard of comparison is an object, measure, or model with which evidence is compared to determine whether both came from the same source.

　　4. Forensic light sources (FLSs), which work on the principle of ultraviolet fluorescence, infrared luminescence, or laser light, can make evidence visible that is not otherwise detectable to the naked eye, such as latent prints, body fluids, and even altered signatures.

　　　　a. Ultraviolet (UV) light is the invisible energy at the violet end of the color spectrum that causes substances to emit visible light, commonly called *fluorescence*.

　　　　b. Lasers can also assist in investigations through trajectory analysis, measurement and evidence collection.

　　　　c. TracER stands for Trace Evidence Recovery.

B. Collecting, marking, and identifying evidence

　　1. Some of the common errors in collecting evidence include

        a. Not collecting enough of the sample

        b. Not obtaining standards of comparison

        c. Not maintaining the integrity of the evidence

    2. Mark or identify each item of evidence in a way that can be recognized later. Indicate the date and case number as well as your personal identifying mark or initials. Record in your notes the date and time of collection, where the evidence was found and by whom, the case number, a description of the item, and who took custody.

C. Packaging and preserving evidence: Package each item separately in a durable container to maintain the integrity of evidence.

D. Transporting evidence

    1. Personal delivery, registered mail, insured parcel post, air express, Federal Express, and United Parcel Service are legal ways to transport evidence.

    2. Always specify that the person receiving the evidence is to sign for it.

E. Protecting and storing evidence

    1. Storage must be secure and free from pests, insects, and excessive heat or moisture.

    2. Property management

        a. Managing the growing mass of evidence is becoming increasingly challenging because there is a growing need for more storage space to accommodate the seemingly exponential increase in the quantity of evidence they must store for longer periods of time, as scientific advances in DNA technology have caused many state legislatures to extend or eliminate their statutes of limitation.

        b. A major crime scene investigation might generate more than 200 pieces of evidence.

        c. The amount of property that must be tracked and stored in metropolitan departments is typically 100,000 to 400,000 or more items.

        d. Automated systems, barcodes, handheld computers, and portable printers are helping manage evidence and property.

F. Exhibiting evidence in court

    1. To ensure admissibility of evidence in court, be able to

        a. Identify the evidence as that found at the crime scene.

        b. Describe exactly where it was found.

        c. Establish its custody from discovery to the present.

        d. Voluntarily explain any changes that have occurred in the evidence.

    2. *Frye* and *Daubert* cases

        a.   Under *Frye v. United States* (1923), whether the science to process the evidence was acceptable under the "general acceptance" of the scientific community was a precondition to the admissibility of scientific evidence.

        b.   However, under *Daubert v. Merrell Dow Pharmaceuticals* (1993), which uses Federal Rules of Evidence rather than *Frye*, the material issue is that an expert's testimony must be both reliable and relevant. This is known as the two-pronged *Daubert* standard.

  G. Final disposition of evidence

     1. Legally disposing of evidence when the case is closed

     2. Evidence is either returned to the owner, auctioned, or destroyed.

V.   Frequently Examined Evidence

  A. Examining physical evidence often involves the use of biometrics, the statistical study of biological data.

  B. The labs themselves should be accredited.

  C. The lab also uses class and individual characteristics.

     1. Class characteristics are the features that place an item into a specific category.

     2. Individual characteristics are the features that distinguish one item from another of the same type.

  D. Fingerprints: At the end of each human finger, on the palm side, there is a unique arrangement of small lines called friction ridges. These ridges leave prints that are unique to the person.

     1. Latent prints are not readily seen but can be developed through powders or chemicals. They are normally left on nonporous surfaces.

     2. Visible fingerprints are made when fingers are dirty or stained. They occur primarily on glossy or light-colored surfaces and can be dusted and lifted.

     3. Plastic fingerprints, one form of visible print, are impressions left in soft substances such as putty, grease, tar, butter, or soft soap. These prints are photographed, not dusted.

     4. Dusting latent fingerprints: be careful not to use too much powder and thus over-process latent fingerprints.

     5. Lifting prints: use black lifters for light powders and light lifters for black powders.

     6. Chemical development of latent fingerprints: Use for unpainted wood, paper, cardboard, or other absorbent surfaces.

     7. Other methods of lifting prints: Magnabrush techniques, laser technology, gelatin lifters, and cyanoacrylate (superglue).

       a.   Caution: Dusting for fingerprints can sometimes destroy parts of the prints. In addition, conventional fingerprinting methods may use liquids or vapors that might alter the prints.

8. New technology: using microbeam X-ray fluorescence (MXRF) to rapidly reveal a sample's elemental composition by irradiating the sample with a thin beam of X-rays; this doesn't disturb the sample.

9. Elimination prints: If fingerprint evidence is found, it is important to know whose prints "belong" at the scene.

10. Inked prints: Standard procedure is to fingerprint all adults who have been arrested, either at the time of booking or at the time of release.

11. Digital fingerprinting: Advances in computer technology are allowing digital fingerprinting to replace inked printing.

       a.   Inkless fingerprints that are stored in a database for rapid retrieval.

       b.   Automated fingerprint identification system (AFIS)

       c.   Integrated Automated Fingerprint Identification System (IAFIS): developed by the FBI and Department of Homeland Security.

       d.   Fingerprint patterns, analysis, and identification: Normally 12 matchable characteristics on a single fingerprint are required for positive identification.

12. Fingerprint patterns, analysis, and identification: arched, looped, or whorled

13. Usefulness of fingerprints: positive evidence of identity

14. Admissibility in court

15. Other types of prints: palm, foot, lips, writer's edge (side of hand)

E. Voiceprints: a graphic record by a sound spectrograph of the energy patterns emitted by speech. Like fingerprints, no two voiceprints are alike.

F. Language analysis: The actual language is often an overlooked type of evidence. This evidence can be captured using digital recorders.

1. Excited utterances made by persons at a crime scene can, upon analysis, reveal the speaker's state-of-mind and may be admitted into testimony even if the person does not testify.

2. To qualify for this exception to the hearsay rule, the victim or witness must have seen an exciting or startling event and made the statement while still under the stress of the event. This is similar to *res gestae* statement.

3. One area of language analysis involves psycholinguistics, the study of the mental processes involved in comprehending, producing, and acquiring language.

G. Human DNA profiling: deoxyribonucleic acid (DNA) is the building block of chromosomes. This substance is individual to the specific person.

1. Genetic code can be used to create a genetic fingerprint to positively identify a person.

a. Except for identical twins, no two individuals have the same DNA structure.

b. DNA profiling uses material from which chromosomes are made to identify individuals positively.

c. Law enforcement should use DNA's full potential because the low cost per test today can also aid in solving high-volume crimes such as burglaries and car break-ins.

2. Collecting and preserving DNA evidence

a. Collection is simple to conduct. The supplies are inexpensive. Processing time in the field is minimal. Standards are easily obtained.

b. Sterile, cotton-tipped applicator swabs, which are inexpensive, easily obtained, and easy to carry and store, are used to collect four DNA samples by rubbing the inside surfaces of the cheeks thoroughly and then air-drying the swabs and placing them back into the original paper packaging or an envelope with sealed corners.

c. Plastic containers should not be used because they can retain moisture, which may damage the integrity of the DNA sample.

d. In some cases, DNA analysis has been rendered worthless by the defense's successful attack on the methods used to collect and store the evidence on which DNA analysis was performed.

3. DNA testing

a. Two types of DNA are used in forensic analyses: nuclear DNA (nDNA) and mitochondrial DNA (mtDNA)

(1) Nuclear DNA (nDNA) from blood, semen, saliva, body tissues, and hairs that have tissue at their root ends

(2) Mitochondrial DNA (mtDNA) from naturally shed hairs, hair fragments, bones, and teeth

b. DNA analysis is difficult with a mixed profile sample (where DNA from more than one individual is in the sample).

(1) A new technique called Y-STR analysis is being used in such cases. It uses the Y chromosome as a male-specific identifier, and typing techniques are now available that develop profiles specific to the male contributor of the DNA

(2) A limitation of Y-STR analysis is that the DNA profile obtained will be identical for all males within the same paternal lineage

4. Biogeographical ancestry DNA testing can be used to include or exclude certain people from an investigation based on their ancestry.

a. Can suspects be identified by race with DNA? Because DNA evidence has scientifically rigorous probabilities, the chances are far less than 1 in 10 billion for a full DNA profile from a single individual matching that of another individual.

5. DNA Database: Combined DNA Index System (CODIS):

    a. Since its inception, more than 4.2 million forensic and convicted offender profiles have been entered into CODIS.

    b. The *forensic index* contains DNA profiles from crime scene evidence where the offender's identity is unknown.

    c. The *offender index* contains DNA profiles of individuals convicted of sex offenses and other violent crimes.

6. Backlog of DNA awaiting testing: More than 450,000 cases have not yet been entered in CODIS.

7. DNA admissibility in court: "Today a DNA match is virtually undisputable in court." (Ivy and Orput, 2007, p.30)

8. Exoneration of incarcerated individuals: More than 200 convicts have been exonerated by 2007 after being convicted with wrongful misidentification.

9. Moral and ethical issues: The needs of the law enforcement community must be weighed with the public's interest in preserving its own civil liberties.

H. Blood and other body fluids: Blood and other body fluids, including semen and urine, can provide valuable information. Semen and saliva may be detected with fluorescent lights (FLS) and blood trails or blood "spatter" can also be useful as evidence. New software programs such as Backtrack can help analyze blood spatter patterns.

I. Scent: Every person has a unique scent that cannot be masked or eliminated, not even by the most potent perfume. Scent can establish probable cause for an arrest.

J. Hairs and fibers: Hairs and fibers can place an individual at the crime scene, especially in violent crimes in which evidence is generally transferred or exchanged. Secondary ion mass spectrometry (SIMS) chemicals can distinguish trace hair samples using consumer chemicals as identifiers. Although chemical colorants and other products commonly applied to hair can thwart microscopic analysis, SIMS is not affected by such substances and can capitalize on their presence to improve identification.

K. Shoe and tire impressions: Tracks or marks left by shoes or tires can be specific to the shoe or tire.

L. Bite marks: Bite marks can be found on the suspect or victim's body or on anything else placed in the mouth such as food.

1. Bite mark identification is based on the "supposed" individuality of teeth and is legally admissible in court, having endured a number of legal challenges.

2. Teeth may also be an excellent source of genomic DNA.

3. A forensic odontologist is recommended.

M. Tools and tool marks: Tools are often used in the commission of a crime. They can be traced if broken parts are left behind or by marks caused by the use of the tool.

N. Firearms and ammunition: Gunpowder tests, shot pattern tests, and functional tests of a weapon can be made and compared.

   1. Firearm evidence can include bullets, shell casings, slugs, shot pellets, and gunshot residue including serial numbers, blood, fingerprints, or other biological evidence.

   2. A new bill in California requires that beginning in 2010, all semi-automatic handguns purchased have the ability to imprint identifying information on cartridges fired by the weapon, which could turn spent cartridges into potential evidence in civil and criminal cases.

O. Glass: Glass can be used for transfer of evidence and to show where a piece of glass came from at the crime scene.

   1. The Glass Evidence Reference Database contains more than 700 glass samples from manufacturers, distributors, and vehicle junkyards and is a useful resource for investigators.

   2. Although it cannot determine the source of an unknown piece of glass, the database can assess the relative frequency that two glass samples from different sources would have the same elemental profile.

P. Soils and minerals: This circumstantial evidence can place a suspect at a crime scene.

Q. Safe insulation: Safes contain insulation that can transfer to the suspect's clothing.

R. Ropes, strings and tapes: These items can be compared, either by type or the cut ends.

S. Drugs: Drug identification kits can be used to make a preliminary analysis of a suspicious substance, but a full analysis must be done at a laboratory.

T. Weaons of mass destruction (WMDs) include nuclear weapons, radiological, biological, or chemical agents, or explosives.

   1. Testing matrixes include aerosols (or air), liquids, solids, surfaces, and dermal samples.

   2. At any WMD crime scene, however, the public's safety takes precedence over evidence collection.

U. Documents: Typing, handwriting, and printing can be compared.

   1. Resource: Forensic Information System for Handwriting (FISH), which is maintained by the U.S. Secret Service.

   2. This database merges federal and Interpol databases of genuine and counterfeit identification documents, such as passports, driver's licenses, and credit cards.

V. Digital evidence: The digital revolution and preponderance of electronic devices pervading everyday life, such as cell phones, pagers, personal digital assistants (PDAs), computers, and global positioning systems (GPSs), has generated a new class of evidence and requirements for handling it.

1. Perhaps the greatest challenge in electronic crimes is the absence of geographic boundaries and the question of jurisdiction.

2. The first part of collecting evidence from a cell phone is the actual handling of the device. Dunnagan and Schroader (2006, p.47) suggest the following basic rules:

    a. Do not change the condition of the evidence. If it's off, leave it off; if it's on, leave it on.

    b. Look for more devices. Remove any other potential points of evidence, which can include SIM cards, external media, power cables, and data cables.

    c. Make sure you have a search warrant before searching the device.

    d. Return the device to a lab for proper processing.

    e. Use forensically sound software and processing tools, and validate your evidence.

3. Only a person with training should analyze a cell phone.

4. All cell phones leave a trail.

5. Global positioning system chips built into cell phones allow authorities to track criminals as well as people in need of help.

6. Each cell phone provider stores and maintains subscriber records, which include subscriber information, such as name, address, and birth date, as well as call-detail records containing data regarding incoming and outgoing phone numbers and the towers that transmitted these calls.

W. Laundry and dry-cleaning marks: Many launderers and dry cleaners use specific marking systems. These can be used for comparisons and to find the business.

X. Paint: Paint colors and samples can lead to the identification of an automobile and can offer many leads.

Y. Skeletal remains: Laboratories can determine whether skeletal remains are animal or human. Dental comparisons and X-rays of old fractures are other important identifying features of individual characteristics.

Z. Wood: Wood comparisons are possible regarding the type of wood and origin.

AA. Other types of evidence: Prescription eyeglasses, broken buttons, glove prints, and other personal evidence found at a crime scene can also be examined and compared.

1. Investigators should learn to read "product DNA," the printed code that appears on nearly every manufactured, mass-produced item, because it can provide valuable leads.

2. Other discarded items at a crime scene that may yield useful information include store and restaurant receipts, bank deposit slips, beverage containers, cigarette packages, membership and check-cashing cards, clothing manufacturer labels and laundry tags, and footwear.

VI.   Evidence Handling and Infectious Disease

A.   Consider all body secretions as potential health hazards.

B.   AIDS is not spread through casual contact such as touching an infected person or sharing equipment.

C.   Tuberculosis (TB) is of greater concern.

D.   MRSA is a staph infection that is resistant to most antibiotics. It is very infectious, severe, and sometimes deadly.

E.   Use "universal precautions" when collecting blood evidence and other bodily fluids.

F.   Wash hands thoroughly with soap and water.

G.   While processing the crime scene, constantly be alert for sharp objects, such as hypodermic needles and syringes.

VII.   Summary

Chapter Questions

1. A mobile crime lab could provide the following:
   a. radio equipment.
   b. equipment for disaster scenes.
   c. stakeouts.
   d. all of these.

2. Ultraviolet light is good for
   a. finding traces of evidence.
   b. finding items when it is dark.
   c. finding stains, such as alcohol.
   d. none of these.

3. Markings should be easily recognizable and
   a. as small as possible.
   b. be marked on the evidence as it is received.
   c. one should not destroy evidence with markings without court approval.
   d. all of these.

4. Your notes should include
   a. the time the item was found and the disposition of the item.
   b. the time and date the item was found.
   c. the time, date, and location the item was found.
   d. the time, date, and location the item was found, as well as the case number, the description of the item, the name of the individual who found the evidence, and the individual who took it into custody.

5. To ensure admissibility of evidence in court, the department must be able to
   a. identify the evidence as that found at the crime scene.
   b. describe exactly where it was found.
   c. establish its custody from discovery to the present and voluntarily explain any changes that have occurred in the evidence.
   d. all of these.

6. Latent fingerprints are
   a. prints that are lifted by the crime scene processor.
   b. transferred to a surface by dirt/soil on the ridges of the fingers or residue oil.
   c. what is used to convict people in court.
   d. markings left at the scene.

7. Fingerprints may be developed using
   a. fingerprint powder.
   b. magana brush techniques, laser technology, gelatin lifters, and cyanoacrylate.
   c. both a and b.
   d. none of these.

8. AFIS stands for:
   a. automated fingerprint issuing system.
   b. automatic fingerprint intake system.
   c. automatic fiber identification system.
   d. automated fingerprint identification system.

9. DNA testing is expensive and takes a lot of time. Because of this fact, it is important that
   a. the samples are large enough to test.
   b. there is sufficient material from both the suspect and the victim, and the evidence must be probative.
   c. there is sufficient material from the suspect, and the evidence must be probative.
   d. none of these.

10. Advances in computer technology now allow investigators to process latent fingerprints much more quickly and with an increased degree of accuracy than ever before. What process best describes this digital fingerprint technology?
    a. Ninhydrin-development technology (NDT)
    b. Cyanoacrylate gelatin lifting (CGL)
    c. Automated fingerprint identification system (AFIS)
    d. Coded Information System (CODIS)

11. It does not matter what type of container you put equipment in for transport.   True or False

12. A mobile crime lab is usually a commercially customized van that provides compartments for holding equipment and countertops for processing evidence.   True or False

13. Having the equipment available is important, but having training on the use of the equipment is the most important.   True or False

14. During the search of a crime scene, it is generally easy to tell which items at the scene are evidence, so the primary difficulty is in collecting the items.   True or False

15. Probability serves no purpose in evidence; the lab must prove whether an item is the item and know the comparison standard.   True or False

16. To simplify testimony in court, it is practical to have one officer collect the item of evidence and another take notes.   True or False

17. Before, during and after its examination, evidence must be securely protected and properly stored. However, once it is ready for court, there are not any issues about how it is stored.   True or False

18. Automating evidence can prevent many problems.   True or False

19. Evidence destruction can occur continuously.   True or False

20. It does not matter what color fingerprint power you use when
    dusting for prints.   True or False

21. _____ evidence is anything real—that is, which has substance—
    that helps to establish the facts of a case.

22. _____ evidence establishes proof of a fact without any other
    evidence.

23. Indirect evidence is also called _____ evidence.

24. _____ of evidence refers to the requirement that any item introduced in
    court must be in the same condition as when it was found at the crime scene.

25. Chain of evidence is also called the chain of _____.

26. DNA _____ uses material from which chromosomes are made to
    identify individuals positively.

27. Allowing items of evidence to touch one another and thus exchange matter is
    called _____-contamination.

28. _____ examinations compare an unknown recorded
    voice sample with a known verbatim voice exemplar produced on a similar
    transmission-and-recording device such as the telephone.

29. A _____ is a graphic record made by a sound spectrograph of
    the energy patterns emitted by speech.

30. Fingerprints are _____ evidence of a person's identity. They cannot,
    however, indicate a person's age, sex, or race.

31. Describe the basic types of equipment that a department would need to
    process a crime scene.

32. Once evidence is discovered, photographed, and sketched, it is ready for collecting. How could you best collect several different items without risking cross-contamination?

33. Why is the quality of the rolled fingerprint important?

34. Why did the jury seem to disregard the DNA evidence in the O. J. Simpson case? What would you suggest to avoid such problems?

35. How is it possible to collect scent evidence from a crime scene?

Case Study

36. As the leader of a Crime Scene Unit team, you are confronted with a crime scene that involves a murder and a suicide. The victim in the case seems to have attempted to escape and in the process fallen out of the second-story window into a small fish pond. What actions would be important for you to take?

_____

_____

_____

_____

_____

_____

_____

_____

_____

_____

_____

_____

_____

_____

_____

Answer Key

1. d	11. False
2. a	12. True
3. d	13. True
4. d	14. False
5. d	15. False
6. b	16. True
7. c	17. False
8. d	18. False
9. b	19. True
10. c	20. False

21. Physical

22. Direct

23. circumstantial

24. Integrity

25. custody

26. profiling

27. cross

28. Spectrographic

29. voiceprint

30. positive

31. Camera, chalk, compass, magic marker, envelopes, fingerprint kit, first-aid kit, knife, labels, magnifier, measuring tape, mirror, notebook, paper, pencils, pens, picks, plaster, tools, protractor, rope, ruler, scissors, scribe, sketching supplies, string, tags, wrecking bar and other items.

32. By putting items in different containers and preventing them from coming into contact with each other.

33. Poorly rolled fingerprints cannot be compared with the suspect's prints.

34. The jury in the case was shown that there were questions about how the samples were collected, preserved, and examined. To avoid such problems, you need to be able to show how the samples were correctly collected, preserved, and examined.

35. One could locate an item with the same scent or use a Scent Transfer Unit.

Case Study Answer

36. This complex case will stretch the skills of the unit. Although the crime may seem to be a murder and a suicide, that fact is not known at the time the crime scene is being processed. This case involves a rather large crime scene that includes much blood (probably), other fluids, damage inside the house, and much more. The information and evidence that is gathered by the crime scene team will be critical. The team will need to gather samples of water, blood, hairs, and fibers; take many pictures of the interior part of the house; and examine both bodies thoroughly for indications of defensive wounds or other marks. Although the evidence gathered may not immediately show that what happened was a murder-suicide, the different pieces of evidence may support other information or evidence gathered by the investigators. The crime scene investigators will not know how critical the different bits of evidence may be at the time they gather them.

OBTAINING INFORMATION AND INTELLIGENCE

OUTLINE

- Sources of Information
- Interviewing and Interrogating
- The Interview
- The Interrogation
- Questioning Children and Juveniles
- Evaluating and Corroborating Information
- Scientific Aids to Obtaining and Evaluating Information
- Use of Psychics and Profilers
- Sharing Information
- Information Versus Intelligence

Chapter 6
Obtaining Information and Intelligence

By the end of this chapter, you should know how to define the terms and understand the application of the following concepts. Test your understanding of the chapter by verifying that you know this information. If you do not know it, review the chapter.

Can You Define?

admission	in custody	polygraph
adoptive admission	indirect question	public safety exception
beachheading	informant	rapport
cognitive interview	information age	sources-of-information file
complainant	interrogation	statement
confession	interview	testimonial hearsay
custodial arrest	*Miranda* warning	third degree
custodial interrogation	network	waiver
direct question	nonverbal	
field interview	communication	

Do you know?

- What sources of information are available to investigators?
- What a sources-of-information file is and what it contains?
- What the goal of interviewing and interrogation is?
- What the characteristics of an effective interviewer or interrogator are?
- How to improve communication?
- What the emotional barriers to communication are?
- What two requirements are needed to obtain information?
- What the difference between direct and indirect questions is and when to use each?

- What technique is likely to assist recall as well as uncover lies?
- When and in what order individuals are interviewed?
- What basic approaches to use in questioning reluctant interviewees?
- What the *Miranda* warning is and when to give it?
- What the two requirements of a place for conducting interrogations are?
- What techniques to use in an interrogation?
- What third-degree tactics are and what their place in interrogation is?
- What restrictions are placed on obtaining a confession?

(continued)

(continued)

• What significance a confession has in an investigation? • What to consider when questioning a juvenile?	• What a polygraph is and what its role in investigation and the acceptability of its results in court are? • How to differentiate information from intelligence?

Chapter Outline

I.   Sources of Information

    A.   Reports, records and databases

        1. Local resources

        2. Auto track systems

        3. Caller ID

        4. Pen registers

        5. Dialed number recorders (DNR)

        6. State resources

        7. Federal resources

    B.   The Internet

    C.   Victims, complainants, and witnesses

        1. The neighborhood canvass

        2. The knock and talk

        3. Caution: Suspect and witness statements are not always reliable.

    D.   Informants

        1. Anyone else who can provide information about a crime who has not been listed previously.

            a.   Confidential informants

            b.   Establishing reliability

            c.   Possible dangers faced by informants

    E.   Suspects: A suspect is a person considered to be directly or indirectly connected with a crime, either through their own actions or by planning or directing it.

II.   Interviewing and Interrogating: The ultimate goal of interviewing and interrogation is to determine the truth—that is, to identify those responsible for a crime and to clear the innocent of suspicion.

    A.   Characteristics of an interviewer/interrogator are the following:

        1. Adaptable and culturally adroit

        2. Self-controlled and patient

3. Confident and optimistic
4. Objective
5. Sensitive to individual rights
6. Knowledgeable about the elements of crimes

B. Communication can be enhanced by the following:
   1. Preparing in advance
   2. Obtaining information as soon after the incident as possible
   3. Being considerate and friendly
   4. Using a private setting
   5. Eliminating physical barriers
   6. Sitting rather than standing
   7. Encouraging conversation
   8. Asking simple questions one at a time
   9. Listen and observing
   10. Emotional barriers to communication include these:
       a. Fear
       b. Anger
       c. Ingrained attitudes and prejudices
       d. The instinct for self-preservation
   11. Other barriers to communication may include language.

C. Effective questioning techniques.
   1. Guidelines for effective questioning:
      a. Be positive in your approach.
      b. Ask one question at a time, and keep your responses simple and direct.
      c. Give the person time to answer.
      d. Listen to answers, but at the same time anticipate your next question.
      e. Watch your body language and tone of voice.
      f. Start the conversation on neutral territory.
      g. The use of tape recorders can be frightening to anyone being interviewed; so the investigator needs to work with these people about the interview.
      h. React to what you hear.
      i. As you move into difficult territory, slow down.
      j. Don't rush to fill silences.
      k. Pose the toughest questions simply and directly.
      l. Avoid showing emotion; you must establish a professional demeanor. Maintain some distance and keep your role clear.
   2. Direct versus indirect questions

      a.   Avoid questions that can be answered "yes" or "no." A narrative account provides more information and may reveal inconsistencies in a person's story.

      b.   Ask direct questions, that is, questions that come right to the point. Use indirect questions (ones that skirt the point) sparingly.

   3. Repetition is an effective technique for improving recall and uncovering lies.

   4. Taping and videotaping interviews and interrogations. Benefits include

      a.   Reduced need for copious note taking.

      b.   Increased focus on suspect dialogue and mannerism.

      c.   Greater accuracy in documenting suspect's statements.

      d.   Increased transparency of detective behavior and line of questioning.

      e.   Use of the interview tapes for review and training.

III.   The Interview

  A. Advance planning

  B. Selecting the time and place

  C. Beginning the interview

  D. Establishing rapport

  E. Networking an interview

    1. Reluctant interviewees

      a.   Most people who are reluctant to be questioned respond to one of two approaches: logical or emotional.

      b.   Appeal to a reluctant interviewee's reason or emotion.

    2. The cognitive interview

      a.   This method tries to get the interviewee to recall the scene mentally by using simple mnemonic techniques aimed at encouraging focused retrieval.

      b.   These techniques include allowing interviewees to do most of the talking, asking open-ended questions, allowing ample time for answers, avoiding interruptions, and encouraging the person to report all details, no matter how trivial.

  F. Avoiding contaminating the interview

    1. Testimonial hearsay includes prior testimony as well as statements made as a result of police interrogation.

  G. Statements: legal narrative description of events related to a crime.

  H. Closing the interview

IV.   The Interrogation

  A. The *Miranda* warning

1. When *Miranda* does not apply
2. Waiving the rights
   a. *Davis v. United States* (1994) established that it is not the burden of the police to resolve the ambiguity when a suspect has waived *Miranda* rights and ambiguously asks for a lawyer, for example, "Maybe I should talk to a lawyer."
   b. *Miranda* reinitiation checklist (Rutledge, 2007c, p.71):
      (1) After a waiver, OK to question.
      (2) After suspect reinitiates and waives, OK to question.
      (3) After invocation of silence on Case A, OK to seek later waiver and question.
      (4) After invocation of counsel, no police-initiated questioning on any case during continuous custody.
3. The effects of *Miranda*
4. *Miranda* challenged

B. The "question first" or "beachheading" technique
C. The interplay of the Fourth and Fifth amendments
   1. The right to counsel under the Fifth and Sixth amendments
D. Foreign nationals, the Vienna Convention treaty, and diplomatic immunity
E. Selecting the time and place
F. Starting the interrogation
G. Establishing rapport
H. Approaches to interrogation
   1. Inquiring indirectly or directly
   2. Forcing responses
   3. Deflating or inflating the ego
   4. Minimizing or maximizing the crime
   5. Projecting the blame
   6. Rationalizing
   7. Combining approaches
I. Using persuasion during interrogation
   1. Investigative questionnaires
J. Ethics and the use of deception
   1. OK to use deception or trickery
K. Third-degree tactics
   1. Not OK to use force, fear, threats, intimidation, or promises
L. Admissions and confessions
   1. Admissions contain some information concerning the elements of a crime but fall short of a full confession

a. "An adoptive admission occurs when someone else makes a statement in a person's presence and under circumstances where it would be logical to expect the person to make a denial if the statement falsely implicated him, but he does not deny the allegations." (Rutledge, 2008, p.63)

2. Confessions are information supporting the elements of a crime given by a person involved in committing it.

3. A confession is only one part of an investigation. Corroborate it by independent evidence.

V. Questioning Children and Juveniles

A. Special considerations exist when questioning children and juveniles.

B. As in any interview, the first step is to build rapport.

C. Investigators must obtain parental permission before questioning a juvenile, unless the situation warrants immediate questioning at the scene.

VI. Evaluating and Corroborating Information

A. To break a "pat" story, ask questions that require slightly different answers and alter memorized responses.

VII. Scientific Aids to Obtaining and Evaluating Information.

A. The polygraph and voice stress tests

B. Hypnosis and truth serums

1. Hypnosis
   a. Used with crime victims and witnesses to crimes, not with suspects.
   b. Courts have established guidelines for using testimony gained from hypnosis that require that a trained professional perform it and that the professional be independent of, rather than responsible to, the prosecution.

2. Truth serums
   a. Truth serums are fast-acting barbiturates of the type used to produce sleep at the approximate level of surgical anesthesia.
   b. Truth serums are not used extensively by the police because the accuracy of the information obtained with them is questionable.
   c. The courts do not officially recognize truth serums or their reliability, nor do they admit the results as evidence.

VIII. Use of Psychics and Profilers

A. Psychics: Although use of psychics in criminal investigations is controversial, some agencies are willing to consider any possible lead or source of information, including psychics.

B. Profilers: Effective profiling relies on the profiler's ability to combine investigative experience, training in forensic and behavioral sciences, and information about the characteristics of known offenders.

IX. Sharing Information

A. "Substantial obstacles" that prevent police agencies from sharing information include competing local systems, incompatible data formats, issues of who controls the data, security questions, cost, and training time and resources

B. To overcome the obstacle of incompatible data formats and enable federal, state, and local justice and public safety agencies to exchange data in a common, replicable format, the Global Justice XML Data Model (GJSCM) was developed.

C. Over the past several years, GJSCM has become the national standard.

D. Other resources include

1. The OneDOJ Initiative allows state, local, and tribal law enforcement partners to obtain information from all the department's investigative components with a single query.

2. Law Enforcement National Data Exchange (N-DEx) is being developed by the Raytheon Corporation. This Internet-based information system will eventually link the more than 18,000 law enforcement agencies in the nation electronically.

X. Information Versus Intelligence

A. Information or data is not intelligence. Information plus analysis is intelligence.

B. Fusion centers

1. A fusion center is used to exchange information and intelligence and merges data from many sources.

C. Technology

1. Memex allows users to rank reliability of intel sources and links tips to map out intel. It automatically alerts users when new, relevant data is posted.

D. Intelligence-led policing models

XI. Summary

Chapter Questions

1. Which of the following is true about repetition in an interview?
   a. A person who is telling the truth will tell exactly the same story each time.
   b. A person who is lying will tell the story exactly the same way each time.
   c. Repetition does not help to uncover lies.
   d. Repetition does not help to obtain recall and to uncover lies.

2. The ultimate goal of interviewing and interrogating is to
   a. identify the person who is to be arrested.
   b. determine the truth; that is, to identify those responsible for a crime and to eliminate the innocent from suspicion.
   c. present a good case to the prosecutor.
   d. none of these.

3. The two most important basic requirements for obtaining information are to
   a. listen and observe.
   b. listen and respond.
   c. observe and analyze.
   d. listen and record.

4. Which is an example of a direct question?
   a. "Were you around the area of the corner of 5th and Main last night?"
   b. "Where were you last night?"
   c. "Did you assault George Smith at 5th and Main last night?"
   d. none of these

5. Which of the following figures of speech may indicate deception?
   a. "I believe . . ."
   b. "Kind of . . ."
   c. "To the best of my recollection . . ."
   d. all of these

6. Most people who are reluctant to be questioned respond to one of two approaches:
   a. third degree or cognitive
   b. logical or emotional
   c. direct or indirect
   d. call or response

7. Which of the following best describe a person who requests that some action be taken by the police?
   a. witness
   b. complainant
   c. victim
   d. informant

8. Often the questioning of a suspect may occur spontaneously on the street and can be advantageous to officers, allowing them to pose questions right after the crime has occurred. What best describes this scenario?
   a. interrogative stop
   b. probing interview
   c. field interview
   d. streetside interrogation

9. Which kind of interview test records several measurements on a visible graph?
   a. Memex
   b. fusion center
   c. polygraph
   d. N-DEx

10. "When did you and your wife leave the restaurant?" is best classified as what?
    a. indirect question
    b. direct question
    c. repetitive question
    d. declarative statement

11. Witness statements are almost always reliable.   True or False

12. Emotional barriers to communication include ingrained attitudes, prejudices, fear, anger, and self-preservation.   True or False

13. The interviewer should watch his or her body language and tone of voice.   True or False

14. If time permits, investigators need to plan carefully for interviews.   True or False

15. There are three critical dimensions of an interview: (1) the environment, (2) the interviewer's behavior, and (3) the questions asked.   True or False

16. To encourage interviewees to talk, use an erect posture and do not respond when the individual speaks because you may stop their chain of thought.   True or False

17. The *Miranda* warning advises suspects of their Fourth Amendment rights.   True or False

18. When conducting an interrogation, you should seek a place where the individual will feel the most stress.   True or False

19. Officers may use deception during interviews.   True or False

20. Audio and video recordings are becoming more popular.   True or False

21. Avoid asking questions that can simply be answered _____ or _____; a narrative account provides more information and may reveal inconsistencies in the person's story.

22. Interviewers should ask _____questions.

23. A(n) _____ is a person injured by a crime.

24. A(n) _____ is a person who requests that some action be taken.

25. A(n) _____ is a person who saw a crime or some part of it being committed.

26. GOYAKOD stands for "Get off your ass and _____ ___ _____."

27. _____ is a legitimate investigative technique where an officer goes to a home of a suspect or witness to ask them information about an investigation.

28. A(n) _____ is anyone who can provide information about a case but who is not a complainant, witness, victim, or suspect.

29. Of importance to investigators is the _____ informant or CI, an informant who is registered with the department and who is paid for supplying information or for performing a service.

30. A _____ is a person considered to be directly or indirectly connected with a crime, either by overt act or by planning or directing it.

31. How does the Internet serve as a resource for investigators?

32. What are the qualities of an effective interview?

33. Describe a cognitive interview.

34. Compare and contrast the purposes of an interview and an interrogation.

35. Investigators may find on occasion that an individual may be reluctant to be interviewed. Name the emotional barriers that often times must be overcome to have a successful interview.

Case Study

36. You suspect that the individual you are about to interview is responsible for more than 200 burglaries. There is minimal evidence connecting him to the crime that he was arrested for, so the current case against him is very weak. However, the crime analyst has found some similarities between the MO of the crime he was taken into custody for and the MO of many others. What would you do?

_____

_____

_____

_____

_____

_____

_____

_____

_____

_____

_____

_____

_____

_____

_____

_____

Answer Key

1. b

2. b

3. a

4. c

5. d

6. b

7. b

8. c

9. c

10. b

11. False

12. True

13. True

14. True

15. True

16. False

17. False

18. False

19. True

20. True

21. "yes," "no"

22. direct

23. victim

24. complainant

25. witness

26. knock on doors

27. knock and talk

28. informant

29. confidential

30. suspect

31. The Internet is an extremely valuable source of information. Fast-breaking cases, such as kidnappings, can be aided by an investigator's ability to distribute photographs and detail efficiently and quickly. In addition to reports and records, databases, and Internet resources, investigators obtain information from people associated with the investigation: witnesses, victims, and so on.

32. An effective interviewer is adaptable and culturally adroit, self-controlled and patient, confident and optimistic, objective, sensitive to individual rights, and knowledgeable about the elements of crimes.

33. Cognitive interview techniques call for the interview to take place in a secluded, quiet place without distractions. The interviewer should encourage the subject to speak slowly and freely. The interviewer helps the interviewee to reconstruct the circumstances of an event by asking interviewees how they felt at the time, and other details such as the weather, the surroundings, objects, people, and smells. Interviewees are encouraged to report everything, even things that seem unimportant to them.

34. An interviewer asks questions of people who are not suspects in a crime but who may know something about it or the people involved. An interrogation involves those who are suspected of having direct or indirect involvement in a crime. The ultimate goal of each is to determine the truth surrounding an incident and identify those responsible for the crime.

35. Emotional barriers to communication include ingrained attitudes and prejudices, fear, anger, and self-preservation.

Case Study Answer

36. The case is important. You will need to be thoroughly familiar with the previous burglaries and the patterns that connect them to this case. You will also need to know the details of the circumstances that brought about the suspect's arrest and the strength of the case against him, including any evidence that could prove he committed the crime. You will want to know about his conduct toward the arresting officers and his past crimes or arrests. You need to prepare for this case and need to gather all of the information that you can (analysis evidence, reports, victim statement, etc.) in the time available. If you take an approach with the interview that does not work, be prepared to change your approach, or to turn the interrogation over to someone else. Approaches may vary from friendly to forceful to threatening. Your choice of an approach depends on your judgment of what will work, and this needs to be based on what the arresting officers have told you about the suspect. Use all the tools at your disposal, and do not give up if one approach does not work.

IDENTIFYING AND ARRESTING SUSPECTS

OUTLINE

- Identifying Suspects at the Scene
- Locating Suspects
- Identifying Suspects
- Surveillance, Undercover Assignments and Raids: The Last Resort
- Surveillance
- Undercover Assignments
- Raids
- Legal Arrests
- Avoiding Civil Liability When Making Arrests

Chapter 7
Identifying and Arresting Suspects

By the end of this chapter, you should know how to define the terms and understand the application of the following concepts. Test your understanding of the chapter by verifying that you know this information. If you do not know it, review the chapter.

Can You Define?

arrest	geographic profiling	show-up identification
bugging	loose tail	solvability factors
close tail	nightcap provision	stakeout
cover	open tail	subject
criminal profiling	plant	surveillance
de facto arrest	pretextual traffic stops	surveillant
entrapment	psychological profiling	tail
excessive force	racial profiling	tight tail
field identification	raid	undercover
fixed surveillance	reasonable force	wiretapping
force	rough tail	

Do you know?

- What field identification or show-up identification is and when it is used?
- What rights a suspect has during field (show-up) identification and what case established these rights?
- How a suspect is developed?
- How to help witnesses describe a suspect or a vehicle?
- When mug shots are used?
- What the four basic means of identifying a suspect are?
- What photographic identification requires and when it is used?
- What a lineup requires and when it is used?

- What rights suspects have regarding participation in a lineup and which cases established these rights?
- When surveillance is used? What its objectives are?
- What the types of surveillance are?
- When wiretapping is legal and what the precedent case is?
- What the objectives of undercover assignments are? What precautions you should take?
- What the objectives of a raid are?
- When raids are legal?
- What precautions should be taken when conducting a raid?

(continued)

(continued)

• When a lawful arrest can be made? • When probable cause must exist for believing that a suspect has committed a crime? • What constitutes an arrest?	• In what areas officers leave themselves open to civil liability when making an arrest? • When force is justified in making an arrest? How much force is justified?

Chapter Outline

I.   Identifying Suspects at the Scene

    A.   Identification by driver's license

        1.   The REAL ID Act requires states to take new steps to verify the identity of applicants before issuing drivers' licenses and other ID cards.

        2.   Use of Reality Mobile's Reality Vision software

    B.   Mobile identification technology

        1.   Mobile Identifier™

    C.   Biometric identification

        1.   Facial recognition systems

    D.   Field identification or show-up identification

    E.   Developing a suspect

        1.   Information provided by victims, witnesses, and other persons likely to know about the crime or the suspect

        2.   Physical evidence left at the crime scene

        3.   Psychological or criminal profiling

        4.   Information in police files

        5.   Information in the files of other agencies

        6.   Informants

    F.   Victims and witnesses

    G.   Mug shots

    H.   Composite drawings and sketches

    I.   Developing a suspect through modus operandi (MO) information

    J.   Psychological or criminal profiling and geographic profiling

        1.   Geographic profiling is based on everyone having a pattern to their lives, particularly in relation to the geographical areas they frequent.

    K.   Racial profiling

    L.   Tracking

        1.   Footprints

        2.   Tire tracks

3. Other impressions

M. Other identification aids

1. Newspaper photos
2. Video
3. Newsfilms
4. Yearbook photos
5. Dental and orthopedic records
6. Facial reconstruction

N. Information in police files and files of other agencies

II. Locating Suspects

A. Information sources

1. Many information sources used to develop a suspect can also help to locate the suspect.
2. Potential methods for locating a suspect include:

    a. Telephoning other investigative agencies.
    b. Inquiring around a suspect's last known address.
    c. Checking the address on a prison release form.
    d. Questioning relatives.
    e. Checking with utility companies.
    f. Checking with other contacts.

III. Identifying Suspects

A. Photographic identification
B. Lineup identification

1. *United States v. Wade* (1967): No right to attorney during field identification, but suspects have a right to have counsel present at a lineup.
2. Suspects may refuse to participate in a lineup, but such refusals can be used against them in court (*Schmerber v. California,* 1966).
3. Level of certainty in making an ID

    a. A study on eyewitness identification by the Illinois State Police found that the sequential double-blind procedures resulted in a *higher* rate of false identification than did the simultaneous lineup.

IV. Surveillance, Undercover Assignments and Raids: The Last Resort

A. Surveillance, undercover assignments, and raids are used only when normal methods of continuing the investigation fail to produce results.

V. Surveillance

A. Purposes of surveillance:
   1. Gain information required for building a criminal complaint
   2. Determine an informant's loyalty
   3. Verify a witness's statement about a crime
   4. Gain information required for obtaining a search or arrest warrant
   5. Gain information necessary for interrogation of a suspect
   6. Identify a suspect's associates
   7. Observe members of terrorist organizations
   8. Find a person wanted for a crime
   9. Observe criminal activities in progress
   10. Make a legal arrest
   11. Apprehend a criminal in the act of committing a crime
   12. Prevent a crime
   13. Recover stolen property
   14. Protect witnesses

B. The surveillant
   1. The police investigator

C. The subject
   1. The target of the surveillance

D. Types of surveillance
   1. Stationary surveillance (fixed, plant, or stakeout)
   2. Moving surveillance (tight or close, loose, rough, on foot or by vehicle)
      a. Also known as "the tail"

E. Avoiding detection

F. Surveillance equipment

G. Aerial surveillance

H. Visual/video surveillance
   1. Video analysis
   2. Through-the-wall-surveillance (TWS)

I. Audio or electronic surveillance
   1. "Bugging" or wiretapping
      a. *Katz v. United States* (1967): "The Fourth Amendment protects people, not places."

J. Surveillance and the constitution.
   1. Thermal imaging (*Kyllo* case—requires warrants)

VI. Undercover Assignments

A. The objective of an undercover assignment may be to gain a person's confidence or to infiltrate an organization or group by using an assumed identity and to thereby obtain information or evidence connecting the subject with criminal activity.

  B. Undercover assignments can be designed to

     1. Obtain evidence for prosecution.

     2. Obtain leads into criminal activities.

     3. Check the reliability of witnesses or informants.

     4. Gain information about premises for use later in conducting a raid or an arrest.

     5. Check the security of a person in a highly sensitive position.

     6. Obtain information on or evidence against subversive groups.

  C. Precautions for undercover agents:

     1. Write no notes the suspect can read.

     2. Carry no identification other than the cover ID.

     3. Ensure that any communication with headquarters is covert.

     4. Do not suggest, plan, initiate, or participate in criminal activity.

  D. Entrapment

     1. Entrapment occurs only when the criminal conduct was "the product of the creative activity" of law enforcement officials.

     2. *Sorrells v. United States* (1932): "the conception and planning of an offense by an officer, and his procurement of its commission by one who would not have perpetrated it except for the trickery, persuasion or fraud of the officer."

  E. Sting operations

VII. Raids

  A. The objectives of a raid are to recover stolen property, seize evidence, or arrest a suspect. A raid must be the result of a hot pursuit or be under the authority of a no-knock arrest or search warrant.

  B. Planning a raid.

  C. Executing a raid.

  D. Precautions in conducting raids:

     1. Ensure that the raid is legal.

     2. Plan carefully.

     3. Assign adequate personnel and equipment.

     4. Thoroughly brief every member of the raiding party.

     5. Be aware of the possibility of surreptitious surveillance devices at the raid site.

  E. SWAT teams

VIII. Legal Arrests

  A. Police officers are authorized to make an arrest

1. For any crime committed in their presence

2. For a felony (or a misdemeanor, in some states) not committed in their presence, if they have probable cause to believe the person committed the crime

3. Under the authority of an arrest warrant

4. Sometimes a suspect will refuse to identify himself or herself. Pursuant to the Supreme Court's opinion in *Hiibel v. Sixth Judicial District Court of Nevada* (2004), a state law requiring a subject to disclose his name during a *Terry* stop does not violate the Fourth Amendment's ban on unreasonable search and seizure.

B. Residential entry after outdoors arrest is unconstitutional (*James v. Louisiana*, 1965)

C. Arresting a group of companions

   1. *Maryland v. Pringle* (2003): OK with probable cause when all suspects deny possession

D. Off-duty arrests

   1. Every department needs a policy that allows off-duty officers to make arrests. A suggested policy for off-duty arrests requires officers to

      a. Be within the legal jurisdiction of their agency.

      b. Not be personally involved.

      c. Perceive an immediate need for preventing crime or arresting a suspect.

      d. Possess the proper identification.

IX. Avoiding Civil Liability When Making Arrests

   A. False arrest

   B. Use of force

      1. When making an arrest, use only as much force as is necessary to overcome any resistance. If no resistance occurs, you may not use any force.

      2. *Graham v. Connor* (1989): five factors to evaluate alleged cases of excessive force:

         a. The severity of the crime

         b. Whether the suspect posed an immediate threat to the officer or others

         c. Whether the circumstances were tense, uncertain, and rapidly evolving

         d. Whether the suspect was attempting to evade arrest by flight

         e. Whether the suspect was actively resisting arrest

      3. Use-of-force continuums

   C. Less-lethal weapons

1. "Less-lethal does not imply never-lethal. Munitions fired from most less-lethal weapons can cause death if vital areas are struck: head, eyes, throat and possibly the upper abdomen." (Page, 2007, p.144)

   D. Restraints

      1. Handcuffs

      2. Aerosols

      3. Impact weapons

      4. Controlled electronic devices (CEDs)

         a. TASERs

         b. Stun guns

      5. Other less-lethal options: capture nets

   E. Use of deadly force

      1. Combating edged weapons

         a. Threat of knives or other edged weapons.

         b. Tests show it may be difficult to draw and fire before a suspect can clear the distance between officers and themselves.

         c. The "21-foot rule" versus "45-foot" rule.

      2. "Ramming" in pursuit as use of force

         a. *Scott v. Harris* (2007): The court concluded the suspect was liable, not the police.

      3. In-custody death: excited delirium

      4. Use of force and the mentally ill

      5. Suicide by police

   F. Use-of-force reports

X.   Summary

Chapter Questions

1. Field identification or show-up identification is the identification of a suspect by a victim or witness of a crime at the crime scene. The show-up must be
   a. close in time to the incident.
   b. close in location to the incident.
   c. always done when possible.
   d. none of these.

2. Suspects can be identified using
   a. field or show-up identification
   b. mug shots
   c. photographic identification or lineups
   d. all of these

3. Which of the following is a factor that courts use to evaluate alleged cases of excessive force?
   a. the severity of the crime
   b. whether the suspect posed an immediate threat to the officer or others
   c. whether the circumstances were tense, uncertain and rapidly evolving
   d. all of the above

4. Surveillance, undercover assignments and raids are used only
   a. when the case is important.
   b. when the case is a felony.
   c. when normal methods of continuing the investigation fail to produce results.
   d. occasionally.

5. The objective of surveillance is to
   a. only obtain information that can be used to solve narcotics-related crimes.
   b. obtain information about people, their associates, and their activities that may help to solve a criminal case or to protect a witness.
   c. obtain information about anyone and anything.
   d. none of these.

6. Undercover agents should take the following precautions:
   a. Write no notes that the subject can read.
   b. Carry police identification in case you need to make an arrest.
   c. Ensure that communication with headquarters is covert.
   d. Answers a and c.

7. SWAT stands for
   a. Special Weapons, Assault and Tactics
   b. Special Weapons and Tactics
   c. Secret Weapons, Arrest and Tracking
   d. None of the preceding

8. Police officers may make arrests for
   a. any criminal activity they are aware is occurring.
   b. any crime committed in their presence.
   c. any felony crime, whether committed in their presence or not.
   d. none of these.

9. These factors should be considered when deciding whether to investigate a crime:
   a. control factors
   b. solvability factors
   c. checklist factors
   d. whodunit factors

10. *United States v. Ash, Jr.* (1973) established that a suspect does not have the right to have an attorney present at a
    a. voice comparison
    b. lineup
    c. field identification
    d. handwriting exemplar

11. The amount of time it takes to identify a suspect is directly correlated to the length of time it takes to solve a crime.   True or False

12. *United States v. Ash, Jr.* established that a suspect does have the right to have counsel present at a field identification.   True or False

13. Investigators should never show witnesses mug shots since they will taint any future court identification.   True or False

14. Visatex is becoming more popular for drafting computer-generated composites.   True or False

15. Racial profiling is defined as the use of discretionary authority by law enforcement officers in encounters with minority motorists, typically within the context of a traffic stop, that result in disparate treatment of minorities.   True or False

16. Suicide by police is a phenomenon in which someone commits suicide directly in front of an officer.   True or False

17. Officers should tell witnesses viewing photographic lineups that the suspect may not be in the photographs.   True or False

18. Investigators should avoid having the same person make both a photographic and a lineup identification.   True or False

19. The objective of an undercover assignment may be to gain a person's confidence or to infiltrate an organization or group by using an assumed identity and to thereby obtain information or evidence connecting the subject with criminal activity.　　　True or False

20. The objective of a raid is only to arrest a suspect, so no warrant is needed.　　　True or False

21. One aid in determining authenticity of a driver's license is the *Drivers License* _____.

22. Investigators need to ask _____ questions and use an identification diagram to assist witnesses in describing suspects and vehicles.

23. _____ weapons are those used with the intent to avoid the use of deadly force.

24. Suspects may _____ to participate in a lineup, but such _____ can be used against them in court.

25. Factors crucial to resolving criminal investigations are called _____ _____.

26. Read suspects the _____ warning before questioning them.

27. Developing a suspect is much easier if the victim or _____ can describe and identify the person who committed the crime.

28. A composite image's main objective is to generate _____ for the investigating detectives

29. _____ profiling, which attempts to identify an individual's mental, emotional, and psychological characteristics, is most often used in crimes against people in which a motive is unknown.

30. Another viable alternative to racial profiling is "_____ a case."

31. What are some precautions that officers should take before conducting a raid?

32. Define reasonable force.

33. Define what a field identification or "show-up" identification, is, and how critical the time element is to this process.

34. One method of suspect identification is psychological or criminal profiling. Describe this process and the crimes that it is most commonly used to help solve.

35. Discuss the meaning of a pretextual traffic stop as it relates to profiling and any court decisions surrounding this procedure.

Case Study

36. An officer needs to complete a case involving an armed robbery. The victim was able to see the suspect enter a car without a mask when the victim was 25 feet away at 6:00 pm. What issues will develop with this identification and how would you work to overcome the issues?

_____

_____

_____

_____

_____

_____

_____

_____

_____

_____

_____

_____

Answer Key

1.	a	11.	True
2.	d	12.	False
3.	d	13.	False
4.	c	14.	True
5.	b	15.	True
6.	d	16.	False
7.	b	17.	True
8.	b	18.	True
9.	b	19.	True
10.	c	20.	False

21. (*Driver's License*) Guide

22. specific

23. Less-lethal

24. refuse, refusal

25. solvability factors

26. *Miranda*

27. witness

28. leads

29. Psychological

30. building

31. Officers must ensure that the raid is legal, plan carefully, assign adequate personnel and equipment, thoroughly brief every member of the raiding party, be aware of the possibility of surreptitious surveillance devices or booby traps at the raid site.

32. The amount of force a prudent person would use in similar circumstances.

33. Field identification is also referred to as a show-up identification. It involves an on-the-scene identification of a suspect by a victim of or a witness to a

crime. The identification must be made within a short period after the crime was committed, usually within 15 to 20 minutes. Some experts suggest that if a suspect has been temporarily detained, the show-up may occur as much as 2 hours after the crime occurred.

34. Psychological profiling attempts to identify an individual's mental, emotional, and psychological characteristics. It provides corroborative leads to a known suspect or possibly to an unknown suspect. It is primarily developed for violent crimes such as homicides, sex crimes, and crimes of ritual or serial sequence.

35. A pretextual traffic stop is when an officer stops a car and his intent (pretext) was not the real reason for the stop. An example is when an officer finds a reason to stop a vehicle for a minor traffic violation because he really suspects that the person in the car is in possession of illegal drugs but has no reasonable suspicion to make the stop for drug possession. *Whren v. United States* affirmed that officers could stop vehicles to allay any suspicions even though they have no evidence of criminal behavior. The legality of the stop will be gauged by its objective reasonableness.

Case Study Answer

36. There are many variables in this situation to affect the reliability of an eyewitness identification. These might include what time of year it was, how dark it was at 6:00 pm, what type of weather existed at that time, how well the victim could see, whether the victim required glasses to see (and if so, whether the victim was wearing his or her glasses), whether the suspect ever left the victim's field of vision, what visual obstacles existed, and what other confounding circumstances exist. Supporting the identification would depend on factors such as the details given in the victim's description of the suspect, whether this contained any individual characteristics of the suspect, and the length of time the victim observed the suspect.

DEATH INVESTIGATIONS

OUTLINE

- Classification of Deaths
- Elements of the Crime
- The Declining Clearance Rate
- Challenges in Investigation
- Equivocal Death
- Suicide
- Preliminary Investigation of Homicide
- Discovering and Identifying the Victim
- Estimating the Time of Death (ToD)
- The Medical Examination or Autopsy
- Unnatural Causes of Death and Method Used
- The Homicide Victim
- Witnesses
- Suspects
- Cold Cases
- Death Notification
- Strategies for Reducing Homicide
- The 10 Most Common Errors in Death Investigations
- A Case Study

Chapter 8
Death Investigations

By the end of this chapter, you should know how to define the terms and understand the application of the following concepts. Test your understanding of the chapter by verifying that you know this information. If you do not know it, review the chapter.

Can You Define?

adipocere	heat of passion	murder
algor mortis	hesitation wounds	noncriminal homicide
asphyxiation	homicide	postmortem lividity
autoerotic asphyxiation	instrumental violence	premeditation
cadaveric spasm	involuntary manslaughter	rigor mortis
criminal homicide	justifiable homicide	second-degree murder
criminal negligence	livor mortis	serial murder
defense wounds	lust murder	suicide
equivocal death	malicious intent	suicide by police
excusable homicide	manslaughter	third-degree murder
expressive violence	mass murder	toxicology
first-degree murder	mummification	voluntary manslaughter

Do you know?

- What a basic requirement in a homicide investigation is?
- What the four categories of death are?
- How to define and classify homicide, murder and manslaughter?
- What degrees of murder are frequently specified?
- How criminal and noncriminal homicide differ?
- How excusable and justifiable homicide differ?
- What the elements of each category of murder and manslaughter are?
- What special challenges a homicide investigation presents?

- What the first priority in a homicide investigation is?
- How to establish that death has occurred?
- What physical evidence is usually found in homicides?
- How to identify an unknown homicide victim?
- What factors help in estimating the time of death?
- What cadaveric spasm is and why it is important?
- What effect water has on a dead body?
- What information is provided by the medical examiner or coroner?

(continued)

(continued)

• What the most frequent causes of unnatural death are and what indicates whether a death is a suicide or a homicide? • What information and evidence are obtained from a victim? • Why determining a motive is important in homicide investigations?	• What similarities exist between school and workplace mass murders? • How the conventional wisdom about homicide has changed in some departments?

Chapter Outline

I.   Classification of Deaths

    A.   Natural causes

    B.   Accidental death

    C.   Suicide

    D.   Homicide

        1.   Criminal homicide

           a.   Murder

           b.   Manslaughter

        2.   Noncriminal homicide

           a.   Excusable

           b.   Justifiable

II.   Elements of the Crime

    A.   Causing the death of another human

    B.   Premeditation

    C.   Intent to effect the death of another person

    D.   Adequately provoked intent resulting from heat of passion

    E.   While committing or attempting to commit a felony

    F.   While committing or attempting to commit a crime not a felony

    G.   Culpable negligence or depravity

    H.   Negligence

III.   The Declining Clearance Rate

    A.   Crimes are either cleared, closed, or solved. The terms are used interchangeably.

1. In 2006, 60.7 percent of murders were cleared by arrest or exceptional means.
2. Homicide clearance rates in police departments are decreasing.
    a. In 1965, the average national clearance rate for homicide was 91 percent; in 1976, it was 79 percent; and in 2002, it was 64 percent.
    b. Some possible reasons: an increase in stranger-to-stranger homicides, which are difficult to solve; an increase in gang-related offenses that turn fatal; community and witness intimidation; and reductions in witness cooperation.
    c. Police departments also report an increasing number of "petty arguments" and incidents of "disrespect" that lead to homicides and an increase of the reentry of prisoners [650,000 per year] into communities.
    d. Backlogs and heavy caseloads in crime labs and coroners' offices may reduce investigative effectiveness.
    e. Increases in illegal immigration from countries where residents fear and do not trust the local police decrease the police department's effectiveness within these communities.
    f. The growth of "Thug Culture" and "Stop Snitchin'" campaigns reduces witness cooperation.
B. Aspects of the offense associated with likelihood of clearing a case
    1. Homicide circumstances: felony-related homicides are more difficult to clear than those with other circumstances.
    2. Weapons: homicides committed with weapons that bring the offender and victim into contact with one another increase the likelihood of clearing.
    3. Location: homicides committed in residences increases the likelihood of clearing.
C. Law enforcement actions affecting clearance
    1. The initial response
        a. The first officer on the scene immediately notifies the homicide unit, the medical examiner's office and the crime lab.
        b. The first officer on the scene immediately secures the area and attempts to locate witnesses.
        c. The detective assigned to the case arrives at the scene within 30 minutes of being notified.
    2. Actions of the detectives
        a. Three or four detectives, instead of one or two, were assigned to the case.
        b. The detectives took detailed notes describing the crime scene, including measurements.
        c. Detectives followed up on all information provided by witnesses.

   d. At least one detective assigned to the case attended the postmortem examination.

  3. Other police actions

   a. A computer check using the local criminal justice information system was conducted on the suspect or on any guns found.

   b. A witness interviewed at the crime scene provided valuable evidence such as information about circumstances of the death or the perpetrator's motivation, an identification of the suspect or victim, or the whereabouts of the suspect.

   c. Witnesses, friends, acquaintances, and neighbors of the victim were interviewed.

   d. The medical examiner prepared a body chart of the victim and it was included in the case file.

   e. The attending physician and medical personnel were interviewed.

   f. Confidential informants provided information.

   g. Many departments use a homicide case review solvability chart to determine which cases to focus on.

 D. Impact of Unsolved Homicides

 E. Cases exceptionally cleared: In certain situations, elements beyond law enforcement's control prevent the agency from arresting and formally charging the offender. When this occurs, the agency can clear the offenses exceptionally.

IV. Challenges in Investigation

 A. Include pressure by the media and the public, the difficulty of establishing that a crime has been committed, identifying the victim and establishing the cause and time of death.

V. Equivocal Death

 A. Investigations are situations that are open to interpretation.

  1. Cause may be homicide, suicide, or accidental death

  2. Staged crime scene

  3. Sudden, unexplained infant death

 B. In-custody deaths

  1. Equivocal?

  2. Excited delirium?

  3. Homicide?

  4. Suicide?

  5. Natural causes?

  6. Abuse of force?

  7. Overdose?

       a.   Often associated with chronic drug use

   8. Because police are involved in the death, a thorough but objective investigation is critical. Some of the things an investigator should look for are

       a.   Was the person sweating?

       b.   Was the person restrained prior to his or her death or at the time of his or her death?

       c.   Does the person have a callous on the underside of his or her thumb, indicative of crack cocaine use.

VI.   Suicide

  A. The following warning signs are often observable in someone contemplating suicide:

    1. Talking, writing, or joking about suicide or death

    2. Giving away prized possessions

    3. Making final arrangements

    4. Depressive symptoms

    5. Sudden, unexplained recovery from a profound depression

    6. Marked feelings of helplessness and hopelessness

    7. Risk-taking behavior

    8. Self-mutilating behavior

    9. Organizing a suicidal plan or gathering the means

   10. Previous suicide attempts

   11. Anxiety over impending or anticipated discipline

   12. Chemical abuse

  B. Suicide by police

    1. Causative factors may include the following:

       a.   Financial concerns

       b.   Divorce or serious relationship issues

       c.   Loss of a job or retirement

       d.   Being investigated

       e.   Health problems

  C. Suicide of police officers

    1. Each year, as many officers kill themselves each year (about 300) as are killed by criminals in the line of duty, making suicide the most lethal factor in a police officer's line of work.

    2. Exact statistics vary, but police officers have a much greater chance of killing themselves than of dying in the line of duty and are much more likely to kill themselves than are other municipal workers.

    3. About 97 percent of officer suicides involve their own duty weapon.

VII.   Preliminary Investigation of Homicide

    A.   "The homicide crime scene is, without a doubt, the most important crime scene to which a police officer or investigator will be called upon to respond." (Geberth, 2006, p.140)

    B.   Determining that death has occurred

        1.   Signs of death include lack of breathing, lack of heartbeat, lack of flushing of the fingernail bed when pressure is applied to the nail and then released, and failure of the eyelids to close after being gently lifted.

    C.   The focus of the homicide investigation

        1.   Crime scene priorities:

            a.   Identify the victim

            b.   Establish the time of death

            c.   Establish the cause of and the method used to produce death

            d.   Develop a suspect

        2.   The "fact-finding capsule": Three important rules for investigative tactics:

            a.   Specificity

            b.   Element of surprise

            c.   Haste

VIII.   Discovering and Identifying the Victim

    A.   In some cases, identification may be difficult because of decomposition, burning or other accidental or deliberate damage.

    B.   Technologies such as ground-penetrating radar, magnetometers, metal detectors, and infrared thermography may be used.

    C.   Specially trained cadaver dogs may be used.

    D.   Homicide victims may be identified by

        1.   Immediate family members.

        2.   Relatives.

        3.   Acquaintances.

        4.   Personal effects.

        5.   Fingerprints.

        6.   DNA analysis.

        7.   Dental and skeletal studies.

        8.   Clothing and laundry marks.

        9.   Missing person files.

        10.   Record a complete description and take photographs if possible.

IX.   Estimating the Time of Death (TOD)

A. In many homicides, there is a delay between the commission of the crime and the discovery of the body, sometimes only minutes, other times years.

B. Time of death relates directly to whether the suspect could have been at the scene of the crime.

C. Recent death: within one half hour.

D. Death that occurred half an hour to 4 days prior can be determined to within 4 hours.

    1. Body temperature

    2. Rigor mortis

    3. Postmortem lividity

    4. Examination of the eyes

    5. Examination of stomach contents

E. Many days after death

    1. Decomposition

F. Effects of water

G. Factors suggesting a change in the victim's routine

X.   The Medical Examination or Autopsy

A. Exhuming a body for medical examination

XI.   Unnatural Causes of Death and Method Used

A. Gunshot wounds

    1. Suicide indicators:

        a. Gun held against the skin

        b. Wound in mouth or in right temple if victim is right-handed and left temple if left-handed

        c. Not shot through clothing, unless shot in the chest

        d. Weapon present, especially if tightly held in the hand

    2. Murder indicators:

        a. Gun fired from more than a few inches away

        b. Angle or location that rules out self-infliction

        c. Shot through clothing

        d. No weapon present

B. Stabbing and cutting wounds

    1. Stab wounds

    2. Cutting wounds

    3. Suicide indicators:

        a. Hesitation wounds

        b. Wounds under clothing

        c. Weapon present, especially if tightly clutched

        d. Usually wounds at throat, wrists, or ankles

        e. Seldom disfigurement

        f. Body not moved

    4. Murder indicators:

        a. Defense wounds

        b. Wounds through clothing

        c. No weapon present

        d. Usually injuries to vital organs

        e. Disfigurement

        f. Body moved

C. Blows from blunt objects

D. Asphyxia

    1. Choking

    2. Drowning

    3. Smothering

    4. Hanging

    5. Strangulation

    6. Poisons, chemicals, and overdoses of sleeping pills

    7. Autoerotic asphyxiation

    8. Indicators of accidental death during autoerotic practices include

        a. Nude or sexually exposed victim.

        b. Evidence of solo sexual activity.

        c. Mirrors placed to observe the ritual.

        d. Evidence of masturbation and presence of such items as tissues or towels for cleanup.

        e. Presence of sexual fantasy aids or sexually stimulating paraphernalia (vibrators, dildos, sex aids, and pornographic magazines).

        f. Presence of bondage.

    9. Other types of autoerotic death

        a. Such fatalities have involved electrocution, crushing, sepsis following perforation of the bowel, and accidental self-impalement.

E. Poisoning

    1. Poisoning, one of the oldest methods of murder, can occur from an overwhelming dose that causes immediate death or from small doses that accumulate over time and cause death.

2. Poisons can be injected into the blood or muscles, inhaled as gases, absorbed through the skin surface, taken in foods or liquids, or inserted into the rectum or vagina.

3. Look for signs of accidental poisoning, signs of possible toxins, and use the forensic tests used to prove homicidal poisoning took place.

4. Those at the highest risk of poisoning are the terminally ill, mentally incapacitated, drug addicts, the elderly, and the very young.

5. "The other high-risk group is the unwanted spouse or lover." (Steck-Flynn, 2007, p.118)

6. Perpetrators of homicidal poisonings are often employed in the medical or care giving fields.

7. Homicidal poisoning can be accomplished with any one of thousands of substances, but some are far more common that others.

8. Among the most commonly used is arsenic, known as the King of Poisons and the Poison of Kings.

9. Cyanide, also commonly used, is a favorite in mass homicides, suicides, and politically motivated killings.

10. Strychnine, given in large enough doses, produces "a dramatic and horrifying death with the victim's body frozen in mid-convulsion, eyes wide open" (Steck-Flynn, 2007, pp.121–124).

11. Experts in toxicology (the study of poisons) can determine the type of poison, the amount ingested, the approximate time ingested, and the effect on the body.

12. Investigators should ask the following questions to help determine if a homicidal poisoning has occurred:

    a. Was the death sudden?

    b. Is there a caregiver who has been associated with other illnesses or death?

    c. Did the victim receive medical treatment and appear to recover only to die later?

    d. Did the caregiver have access to restricted drugs or other chemicals?

    e. Was the victim isolated by the caregiver? Did the caregiver position himself to be the only one with access to the victim's food or medications?

    f. Was there a history of infidelity of either the victim or spouse?

    g. Is there a history of the deaths of more than one child?

F. Burning

G. Explosions, electrocution, and lightning

H. Drug-related deaths

1. Some evidence suggests that the decline in homicides since the early 1990s is partially attributable to declining levels of drug market activity.

 I. Vehicular deaths

  1. Motor vehicle traffic crashes were the leading cause of death for every age 3 through 6 and 8 through 34, in 2005.

XII. The Homicide Victim

 A. Domestic-violence homicides

  1. Determining truth about relationships between family members is key to solving domestic-violence homicides.

  2. Many batterers eventually kill their intimate (one out of six murders is a partner homicide), and women who leave their batterers face a 75 percent greater risk of being killed by them than do those who stay.

  3. In some cases, batterers themselves become victims of homicide.

 B. Law enforcement officers killed in the line of duty

  1. The FBI reports that in 2006, 48 law enforcement officers were feloniously killed as a result of 47 separate incidents (*Officers Feloniously Killed 2006*).

  2. Of these, 12 officers died as a result of felonious attacks during arrest situations, 10 were fatally assaulted when ambushed, 8 were killed while responding to disturbance calls (e.g., bar fights, family quarrels), and 8 were killed while conducting traffic pursuits or stops.

XIII. Witnesses

XIV. Suspects

 A. Mass murder: occurs when multiple victims are killed in a single incident by one or a few suspects

 B. Serial killing: the killing of three or more separate victims, with a "cooling off" period between the killings

 C. Lust murderers

  1. Two types of lust murderers are often described—organized and disorganized.

   a. The organized offender is usually of above-average intelligence, methodical, and cunning. He is socially skilled and tricks his victims into situations in which he can torture and then murder them.

   b. In contrast, the disorganized offender is usually of below-average intelligence, has no car, and is a loner who acts on impulse.

XV. Cold Cases

A. The point at which a case is moved to the cold case shelf varies from agency to agency, depending on the number of cases and the staff available.

B. Before reinterrogating a suspect who is serving time for another crime, make sure the *Miranda* warning is properly issued. If the inmate had previously requested counsel, no interrogation is allowed without counsel.

C. Volunteer cold case squads: use of local retired investigators

D. Benefits of a cold case unit

    1. "Case clearance rates increase, guilty parties are brought to justice, innocent parties are exonerated, victims' survivors get a measure of relief, and investigators benefit from the personal satisfaction associated with solving cold cases." (Cronin et al., 2007, p.116)

XVI. Death Notification

A. Officers must be prepared for a wide range of emotional and physical reactions people may have upon hearing of a death.

B. "Notification should be done in person, in pairs, in private, in plain language, and in time. Avoid words such as *passed on, expired.* And make notification before the family sees it on the news." (Page, 2008, p.20)

C. Notifying the family of an officer who has been killed is even more difficult.

XVII. Strategies for Reducing Homicide

A. Two trends are changing reactive view.

    1. The first trend is crime analysis showing that homicide is greatest for young people in core, inner-city neighborhoods and is often related to drugs, guns, and gangs.

    2. The second trend is the emergence of community policing and a problem-solving approach to crime. In this approach, homicide is viewed as part of a larger, more general problem—violence.

XVIII. The 10 Most Common Errors in Death Investigations.

A. Improper response to the scene

B. Failure to protect the crime scene

C. Not handling suspicious deaths as homicides

D. Responding with a preconceived notion

E. Failure to take sufficient photos

F. Failure to manage the process (maintaining the chain of custody and proper documentation)

G. Failure to evaluate victimology

H. Failure to conduct effective canvass

I. Failure to work as a team

J.   Command Interference or inappropriate action

XIX.   A Case Study

  A.   Lessons learned by the Miami-Dade homicide unit:
    1. Work as a team—having two interviews going at the same time led to success.
    2. Avoid gender prejudice—women can kill too.
    3. Stay attuned to subtle clues.

XX.   Summary

Chapter Questions

1. The four types of death are
   a. natural, accidental, suicide, homicide (noncriminal or criminal).
   b. natural, accidental, suicide, murder.
   c. accidental, suicide, murder, voluntary.
   d. none of these.

2. Premeditation is
   a. planning over a short period (a day or so) of a murder.
   b. consideration, planning, or preparing for an act, no matter how briefly, before committing it.
   c. thinking about a murder and then carrying it out.
   d. none of these.

3. Suicide by police is
   a. when an individual commits suicide in front of officers.
   b. when an individual asks the officers to shoot them.
   c. when an individual wishing to commit suicide purposely forces an officer to shoot him or her.
   d. none of these.

4. The first priority at a scene is to
   a. protect the crime scene.
   b. check the area for suspects.
   c. give emergency aid to the victim or others at the scene.
   d. look for witnesses to the events.

5. Once the priority matters are taken care of, the investigator should
   a. identify the victim, establish time of death, and establish the cause of and the method used to produce death, and develop a suspect.
   b. identify the suspect, look for witnesses, notify relatives.
   c. look for safety issues and solve the crime.
   d. none of the preceding.

6. A cadaveric spasm is
   a. when the dead person spasms for a few minutes.
   b. when a person shouts out during the last few second of the death process.
   c. a condition that occurs in specific muscle groups rather than the entire body.
   d. all of these.

7. An indicator of a suicide using a knife is
   a. no weapon present.
   b. defensive wounds.
   c. wounds through clothing.
   d. hesitation wounds.

8. Serial murder is the separate killing of at least how many victims?
   a. 2
   b. 3
   c. 4
   d. 5

9. A dead body that sinks in water usually remains immersed for
   a. 5 to 7 days in warm water and 3 to 4 weeks in cold water.
   b. 8 to 10 days in warm water and 2 to 3 weeks in cold water.
   c. 2 to 3 weeks in warm water and 5 to 6 weeks in cold water.
   d. None of these.

10. The appearance of the eyes also assists in estimating the time of death. A partial restriction of the pupil occurs in ____ hours.
    a. 1
    b. 2
    c. 5
    d. 7

11. A basic requirement in a homicide investigation is to establish whether death was caused by a criminal act.   True or False

12. First-degree murder requires premeditation and the intent to cause death.   True or False

13. Equivocal deaths are those deaths whose cause is open to interpretation.   True or False

14. In *Flippo v. West Virginia*, the Supreme Court determined that there is a somewhat general, but limited exception to the search and seizure rules for a murder investigation.   True or False

15. Most cases of hanging are suicide whereas most cases of strangulation are murder.   True or False

16. A mass murder occurs when multiple victims are killed in a single incident by one or a few suspects.   True or False

17. A lust murder is a sex-related homicide involving sadistic, deviant assault.   True or False

18. The conventional wisdom about homicide has changed in some departments from viewing it as a series of unconnected, uncontrollable episodes to seeing it as part of the larger, general problem of violence, which can be addressed proactively.   True or False

19. Insects offer valuable clues as to the time a body was left or buried.   True or False

20. All murders are homicides, but not all homicides are
    murders.   True or False

21. A basic requirement in a homicide investigation is to establish whether death
    was caused by a _____ action.

22. Although suicide is not a criminal offense, in most states it is a crime to
    _____ to commit suicide.

23. If another individual is the direct or indirect cause of the death, the death is
    classified as _____.

24. Criminal homicide is subdivided into murder and _____, both of
    which are further subdivided.

25. Noncriminal homicide is subdivided into excusable and _____
    homicide.

26. _____ is the most severe statutory crime, one of the few for which the
    penalty can be life imprisonment or death.

27. First-degree murder requires _____ and the intent to cause
    death.

28. _____-_____ murder includes the intent to cause death, but not
    premeditation.

29. _____ manslaughter is accidental homicide that results from extreme
    (culpable) negligence.

30. A person causing a death while depraved and committing acts evident of
    such depravity is guilty of _____-_____ murder.

31. Describe the Violent Crime Apprehension Program (VICAP) and its benefit to
    law enforcement.

32. Define "heat of passion."

33. How can you tell that a person has died recently?

34. Describe postmortem lividity.

35. Describe autoerotic asphyxiation.

Case Study

36. You have been assigned a case involving what appears to be a murder-suicide. The female seems to be the victim and the male the perpetrator. However, there are some bothersome issues about the case. The weapon was found between the two bodies, but it was closer to the female than the male. The location of the wounds on the male's chest is also curious. It appears that he may have been shot through the chest, a less likely place for suicides to shoot themselves than the mouth or the temple. He seems to have taken some time to die because there is quite a bit of blood around the room. What investigative clues would you initially look for at the scene?

_____

_____

_____

_____

_____

_____

_____

_____

_____

_____

_____

_____

_____

Answer Key

1. a
2. b
3. c
4. c
5. a
6. c
7. d
8. b
9. b
10. d

11. True
12. True
13. True
14. False
15. True
16. True
17. True
18. True
19. True
20. True

21. criminal
22. attempt
23. homicide
24. manslaughter
25. justifiable
26. Murder
27. premeditation
28. Second-degree
29. Involuntary
30. third-degree

31. Violent crime investigations have been greatly enhanced because of this program that coordinates violent crime investigations throughout the United States. Operated by the FBI, this program reviews information submitted and compares it with other agencies about similar cases and MOs. This is especially important in serial killings and major violent crimes.

32. It assumes that the act was committed when the suspect suddenly became extremely emotional, thus precluding premeditation.

33. If the time of death is less than half an hour before examination the body is still warm; mucous membranes are still moist but drying; blood is still moist but drying; the pupils have begun to dilate; and in fair-skinned people, the skin is becoming pale.

34. After death, blood coagulates down to the lowest points of the body. If a body is on its back, lividity appears in the lower portion of the back and legs.

35. The victim has sought to intensify sexual gratification by placing a rope or other ligature around the neck and causing just enough constriction to create hypoxia, or a deficiency of oxygen in the bloodstream that results in semi-consciousness.

Case Study Answer

36. There are many ways that you could try to determine what happened. Establishing a time of death for each individual would be a good place to start, especially if it could be demonstrated that one died after the other, but might not provide a total answer. Many methods can be used to determine time of death, but their results might not be conclusive enough to prove the case. The exact cause of death and the location of wounds on the body would also be helpful, as would the weapon, if one was used. Once the primary evidence has been found and examined, the investigator might want to turn to circumstantial evidence to see if it reveals further useful information. After all this, it may still not be possible to determine the perpetrator, but these would be good ways of starting.

ASSAULT, DOMESTIC VIOLENCE, STALKING AND ELDER ABUSE

OUTLINE

- Assault: An Overview
- Classification
- Elements of the Crime
- Special Challenges in Investigation
- The Preliminary Investigation
- Investigating Domestic Violence
- Investigating Stalking
- Investigating Elder Abuse

Chapter 9
Assault, Domestic Violence, Stalking and Elder Abuse

By the end of this chapter, you should know how to define the terms and understand the application of the following concepts. Test your understanding of the chapter by verifying that you know this information. If you do not know it, review the chapter.

Can You Define?

aggravated assault	elder abuse	indicator crimes
assault	felonious assault	simple assault
battery	femicide	stake in conformity
cyberstalking	full faith and credit	stalker
domestic violence	*in loco parentis*	stalking

Do you know?

• What constitutes assault?	• What evidence is likely to be at the scene of an assault?
• How simple assault differs from aggravated assault?	• To aid in data collection, what offenses might be categorized as separate crimes?
• When force is legal?	
• What the elements of simple assault, aggravated (felonious) assault and attempted assault are?	• What constitutes domestic violence?
• What special challenges are posed in an assault investigation?	• What constitutes stalking?
• How to prove the elements of both simple and aggravated assault?	• What constitutes elder abuse? How prevalent it is?

Chapter Outline

I. Assault: An Overview

    A. Assault is unlawfully threatening to harm another person, actually harming another person, or attempting unsuccessfully to do so.

II. Classification

    A. NCVS data indicates a victimization rate of 20.7 per 1,000 persons age 12 or older in 2006. The rate was 15.2 for simple assault and 5.5 for aggravated assault. FBI data shows 860,853 aggravated assaults in 2006. The rate was estimated at 287.5 offenses per 100,000 inhabitants. The Office for Victims of Crime reports that one person is assaulted every 7.2 seconds. The clearance rate for aggravated assault was 54.0 percent in 2007.

    B. Officers assaulted: The FBI reports that in 2006 58,638 officers were assaulted while performing their duties, at a rate of 11.8 per 100 officers: 30.9 percent were assaulted responding to disturbance calls (family quarrels, bar fights, etc.); 12.2 percent were handling, transporting, or maintaining custody of prisoners; and 11.1 percent were performing traffic stops.

    C. Legal force

        1. Physical force may be used legally in certain instances.
        2. In specific instances, people and law enforcement officers can legally use reasonable physical force.
        3. Force used in self-defense is also justifiable.

III. Elements of the Crime

    A. Simple assault:
        1. Intent to do bodily harm to another
        2. Present ability to commit the act
        3. Commission of an overt act toward carrying out the intention

    B. Aggravated or felonious assault:
        1. High probability of death
        2. Serious, permanent disfigurement
        3. Permanent or protracted loss or impairment of body members or organ or other severe bodily harm

    C. Attempted assault: Requires proof of intent along with some overt act toward committing the crime.

IV. Special Challenges in Investigation

    A. Distinguishing the victim from the suspect
    B. Determining whether the matter is civil or criminal
    C. Determining whether the act was intentional or accidental

145

D. Obtaining a complaint against a simple assault

E. May be dangerous for responding officers

V. The Preliminary Investigation

A. Proving the elements of assault: Establish the intent to cause injury, the severity of the injury inflicted, and whether a dangerous weapon was used.

B. Evidence in assault investigations: photographs of injuries, clothing of the victim or suspect, weapons, broken objects, bloodstains, hairs, fibers, and other signs of an altercation.

VI. Investigating Domestic Violence

A. History of domestic violence: from male privilege to criminal act

1. Police interventions in domestic violence cases have changed from treating wife assault as a matter most appropriately addressed privately within the family to regarding it is a crime appropriate for criminal justice intervention.

B. The cycle of violence

C. Types of assault

1. Physical violence
2. Sexual violence
3. Threats of physical or sexual violence
4. Psychological/emotional violence

D. Prevalence of domestic violence and its victims

1. Domestic violence includes intimate partner violence as well as violence between family members.

2. Intimate relationships involve current or former spouses, boyfriends or girlfriends, including same sex relationships.

3. The OVC "Crime Clock" shows that one woman in victimized by an intimate partner every 1.3 minutes; one man is victimized every 6.7 minutes; and one child is reported abused or neglected every 35 seconds.

4. Some victims choose to stay with their batterers for fear that leaving would further enrage their partner. Statistics document that many batterers eventually kill their intimate. In recent years, one third of female murder victims were killed by their intimate partners.

5. Women as abusers

a. Women who assaulted their male partners were more likely to avoid arrest

b. Four decision points: the decision to file charges (versus rejection for insufficient evidence); to file as a felony (versus a misdemeanor or probation violation); to dismiss for insufficient evidence (versus full prosecution); and to reduce felony charges to a misdemeanor or violation of parole.

    c.   The study found suspect gender to be statistically significant in all four outcomes, in favoring female over male suspects, suggesting that frequently female intimate violence perpetrators are viewed more as victims than offenders.

6. Gay and lesbian domestic violence

    a.   The dynamics of same-sex domestic violence are similar to those of opposite-sex domestic violence in many respects.

    b.   When the law enforcement response to domestic violence incidents involving heterosexual and same-sex couples is compared, the couples receive similar treatment.

    c.   Same-sex victims rarely are afforded the same protection as heterosexuals.

7. When the abuser is a police officer

    a.   Forty percent of officers said they had gotten out of control and acted violently toward their spouse or children in the last 6 months.

    b.   Both officers and wives said that 37 percent to 41 percent of the relationships involved some level of physical violence, a considerably higher figure than comparable studies performed with military families (32 percent) and four times higher than the 10 percent figure for the general public.

    c.   Almost one quarter (24 percent) of the officers reported having used some form of violence against their spouses, roughly the same as the 28 percent provided by the wives.

E. Predicators and precipitators of domestic violence

1. History of family violence

2. Gun ownership by the abuser

3. Unemployment of the batterer

4. Estrangement, where the victim has moved out of the previously shared residence

5. Animal cruelty

    a.   The Humane Society of the United States found that 91 percent of adult victims and 73 percent of children, upon entering the shelter, mention incidents of companion animal abuse. But only about 18 percent of the shelters routinely ask victims about their pets.

    b.   Seventy-five percent of women entering shelters are pet owners. Of those women, 71 percent said their abuser had either injured or killed their family pet.

    c.   In 88 percent of homes with prosecutable animal cruelty, children were also being physically abused.

    d.   In more than two-thirds of cases involving elder abuse, the perpetrator may neglect or abuse the elder's pet as a form of control or retaliation, out of frustration over their caretaking responsibilities, or as a way to extract financial assets from the victim.

    e. Blum (2006) notes, "Many serial killers and even students involved in recent school shootings have histories of abusing animals first before moving on to human targets."

F. The police response

    1. The largest category for officer assaults is response to domestic calls (30.5 percent).

    2. There are usually two principal players: the victim and the suspect.

    3. A third element, the rescuer, occurs when the police arrive.

    4. Always respond with a backup or two, separate people for the interviews, impound all firearms at the scene, and never drop your guard just because you're dealing with a homosexual or lesbian couple.

    5. To arrest or not?

        a. Officers should not base their decisions regarding arrest on their perception of the willingness of the victim or witnesses to testify.

        b. The victim need not sign a complaint.

        c. Dual arrest policies allow officers to arrest both parties when injuries to both sides are observed.

        d. A dual arrest policy does not preclude the single arrest of the primary aggressor only, if the officer is able to make that determination. Factors to consider in making this assessment include

            (1) Prior domestic violence involving either person.

            (2) The relative seriousness of the injuries inflicted upon each person involved.

            (3) The potential for future injury.

            (4) Whether one of the alleged batteries was committed in self-defense.

            (5) Any other factor that helps the officer decide which person was the primary physical aggressor.

        e. Specialized domestic violence may be a positive approach.

    6. Police nonresponse

        a. Several studies have examined whether the police response to domestic violence calls does in fact receive a lower priority than other crime calls.

        b. The results generally show an increasingly high priority being placed on such calls.

G. Effectiveness of various interventions

    1. Results of studies that have examined the effectiveness of batterer intervention program (BIPs) suggest that perhaps the most significant factor in the rehabilitation of a batterer is the offender's stake in

conformity, a constellation of variables that, in effect, comprise "what an offender has to lose," such as marital status, residential stability, or employment.

2. Studies show strong support for the continued emphasis on interagency (and community) coordinated responses to intimate partner abuse.

3. The biggest obstacle to such partnerships is poor officer attitude about partnering, domestic violence, or both.

H. Restraining orders

1. The Violence Against Women Act of 1994 assigns full faith and credit to valid orders of protection, meaning that an order issued anywhere in the country is legally binding and enforceable nationwide.

2. Some studies have found that women who seek restraining orders are well aware of their potential ineffectiveness.

3. A new Massachusetts law that requires an offender who violates a domestic order of protection to wear a global positioning system (GPS) monitoring device.

I. Legislation

1. Mandatory arrest laws
2. Restrictions on firearms

J. Avoiding lawsuits

1. Failure to respond appropriately to domestic violence can result in serious financial liability to local governments.

2. Lawsuits include failure of the police to protect them, particularly when there have been restraining orders issued; *Thurman v. City of Torrington,* (1984).

VII. Investigating Stalking

A. Stalking is a crime of power and control. Stalking is the willful or intentional commission of a series of acts that would cause a reasonable person to fear death or serious bodily injury and that, in fact, does place the victim in fear of death or serious bodily injury.

B. Types of stalking: intimate or former intimate stalking, acquaintance stalking, stranger stalking

1. Stalking behaviors also may include persistent patterns of leaving or sending the victim unwanted items or damaging or threatening to damage the victim's property, defaming the victim's character, or harassing the victim via the Internet by posting personal information or spreading rumors about the victim.

2. A well-kept stalking log, supported by physical evidence (phone recordings, e-mails, etc.), will be strong evidence at a trial and will empower the victim.

3. Cyberstalking

C. Legislation and department policies

D. The police response

VIII. Investigating Elder Abuse

A. Prevalence and nature of elder abuse
B. Elder abuse is the physical and emotional abuse, financial exploitation, and general neglect of the elderly.
C. Between 1 and 2 million Americans age 65 or older have suffered elder abuse.
D. For every one case of elder abuse, neglect, exploitation, or self-neglect reported to authorities, about five more go unreported.
E. The OVC Crime Clock shows that one elderly person is victimized every 2.7 minutes.
F. Types of elder abuse
1. Physical abuse
2. Sexual abuse
3. Emotional or psychological abuse
4. Neglect
5. Financial or material exploitation
6. Self-neglect
G. Indicators of elder abuse
1. Signs of physical abuse of the elderly:
a. Injury incompatible with the given explanation
b. Burns
c. Cuts, pinch marks, scratches, lacerations, or puncture wounds
d. Bruises, welts or discolorations
e. Dehydration or other malnourishment without illness-related causes, unexplained weight loss
f. Pallor, sunken eyes or cheeks
g. Eye injury
h. Soiled clothing or bedding
i. Lack of bandages or injuries or stitches where needed, or evidence of unset bone fractures
j. Injuries hidden under the breast or on the other areas of the body normally covered by clothing
k. Frequent use of the emergency room or clinic
2. Signs of financial abuse of the elderly
a. A recent acquaintance expressed an interest in finances, promises to provide care, or ingratiates him or herself with the elder.
b. A relative or caregiver has no visible means of support or is overtly interested in the elder's financial affairs.

    c.   A relative or caregiver expresses concern over the cost of caring for the elder, or is reluctant to spend money for needed medical treatment.

    d.   The utility and other bills are not being paid.

    e.   The elder's placement, care, or possessions are inconsistent with his or her estate.

    f.   A relative or caregiver isolates the elder, makes excuses when friends or family call or visit, and does not give the elder the messages.

    g.   A relative or caregiver gives implausible explanations about finances, and the elder is unaware of or unable to explain the arrangements made.

    h.   Checking account and credit card statements are sent to a relative or caregiver and are not accessible to the elder.

    i.   At the bank, the elder is accompanied by a relative or caregiver who refuses to let the elder speak for himself or herself, or the elder appears nervous or afraid of the person accompanying him or her.

    j.   The elder is concerned or confused about missing money.

    k.   There are suspicious signatures on the elder's checks, or the elder signs the checks and another party fills in the payee and amount sections.

    l.   There is an unusual amount of banking activity, particularly just after joint accounts are set up or someone new starts helping with the elder's finances.

    m.   A will, power of attorney, or other legal document is drafted, but the elder does not understand its implications.

H. Risk factors for elder abuse

   1. Domestic violence grown old; personal problems of the abuser, especially in the case of adult children; caregiver stress, personal characteristics of the elder (dementia, disruptive behaviors, problematic personality traits); and the cycle of violence.

   2. Domestic violence is a learned problem-solving behavior transmitted from one generation to the next.

I. The police response

   1. The police have the lawful right and the legal duty to check on an elder's welfare regardless of how much their caregiver objects.

     a.   Three potential abusers of the elderly are family members, hired caregivers (in home or in a nursing home), and professional con artists.

   2. Police should be patient with victims, who may be embarrassed, scared, or forgetful.

3. Investigators should take good photographs both during the first response and several days later. A comprehensive video is helpful for neglect cases.

4. Investigators should collect anything that looks like evidence, including financial records.

5. Investigators should observe the general condition of the residence when arriving to investigate an elder abuse complaint.

6. Once inside, investigators should carefully observe the general conditions and interview the alleged victim. Non-verbal cues are as important as verbal ones.

7. Investigators should look for the tell-tale cues, such as whether the suspected perpetrator is hanging around and refusing to leave the senior alone to answer questions, or whether the potential victim is looking the officer in the eye and answering direct questions.

8. Findings from NIJ-funded research projects help caretakers, medical personnel, Adult Protective Services agencies, and law enforcement officers recognize abuse indicators—known as forensic markers—to help distinguish between injuries caused by mistreatment and those that are the result of accidents, illnesses, or aging.

9. One critical aspect of an investigation of physical elder abuse is to determine if bruising is the result of an accident or of abuse.

10. NIJ-funded researchers also examined data from the deaths of elderly residents in long-term care facilities to identify potential markers of abuse:

    a. Physical condition/quality of care

    b. Facility characteristics

    c. Inconsistencies

    d. Staff behaviors

J. Reducing elder abuse

1. Advise senior contacts to remain active in some type of community group (church, social, neighborhood).

2. Provide information about the services and resource centers in neighborhoods.

3. Use Triad, a cooperative effort of the International Association of Chiefs of Police (IACP), AARP (formerly the American Association of Retired Persons), and the National Sheriffs' Association (NSA).

4. Develop a curriculum that provides guidance in building evidence-based cases by drawing from the collective wisdom of law enforcement, elder abuse specialists, prosecutors, and trainers.

IX. Summary

Chapter Questions

1. Simple assault is
   a. a minor assault involving limited touching.
   b. intentionally causing another person to fear immediate bodily harm or death or intentionally inflicting or attempting to inflict bodily harm on the person.
   c. a threat to harm someone.
   d. none of these.

2. Which of the following is not an element of simple assault?
   a. intent to threaten someone
   b. intent to do bodily harm to another
   c. present ability to commit the act
   d. commission of an overt act toward carrying out the intention

3. Which of the following is not an element of aggravated assault?
   a. a high probability of serious injury
   b. a high probability of death
   c. serious, permanent disfiguration
   d. permanent or protracted loss of the function of any body member or organ or other severe bodily harm

4. Which of the items listed are not special challenges of the investigator in assault cases?
   a. distinguishing the victim from the suspect
   b. determining whether the matter is civil or criminal
   c. determining whether the act was accidental or intentional
   d. determining whether the incident involves serious intent

5. The cycle of violence involves
   a. tension building, the battering episode, the honeymoon.
   b. tension, arguments, making up.
   c. tension, release, the honeymoon.
   d. threats, battering, compliance.

6. The term *intimate partner* includes
   a. current or former spouses.
   b. opposite-sex cohabiting partners.
   c. same-sex cohabiting partners.
   d. all of these.

7. Types of stalkers include
   a. intimate or former intimate partner.
   b. stranger stalker.
   c. simple obessional and love obessional.
   d. all of these.

8. Which of the following best describes "intentionally causing another person to fear immediate bodily harm or death or intentionally inflicting or attempting to inflict bodily harm on the person?"
   a. simple assault
   b. aggravated assault
   c. felonious assault
   d. forceful assault

9. Teachers have the authority in many states to use minimum force to maintain discipline, stop fights on school property, or prevent destruction of school property. This authority is derived from a term that means "in the place of the parent." Which of the following terms describes this authority?
   a. *parentis controlsis*
   b. *instructis loco*
   c. *control educaus*
   d. *in loco parentis*

10. Domestic violence is commonly thought of as a three-phase cycle. Which of the following choices is not included in this cycle?
    a. tension-building stage
    b. acute battering stage
    c. assaultive intent stage
    d. honeymoon stage

11. Assault is an intentional or unintentional act of injury caused by force directed toward another person.   True or False

12. Attempted assault requires proof of intent along with some overt act toward committing the crime.   True or False

13. Investigators or detectives generally make the first contact with victims.   True or False

14. Two important pieces of evidence in an assault would be the weapon used and photographs of injuries.   True or False

15. Domestic violence is a pattern of behavior involving physical, sexual, economic, and emotional abuse, alone or in combination by an intimate partner, often to establish and maintain power and control over the other partner.   True or False

16. Research has found that children who witness abuse or are abused themselves are more likely to abuse a spouse or child when they become adults.   True or False

17. Although the majority of abuse victims are women, women may also perpetrate such violence.   True or False

18. Research supports a connection between animal cruelty as a child and domestic violence as an adult.   True or False

19. Officers should not disregard potential attackers, even the victim.   True or False

20. Research has shown that law enforcement agencies do give a high priority to responding to domestic violence calls for service.   True or False

21. _____ is unlawfully threatening to harm another person, actually harming another person, or attempting unsuccessfully to do so.

22. Aggravated or _____ assault is an unlawful attack by one person on another to inflict severe bodily injury.

23. _____ _____ is the intentional use of physical force (e.g., shoving, choking, shaking, slapping, punching, burning, or use of a weapon, restraints, or one's size and strength against another person) with the potential for causing death, disability, injury, or physical harm.

24. Domestic violence is found at all income levels and in all races, but it occurs more often in households facing _____ distress.

25. Some victims choose to stay with their batterers for fear that leaving would further _____ their partner.

26. Research suggests _____ abuse may occur more often in police families than among the general public.

27. Police officers must listen to the facts and determine who the _____ is if the assault is not continuing when they arrive.

28. In any assault, one of the most important kinds of evidence is _____ of any injuries.

29. A _____ is someone who intentionally and repeatedly follows, tries to contact, harasses, or intimidates another person.

30. _____ _____ is the physical and emotional abuse, financial exploitation, and general neglect of the elderly.

31. What is aggravated, or felonious assault?

32. What are some factors that predict or precipitate episodes of domestic violence?

33. When should an officer arrest for a domestic violence case?

34. When responding to a domestic violence arrest, when should an officer make a dual arrest, or a single arrest?

35. Describe the defining characteristics of a stalker.

Case Study

36. A woman has reported that her ex-boyfriend has been harassing her. She has recordings of him calling and telling her that he will kill her. He has been on top of a building near her place of business and has watched her, calling her to tell her what he is doing. He has also slashed the tires on her car. Explain how you would investigate this case and how you would assess its level of danger.

_____

_____

_____

_____

_____

_____

_____

_____

_____

_____

_____

_____

_____

_____

_____

Answer Key

1. b	11. False
2. a	12. True
3. a	13. False
4. d	14. True
5. a	15. True
6. d	16. True
7. d	17. True
8. a	18. True
9. d	19. True
10. c	20. True

21. Assault

22. felonious

23. Physical violence

24. economic

25. enrage

26. domestic

27. offender

28. photographs

29. stalker

30. Elder abuse

31. Aggravated, or felonious assault is an unlawful attack by one person on another to inflict severe bodily injury.

32. Some factors include a history of family violence, gun ownership by the abuser, unemployment of the batterer, estrangement, indicator crimes, and animal cruelty.

33. Basically, any evidence that would lead an officer to make an arrest in any other situation also applies to spousal situations (intimate partners).

34. Officers should consider prior domestic violence involving either person, the relative seriousness of the injuries inflicted upon each person involved, the potential for future injury, whether one of the alleged batteries was committed in self-defense, any other factor that helps the officer decide which person was the primary physical aggressor.

35. A stalker is someone who intentionally and repeatedly follows, tries to contact, harasses, or intimidates another person.

Case Study Answer

36. The case is complex. There are several factors to consider in determining how dangerous this individual is or might be, including the fact that he threatened to kill her, he has watched her from the top of a building, and he has called her to tell her that he is watching her and what she is doing. A restraining order is probably indicated in this case. However, you will need to research the case to see if you can put enough information together to justify a restraining order. You have much information to work with, including the stalking, the threats to kill her, so this will not be difficult. Although restraining orders are difficult to enforce (in terms of catching the individual), they offer limited protection, and if they are violated, an arrest warrant can be obtained for the individual. You will need to investigate the recordings to see if you can get a voice match. In addition, you need to look for proof that he slashed the tires. You have his own statements on tape, and they are the most valuable in terms of building your case. This case will be time-consuming, but he seems to be a clear threat, and the danger should be considered high.

SEX OFFENSES

OUTLINE

- Investigating Obscene Telephone Calls
- Investigating Prostitution
- Investigating Human Trafficking
- Classification of Sex Offenses
- Rape/Sexual Assault
- Sex Offenders
- Challenges to Investigation
- The Police Response
- The Victim's Medical Examination
- Interviewing the Victim
- Interviewing Witnesses
- Taking a Suspect into Custody and Interrogation
- Coordination with Other Agencies
- Prosecution of Rape and Statutory Charges
- Civil Commitment of Sex Offenders after Sentences Served
- Sex Offender Registry and Notification
- Other Means to Monitor Sex Offenders

Chapter 10
Sex Offenses

By the end of this chapter, you should know how to define the terms and understand the application of the following concepts. Test your understanding of the chapter by verifying that you know this information. If you do not know it, review the chapter.

Can You Define?

bigamy	indecent exposure	sadist
blind reporting	intimate parts	sadomasochistic abuse
child molestation	oral copulation	sexual contact
cunnilingus	pedophile	sexual penetration
date rape	penetration	sexually explicit conduct
exhibitionists	prostitution	sodomy
fellatio	rape	statutory rape
forcible rape	Rohypnol	voyeurism
incest		

Do you know?

- What the key distinction between human trafficking and human smuggling is?
- How sex offenses are classified?
- How rape is defined and classified?
- What the elements of sexual assault are?
- What modus operandi factors are important in investigating a sexual assault?
- What special challenges exist in investigating sex offenses?
- What blind reporting is and what its advantages are?
- What evidence is often obtained in sex offense investigations?
- What evidence to seek in date rape cases?
- What agencies can assist in a sexual assault investigation?
- What is generally required to obtain a conviction in sexual assault cases?
- Whether recent laws have reduced or increased the penalties for sexual assault and why?
- Which three federal statutes form the basis for sex offender registries?

Chapter Outline

I. Investigating Obscene Telephone Calls

    A. Making obscene telephone calls is a crime and can be a form of harassing stalking behavior. The calls may or may not be of a sexual nature, but the procedures for investigating either would be the same.

II. Investigating Prostitution

    A. Soliciting sexual intercourse for pay—raises several concerns, including moral and nuisance concerns, public health concerns, personal safety concerns, economic concerns, and civil rights concerns.

    B. Single versus serial murders of prostitutes: serial murderers differed from single murderers in three areas—sexual aggression, deviant sexual interests, and active sexual fantasies.

III. Investigating Human Trafficking

    A. Thirteenth Amendment prohibits slavery or involuntary servitude.

    B. Human trafficking

        1. Global phenomenon that involves obtaining or maintaining the labor or services of another through force, fraud, or coercion in violation of an individual's human rights.

        2. Generates billions of dollars in profit each year; one of the world's fastest growing criminal activities, operating on the same scale as the illegal trade of guns and drugs.

        3. Yields $9.5 billion a year in global profits, of which $3.5 billion is generated in the United States.

        4. As many as 900,000 people are trafficked per year internationally, with 17,000 of these victims trafficked into the United States.

        5. Trafficking in Victims Protection Act (TVPA) was passed in 2000 to address the problem of trafficking in persons and to provide for protection and assistance for victims, prosecution of offenders, and prevention efforts internationally.

    C. Trafficking versus smuggling: Key distinction lies in the individual's freedom of choice. Smuggling occurs when someone is paid to assist another in the illegal crossing of borders.

    D. Myths and misconceptions of human trafficking

        1. The victim knew what he or she was getting into.

        2. The victim committed unlawful acts.

        3. The victim was paid for services.

        4. The victim had freedom of movement.

        5. There were opportunities to escape but the victim didn't.

        6. Trafficking involves the crossing of borders.

        7. U.S. citizens can't be trafficked.

8. The trafficker's actions are culturally appropriate.

9. It can't be trafficking when the trafficker and victim are related or married.

   E.   Challenges to law enforcement

     1. Identifying human trafficking

     2. Moving victims from one jurisdiction to another

     3. Challenges in identification

     4. Jurisdictional venue

     5. Attitudes of law enforcement agencies

     6. Trafficking victims are often unable to communicate in English.

IV.   Classification of Sex Offenses

   A.   Sex crimes

     1. Bigamy

     2. Child molestation

     3. Incest

     4. Indecent exposure

     5. Prostitution

     6. Sodomy

     7. Rape

   B.   Sex offenses

     1. Cunnilingus

     2. Fellatio

     3. Oral copulation

     4. Penetration

     5. Sadomasochistic abuse

     6. Sexually explicit conduct

   C.   Other sex offense terminology

     1. Intimate parts

     2. Sexual contact

     3. Sexual penetration

V.   Rape/Sexual Assault

   A.   The National Violence against Women Survey (NVAWS) reports, "Nearly 18 million women and almost three million men in the United States have been raped at some time in their lives, and in a single year, more than 300,000 women and 93,000 men are estimated to have been raped." Most had been also threatened, assaulted, and battered.

   B.   Nearly two thirds of rape incidents include drugs or alcohol by the offender.

C. According to the Uniform Crime Reports, there were an estimated 92,455 forcible rapes reported to law enforcement in 2006.

D. Most sex crimes continue to go unreported. Women have been reluctant to report offenders, particularly those who involve friends or family.

E. Elements of the crime of rape
    1. An act of sexual intercourse
    2. With a person other than a spouse
    3. Committed without the consent of the victim
    4. Against the victim's will and by force

VI. Sex Offenders

A. MO factors important in investigating sex offenders include type of offense, words spoken, use of a weapon, actual method of attack, time of day, type of location, and victim's age.

B. Rapists can be categorized as motivated by either power or anger, and each category is divided into two subcategories.
    1. Power rapist
        a. Manhood reassurance: plans attack; observes victim; chooses same race, meek, nonassertive victim, probably inside the victim's residence; uses stealth; usually attacks at night; may have erection problems, is relatively nonviolent, is likely to apologize
        b. Manhood assertion: seldom pre-plans; selects victim by chance of same age and race; is a smooth talker; rapes at nighttime; spends a long time at the sex act; has retarded ejaculation; tears clothing off the victim; is likely to threaten
    2. Anger rapist
        a. Retaliatory/punishment: acts spontaneously; chooses victims who resemble females in his life; uses immediate excessive force; attacks at any time of day; engages in violent, painful sex acts and degrading, humiliating acts; spends short time; uses profanity; likely to injury victims
        b. Excitation/sadism: has violent fantasies and plans attack; chooses victims of same age and race; brandishes a weapon; attacks anytime; engages in experimental sex; inserts objects into body cavities; spends a long time; uses excessive, brutal force; cuts clothing off; protects his identity; straightens scene; shows no remorse

C. Information to obtain:
    1. Conduct field identification.
    2. If victim knows assailant, obtain suspect's name, address, complete description, and nature of the relationship with victim.
    3. Obtain arrest and search warrants.

4. If victim doesn't know suspect, check MO files and have victim look at photo files.

VII. Challenges to Investigation

    A. Special challenges to investigating rape include
        1. The sensitive nature of the offense
        2. Social attitudes
        3. The victim's horror or embarrassment
    B. Blind reporting allows sexual assault victims to retain their anonymity and confidentiality while sharing critical information with law enforcement.

VIII. The Police Response

    A. As soon as you arrive at the scene, announce yourself clearly to allay fears the victim may have that the suspect is returning.
    B. Explain to the victim what is being done for her safety. If the rape has just occurred, if there are serious injuries, or if it appears the victim is in shock, call for an ambulance.
    C. Protect the crime scene and broadcast a description of the assailant, means and direction of flight, and the time and exact location of the assault.
    D. Physical evidence
        1. Stained or torn clothing; scratches, bruises, or cuts; evidence of a struggle; semen and bloodstains
        2. How the offender gained access to the victim.
        3. There also may be primary, secondary, or multiple scenes.
        4. Preserve physical evidence by securing the scene, ensuring the safety of the victim and witnesses.
        5. A log of all persons at the scene is important, including emergency personnel.
        6. Medical personnel should be asked to help preserve evidence, such as carrying a stretcher around pools of liquid on the ground or floor.
        7. The victim's clothing can be placed in a clean paper evidence bag and sealed.
        8. Maintain the chain of custody where evidence on the victim is concerned by accompanying the victim to the hospital.
        9. Don't allow civilians or family members access to the scene. (Recall the Jon Benet Ramsey case.)
      10. Search warrants should include a list of materials expected to be recovered from an offender who indulged in sexual fantasies.
    E. Investigating date rape
        1. Also known as acquaintance rape.

2. Presence of alcohol, "club," or "date rape" drugs: Referred to as "drug-facilitated sexual assault."

3. The three most common date rape drugs are Rohypnol, gamma hydroxybutyric acid (GHB), and ketamine.

4. Another date rape drug is Ecstasy, or MDMA (3,4 methylenedioxymethamphetamine).

IX. The Victim's Medical Examination

A. The rape victim should have a medical examination as soon as possible to establish injuries, to determine whether intercourse occurred, and to protect against venereal disease and pregnancy.

B. The victim should be asked to sign a release form that authorizes the medical facility to provide police a copy of the examination record.

X. Interviewing the Victim

A. Basic guidelines for victim interviews:
1. Select a location where the victim will be comfortable.
2. Interview the victim in private.
3. Attempt to establish rapport by using sympathetic body language.
4. Explain the necessity for asking sensitive questions.
5. Make a complete report of the victim's appearance and behavior.
6. Obtain a detailed account of the crime, including the suspect's actions and statements.
7. Determine exactly where and how the attack occurred.
8. Determine the exact details of resistance.
9. Establish lack of consent.
10. Obtain the names of any witnesses.
11. Obtain as much information as possible about the suspect.

B. Establishing the behavior profile in sex offense cases
1. Three types of rapist behavior
   a. Physical (use of force)
   b. Verbal
   c. Sexual
2. Three common approaches
   a. Con
   b. Blitz
   c. Surprise
3. Four common methods of control
   a. Mere presence
   b. Verbal threats
   c. Display of a weapon

            d.   Use of physical force

      4. Four levels of physical force

            a.   Minimal

            b.   Moderate

            c.   Excessive

            d.   Brutal

   C. Ending the victim interview: Explain available services, what will happen next.

   D. Follow-up investigation.

XI.   Interviewing Witnesses

   A. Locate witnesses as soon as possible.

   B. Determine whether a relationship exists between the witness and the victim or the offender.

XII.   Taking a Suspect into Custody and Interrogation

   A. If a suspect is apprehended at the scene, record any spontaneous statements made by the suspect and photograph him.

   B. Do not allow communication among suspect, victim, and witness.

   C. Remove the suspect from the scene as soon as possible.

   D. When interrogating sex offenders, obtain as much information as possible, yet remain nonjudgmental. Interview the suspect last.

XIII.   Coordination with Other Agencies

   A. A number of other agencies and individuals assist in handling rape cases.

   B. Rape cases often involve cooperation with medical personnel, social workers, rape-crisis-center personnel, and the news media.

XIV.   Prosecution of Rape and Statutory Charges

   A. Conviction in sexual assault cases requires

      1. Medical evidence.

      2. Physical evidence such as torn clothing.

      3. Evidence of injuries.

      4. A complaint that is reported reasonably close to the time of the assault.

   B. False reports.

      1. Victims make false reports of sexual assault for a number of reasons, including revenge on former lovers, covering up a pregnancy, or getting attention.

XV.   Civil Commitment of Sex Offenders after Sentences Served

A.   Because sex offenders have a high recidivism rate following their release from jail or prison, many have called for legislation that allows for the civil commitment of sex offenders upon completion of the sentence.

B.   Sex offender civil commitment (SOCC) has been enacted in 16 states amid widespread controversy.

XVI.   Sex Offender Registry and Notification

A.   The evolution of sex offender registries can be traced to a trilogy of federal statutes: the Jacob Wetterling Act, Megan's Law, and the Pam Lychner Act.

1.   In 2006, the Adam Walsh Child Protection and Safety Act was signed into law. Title I of the act was the Sex Offender Registration and Notification Act (SORNA), establishing comprehensive standards for sex offender registration and notification.

2.   National Sex Offender Public Registry (NSOPR) Web site, which incorporates real time public data on sex offenders around the country allowing citizens to view registries outside their own states.

3.   The challenge is to balance the communities' rights to access public information with the protections provided to convicted offenders

B.   The National Association of Criminal Defense Lawyers (NACDL) asserts, "It's a fiction to say that this is a civil matter when this is, in fact, an extension of the criminal punishment" (VanderHart, 2008).

C.   However, in April 1998, the Supreme Court rejected constitutional challenges that claimed that the laws' notification requirements represented an unconstitutional added punishment.

XVII.   Other Means to Monitor Sex Offenders

A.   Satellite GPS

B.   DMV screening motor vehicle databases when sex offenders apply for or renew a driver's license.

XVIII. Summary

Chapter Questions

1. Sex offenses can include
   a. bigamy.
   b. child molestation.
   c. incest, indecent exposure, sodomy, rape (sexual assault).
   d. all of these.

2. The elements of the crime of sexual assault commonly include
   a. an act of sexual intercourse.
   b. with a person other than a spouse.
   c. committed without the victim's consent and against the victim's will.
   d. all of these.

3. Special challenges to the investigation of sex crimes include
   a. the sensitive nature of the offense.
   b. social attitudes.
   c. victim's horror.
   d. all of these.

4. The "date rape drug" is
   a. aspirin.
   b. morphine.
   c. Rohypnol.
   d. none of these.

5. Several specific areas should be covered in the behavior-oriented interview of rape victims. The areas should include
   a. a careful interview of the victim about the rapist's behavior.
   b. an analysis of the behavior to ascertain the motivation underlying the assault.
   c. compilation of a profile of the individual likely to have committed the crime.
   d. all of these.

6. Which of the following terms best describe a person who is sexually attracted to young children?
   a. voyeur
   b. pedophile
   c. sadist
   d. transient

7. When someone is paid to assist another in illegally crossing a border, this is called
   a. smuggling
   b. human trafficking
   c. alligatoring
   d. beachheading

8. Marrying another person when one or both parties are already married is best defined as
   a. indecent exposure.
   b. incest.
   c. bigamy.
   d. rape.

9. An individual who binds and tortures his unwilling victim for sexual gratification is best described as a
   a. peeping Tom.
   b. voyeur.
   c. cunnilingus.
   d. sadomasochist.

10. Which of the following two categories are rapists traditionally categorized under?
    a. power or control
    b. power or anger
    c. sadism or stealth
    d. forcible or nonforcible

11. Bigamy is the marrying of another person when one is already married.   True or False

12. Incest is sexual intercourse with another person more closely related than a second cousin.   True or False

13. Sexual assault and rape mean the same thing legally.   True or False

14. Fellatio is sexual activity involving oral contact with the male genitals.   True or False

15. Statutory rape is not actually or legally rape, because the victim agreed to the act.   True or False

16. The element of sexual intercourse does not require that a complete sex act accompanied by ejaculation occurred.   True or False

17. Police should not accept blind reporting because they do not get to investigate the crime.   True or False

18. Evidence in a rape case shows the amount of force that occurred, establishes that a sex act was performed, and links the act with the suspect.   True or False

19. Officers investigating a sexual assault where the victim cannot give much information about the crime should suspect that a date rape drug is involved.   True or False

20. Medical exams of individuals believed to be victims of sexual assault look for signs of sexual assault in the vagina, anus, or mouth.   True or False

21. The police may use _____ or _____ if given a signed affidavit from the victim stating the facts related to obscene telephone calls.

22. Two types of rapists are _____ rapists and _____ rapists.

23. Additional evidence in date rape cases may include the presence of _____ and/or _____ in the victim's system.

24. If a rapist used _____ force, it may identify the offender as a sadist.

25. _____ is best known as a "date rape drug" and is the oldest drug used in this crime.

26. The term _____ is typically is associated with sexual intercourse with a minor.

27. _____ is the element most difficult to prove in a rape case.

28. The Jacob Wetterling Act, Megan's Law, and the Pam Lychner Act all have to do with registration of _____ _____ .

29. Section 2423 of the _____ Act prohibits "coercion or enticement of minor females and the taking of male or female persons across the state line for immoral purposes."

30. _____ reporting allows sexual assault victims to retain their anonymity and confidentiality while sharing critical information with law enforcement.

31. Describe how the Thirteenth Amendment to the U.S. Constitution affects human trafficking.

32. List and describe the first things that an officer arriving at the scene of a sex crime should do.

33. Human trafficking is a growing problem in America. What are some of the tips investigators can use when attempting to detect these types of crimes?

34. Describe the differences between forcible rape and statutory rape.

35. The modus operandi (MO) factors surrounding the investigation of sex offenses are critically important. List several of these factors that investigators should pay close attention to.

Case Study

36. A victim of a sexual assault comes to the department three days after the assault. What problems are created by her late reporting of the incident? What steps would you take as the investigator to overcome these problems?

_____

_____

_____

_____

_____

_____

_____

_____

_____

_____

_____

_____

_____

_____

_____

_____

Answer Key

1. d	11. True
2. d	12. False
3. d	13. False
4. c	14. True
5. d	15. False
6. b	16. True
7. b	17. False
8. c	18. True
9. d	19. True
10. b	20. True

21. traps or traces

22. power, anger

23. alcohol and/or drugs

24. excessive

25. Rohypnol

26. statutory

27. Force

28. sex offenders

29. Mann

30. Blind

31. The actual clause from the constitution states that "Neither slavery nor involuntary servitude [is allowed], except as punishment for a crime whereof the party shall have been duly convicted." The intent is to define and eliminate the use of slavery. Thus, the clause disallows slavery and involuntary servitude.

32. As soon as officers arrive at the scene, they should announce themselves to allay fears the victim may have that the suspect is returning. At a minimum, officers on the scene should record their arrival time, determine the victim's

location and condition, determine whether the suspect is at the scene, protect the crime scene, identify and separate witnesses, initiate crime broadcast if applicable.

33. Investigators should pay attention to the following leads when investigating human trafficking: They should consider businesses in their community that might serve as fronts for trafficking. They should determine if building security is used to keep people out or to keep them in. What are the working conditions? Do workers have freedom of movement? Do they live and work in the same place? Do they owe a debt to their employers? Do the employers control their workers' immigration documents? Officers should also consider the appearance and mannerisms of the workers. Are there signs of trauma, fatigue, injuries or other evidence of poor care? Are individuals withdrawn, afraid to talk, or is the communication censored?

34. Forcible rape is sexual intercourse against a person's will by the use or threat of force. Statutory rape is sexual intercourse with a minor, with or without consent. Minimum ages regarding consent vary from state to state.

35. When investigating sex offenses, investigators should be aware of the following factors: (1) The type of offense, (2) words spoken by the perpetrator, (3) use of a weapon, (4) the actual method of attack, (5) the time of day the offense occurred, (6) the location of the offense, and (7) the victim's age.

Case Study Answer

36. Investigating this rape case will be more difficult than investigating a rape case reported right away, but it will not be impossible. There may still be evidence at the scene of the crime. The clothing the victim was wearing may also be available. There may be injuries and other marks on the victim's body that can serve as evidence. Other witnesses may exist as well. The reason the victim waited to report the crime will probably prove to be important and should be examined. The time between the act and the reporting may be an issue if the case goes to trial, and the prosecuting attorney will need information about why the delay occurred. The defense attorney will raise this as an issue and probably as part of the defense. Other problems that are created is loss of evidence (DNA, possibly fingerprints at the scene, the crime scene may have been disturbed, and other issues). None of these issues mean that the case will be impossible to prove, but as an investigator, you need to strive to put the pieces together. Even with the time gap, don't give up.

CRIMES AGAINST CHILDREN

OUTLINE

- Maltreatment of Children: Neglect and Abuse
- The Extent of the Problem
- The Effects of Child Abuse and Neglect
- Risk Factors for and Causes of Abuse and Neglect
- Child Abuse and Neglect Laws
- Case Processing
- Challenges in Investigating Maltreatment Cases
- The Initial Report
- The Police Response
- Evidence
- The Suspect
- The Pedophile
- Commercial Sexual Exploitation
- Missing Children: Runaway or Abducted?
- Children as Witnesses in Court
- Preventing Crimes against Children

Chapter 11
Crimes Against Children

By the end of this chapter, you should know how to define the terms and understand the application of the following concepts. Test your understanding of the chapter by verifying that you know this information. If you do not know it, review the chapter.

Can You Define?

chicken hawk	misoped	physical abuse
emotional abuse	molestation	seesaw model
exploitation	Munchausen syndrome	sexual abuse
hebephile	Munchausen syndrome by proxy (MSBP)	sexual exploitation
kidnapping		sexual seduction
lewdness	neglect	sudden infant death syndrome (SIDS)
maltreatment	osteogenesis imperfecta (OI)	temporary custody without hearing
mandated reporters	pedophile	
minor		

Do you know?

• What crimes against children are frequently committed?	• When a child should be taken into protective custody?
• What the four common types of maltreatment are?	• What factors to consider in interviewing child victims?
• What the most common form of child maltreatment is and how serious it is?	• Whether children are generally truthful about abuse?
• What has been identified as the biggest single cause of death of young children?	• Who usually reports crimes against children?
• What effects child abuse can have?	• What evidence is important in these cases?
• What the two leading causes of child abuse are thought to be?	• What things can indicate child neglect or abuse?
• Typically what three components are included in child abuse/neglect laws?	• What types of sex rings exist in the United States?
• What challenges are involved in investigating crimes against children?	• How pedophiles typically react when discovered?
	• What the Child Protection Act involves?

(continued)

(continued)

• What three law enforcement approaches are models to combat child sexual exploitation? • What challenges a missing child report presents?	• What the most common type of child abduction is? • What the AMBER Alert program is? • How crimes against children can be prevented?

Chapter Outline

I.   Maltreatment of Children: Neglect and Abuse

    A.   Maltreatment means to treat roughly or abuse. Maltreatment exists in many forms and along a continuum of severity and chronicity.

    B.   Definitions of the various types of maltreatment vary from state to state and even locality to locality, but all are based on minimum standards set by federal law.

    C.   The federal Child Abuse Prevention and Treatment Act, as amended by the Keeping Children and Families Safe Act of 2003, defines child abuse and neglect as

        1.   Any recent act or failure to act on the part of a parent or caretaker which results in death, serious harm, serious physical or emotional harm, sexual abuse or exploitation; or

        2.   An act or failure to act that presents an imminent risk of serious harm.

    D.   The four common types of maltreatment are neglect, physical abuse, emotional abuse, and sexual abuse.

        1.   Neglect is the most common form of child maltreatment and may be fatal.

            a.   Child neglect often occurs in homes and apartments that house methamphetamine labs.

        2.   Sexual abuse

            a.   Sexual seduction

            b.   Lewdness

            c.   Molestation

II.   The Extent of the Problem

    A.   Children as victims of violent crime:

        1.   One of every four violent crime victims is a juvenile, and most are female.

        2.   More than one-third of juvenile victims of violent crime are under age 12.

        3.   About two-thirds of violent crimes with juvenile victims occur in a residence.

4. Few statutory rapes involve both juvenile victims and juvenile offenders, with the majority of victims being females (95 percent), most of whom were ages 14 or 15. Male offenders were much older than their female victims.

5. The number of juveniles murdered in the U.S. fell 44 percent from 1993 to 2002, to the lowest level since the mid-1980s.

6. Child fatalities: During 2006,

    a. An estimated 1,530 children died because of child abuse or neglect.

    b. The overall rate of child fatalities was 2.04 deaths per 100,000 children.

    c. More than 40 percent (41.1%) of child fatalities were attributed to neglect; physical abuse also was a major contributor to child fatalities.

    d. More than three-quarters (78.0%) of the children who died because child abuse and neglect were younger than 4 years old.

    e. Infant boys (younger than 1 year) had the highest rate of fatalities, at 18.5 deaths per 100,000 boys of the same age in the national population.

    f. Infant girls had a rate of 14.7 deaths per 100,000 girls of the same age.

    g. Child abuse has been identified as the biggest single cause of death of young children.

    h. Child fatalities may be underreported: variation among reporting requirements and definitions of child abuse and neglect, variation in death investigative systems and in training for investigators, variation in state child fatality review processes, and the amount of time it may take to establish the cause of death.

B. Seriousness of the problem, two conflicting views

1. The maximalist alarmist perspective: the problem of child and sexual abuse is reaching epidemic proportions.

2. The minimalist skeptical perspective: maximalist estimates are drastically inflated.

III. The Effects of Child Abuse and Neglect

A. Child abuse and neglect can result in serious and permanent physical, mental, and emotional damage, as well as in future criminal behavior.

IV. Risk Factors for and Causes of Abuse and Neglect

A. Characteristics of children that increase their risk of being abused: premature birth, birth to adolescent parents, colic, congenital deficiencies or abnormalities, hospitalization of the newborn resulting in lack of parental contact, and lack of parent-child bonding.

B. The seesaw model conceptualizes other causes of child abuse, illustrating both functional and nonfunctional families and two critical factors: stress and resources.

C. The two leading causes of child abuse are thought to be poverty and violence between husbands and wives.

D. The cycle of abuse

   1. Childhood abuse is often associated with delinquency.

   2. Abused children may become violent offenders.

V.   Child Abuse and Neglect Laws

A. Typically child abuse/neglect laws have three components:

   1. Criminal definitions and penalties

   2. A mandate to report suspected cases

   3. Civil process for removing the child from the abusive or neglectful environment.

B. Federal legislation

   1. The Federal Child Abuse Prevention and Treatment Act passed in 1974 and amended in 1978.

      a. Any of the following elements constitutes a crime: "The physical or mental injury, sexual abuse or exploitation, negligent treatment, or maltreatment of a child under the age of 18, by a person who is responsible for the child's welfare under circumstances that indicate the child's health or welfare is harmed or threatened."

      b. Federal courts have also ruled that parents are free to strike children because "the custody, care and nurture of the child resides first in the parents."

      c. A determination of "reasonableness" was made in *Ingram v. Wright* (1977) regarding the use of physical punishment of students by teachers: The punishment was not to be "degrading or unduly severe."

   2. The Child Abuse Prevention and Enforcement Act (2000) made more funds available for child abuse and neglect enforcement and prevention initiatives.

   3. The Adam Walsh Child Protection and Safety Act (2006) is aimed at tracking sex crime offenders and subjecting them to stiff, mandatory minimum sentences.

C. State laws

   1. Since the 1960s, every state has enacted child abuse and neglect laws.

2. On the whole, states offer a bit more protection to children by statute than does the federal government.

3. Legal definitions vary from state to state.

VI. Case Processing

A. Most child abuse and neglect cases enter the child welfare system through child protective services (CPS) agencies

B. The term *child protective services* generally refers to services provided by an agency authorized to act on behalf of a child when parents are unable or unwilling to do so.

C. CPS may provide protective custody of a child outside the home or provide protective supervision of the child within the family unit at any point until a case is closed or dismissed.

VII. Challenges in Investigating Maltreatment Cases

A. Protecting the child

1. If the possibility of present or continued danger to the child exists, the child must be removed into protective custody.

2. Temporary custody without hearing usually means for 48 hours.

B. The need to involve other agencies: The multidisciplinary team approach

1. A multidisciplinary team consists of professionals who work together to ensure an effective response to reports of child abuse and neglect.

2. National Fingerprint for Children Identification project provides information to law enforcement agencies about the identification of children who have been fingerprinted and listed in their files.

3. The media can help when speed of information dissemination is critical

C. Difficulty in interviewing children

1. Limited vocabulary of very young children

2. Embarrassment and fear of older children

3. Short attention spans

D. Credibility concerns

1. In most child abuse cases, children tell the truth to the best of their ability.

2. Children frequently lie to get out of trouble, but they seldom lie to get into trouble.

3. A child's motivation for lying may be revenge, efforts to avoid school or parental disapproval, efforts to cover up for other disapproved behavior, or, in the case of sexual abuse, an attempt to explain a pregnancy or to obtain an abortion at state expense.

VIII. The Initial Report

A. Most reports of child neglect or abuse are made by third parties such as teachers, physicians, neighbors, siblings, or parents. Seldom does the victim report the offense.

B. Mandated reporters includes teachers, school authorities, child-care personnel, camp personnel, clergy, physicians, dentists, chiropractors, nurses, psychologists, medical assistants, attorneys, and social workers.

C. Such a report may be made to the welfare department, the juvenile court, or the local police.

D. In most states, action must be taken on a report within a specified time, frequently 3 days.

IX. The Police Response

A. Interviewing abused children
   1. Do not have a family member present.
   2. Investigators must maintain rapport.
   3. Make the child feel comfortable.
   4. Use cognitive interview techniques.

B. To assess the child's credibility, use the following criteria:
   1. Does the child describe acts or experiences to which a child of his or her age would not normally have been exposed?
   2. Does the child describe circumstances and characteristics typical of a sexual assault?
   3. How and under what circumstances did the child tell? What were the child's exact words?
   4. How many times has the child given the history, and how consistent is it regarding the basic facts of the assault?
   5. How much spontaneous information does the child provide? How much prompting is required?
   6. Can the child define the difference between the truth and a lie?

C. A program called "Finding Words" trains officers in conducting child interviews and specifically teaches rapport, anatomy identification, touch inquiry, abuse scenarios, and closure protocols.
   1. *Building rapport* is the critical first step in interviewing children.
   2. *Anatomical identification* then follows, using anatomically correct dolls to establish the names a child victim uses for various body parts.
   3. *Good touch, bad touch* can be done with the dolls.
   4. *The abuse scenario* gives trainees a fictitious abuse report and asks them to construct a plan to interview the victim.
   5. *Finding closure.*

X. Evidence

A. Evidence in child neglect or abuse cases includes the surroundings, the home conditions, clothing, bruises or other body injuries, the medical examination report and other observations.

B. Indicators of child neglect and abuse may be physical or behavioral or both.

C. Neglect indicators:
  1. Physical: frequent hunger, poor hygiene, inappropriate dress, consistent lack of supervision, unattended physical problems or medical needs, abandonment
  2. Behavioral: begging, stealing (especially food), extending school days by arriving early or leaving late, constant fatigue, listlessness or falling asleep in school, poor performance in school, truancy, alcohol or drug abuse, aggressive behavior, delinquency, and stating no one is at home to care for them

D. Emotional abuse indicators:
  1. Physical: speech disorders, lags in physical development, general failure to thrive
  2. Behavioral: habit disorders, conduct disorders, sleep disorders, inhibitions in play, obsessions, compulsion, phobias, hypochondria, behavioral extremes, attempted suicide

E. Physical abuse indicators
  1. Physical: unexplained bruises or welts, burns, fractures, lacerations, abrasions
  2. Behavioral: being wary of adults, being apprehensive when other children cry, extreme aggressiveness or withdrawal, being frightened of parents, being afraid to go home
  3. Parental: contradictory explanations for a child's injury, attempts to conceal a child's injury, routine use of harsh, unreasonable discipline, poor impulse control

F. Sexual abuse indicators
  1. Physical: difficulty urinating and irritation, bruising or tearing around the genital or rectal areas
  2. Behavioral: unwillingness to change clothes for or participate in physical education classes; withdrawal, fantasy, or infantile behavior; bizarre sexual behavior, sexual sophistication beyond the child's age, poor peer relationships, delinquency or running away, reports of being sexually assaulted
  3. Parental: jealousy and overprotectiveness of child

XI. The Suspect

A. Most sexual abuse is committed by persons known to the child.

1. Women comprised a larger percentage of all perpetrators than men, 57.9 percent compared with 42.1 percent. More than 75 percent (77.5%) of all perpetrators were younger than age 40.

2. Of the perpetrators who maltreated children, less than 10 percent (7.0%) committed sexual abuse, and 60.4 percent committed neglect.

3. Of the perpetrators who were parents, more than 90 percent (91.5%) were the biological parent of the victim.

B. The parent as suspect

    1. Munchausen's syndrome: Involves self-induced or self-inflicted injuries to seek attention or sympathy.

    2. Munchausen syndrome by proxy is a form of child abuse in which a parent or adult caregiver deliberately provides false medical histories, manufactures evidence, and causes medical distress in a child.

    3. Osteogenesis imperfecta (OI): A genetic disorder characterized by bones that break easily, often from little or no apparent cause. False accusations of child abuse may occur in families with children who have milder forms of OI and/or in whom OI has not previously been diagnosed

    4. Sudden infant death syndrome: often confused with child abuse

    5. Investigating child fatalities

        a. Tough questions must be asked to grieving parents or caregivers so the investigator may determine whether the fatality results from an unknown medical condition, an accident, or a criminal act.

        b. Successful investigations hinge on three factors

            (1) Effectively conducted, well-documented interviews of witnesses

            (2) Thorough background checks on every witness and suspect

            (3) Competent interrogation of the suspect(s)

C. Sex crimes by other children: An increasing number of child sex crimes are being committed by other children.

D. The non-parent suspect:

    1. Perpetrators other than parents have included babysitters, camp counselors, school personnel, clergy, and others.

    2. Habitual child sex abusers, whether they operate as loners or as part of a sex ring, have been classified into three types.

        a. Misoped: the person who hates children, has sex with them, and then brutally destroys them

        b. Hebephile: a person who selects high school–age youths as his or her sex victims

      c.   Pedophile: sometimes referred to as a chicken hawk, an adult who has either heterosexual or homosexual preferences for young boys or girls of a specific, limited age range

XII.   The Pedophile

    A.   Pedophiles are typically, but not always, male.

    B.   An adult who has either heterosexual or homosexual preference for young boys or girls of a specific, limited age range

    C.   Child sexual abuse rings

       1.   Solo sex rings: organization primarily by the age of the child.

       2.   Transition sex rings: Experiences are exchanged, photographs of children and sexual services may be traded or sold.

       3.   Syndicated sex rings: well-structured organization that recruits children, delivers direct sexual services, and establishes an extensive network of customers.

    D.   Ritualistic abuse by satanic cults: use rituals or ceremonial acts to draw their members together into a certain belief system.

    E.   Victimology: Bond often develops between offender and victims.

    F.   Offender reactions: complete denial, attempt to minimize what they have done, attempt to justify behavior, blame the victims, claim to be sick

XIII.   Commercial Sexual Exploitation

    A.   Refers to taking unfair advantage of children or using them illegally. This includes using children in pornography and prostitution. At the federal level, child abuse statutes pertain mainly to exploitation, but they also set forth important definitions that apply to any type of child abuse.

    B.   Pornography

       1.   An organized, multimillion-dollar industry.

       2.   The Child Protection Act (1984) prohibits child pornography and greatly increases the penalties for adults who engage in it.

    C.   Internet sex crimes against children

       1.   Advances in computer technology and the expansion of the Internet have created an entirely new global forum in which sex offenders can access potential victims and distribute or trade child pornography

       2.   Internet sex crimes against minors can be categorized in three mutually exclusive groups:

          a.   Internet crimes against identified victims involving Internet-related sexual assaults and other sex crimes, such as the production of child pornography committed against identified victims

          b.   Internet solicitations unknowingly to undercover law enforcement officers posing as minors that involved no identified victims

      c.   The possession, distribution, or trading of Internet child pornography by offenders who did not use the Internet to sexually exploit identified victims or unknowingly solicit undercover investigators

   3. The Child Protection and Sexual Predator Punishment Act (1998) prohibits contacting a minor via the Internet to engage in illegal sexual activity and punishes those who knowingly send obscenity to children.

   4. The National Center for Missing and Exploited Children (NCMEC) has a congressionally mandated Cyberline, a reporting mechanism for child sexual exploitation.

   5. Project Safe Childhood (PSC) empowers federal, state, and local law enforcement officers with tools needed to investigate cybercrimes against children.

   6. As a result of task force investigations, 7,328 arrests have been made in the past seven years. In addition, the FBI made 1,648 arrests in 2005 as part of its Innocent Images National Initiative (IINI).

D.   Three models to combat child sexual exploitation:

   1. Special task forces

   2. Strike forces

   3. Law enforcement network

E.   Federal agencies working against child pornography

   1. Innocent Images National Initiative provides coordinated FBI response.

   2. Internet crimes against children task forces: more than 1,000 affiliated state and local organizations.

   3. CyberTipline receives leads in five basic areas:

      a.   Possession, manufacture, and distribution of child pornography

      b.   Online enticement of children for sexual acts

      c.   Child prostitution

      d.   Child sex tourism

      e.   Child sexual molestation outside the family

F.   International initiatives

   1. In 1996, the First World Congress against Commercial Exploitation of Children adopted a Declaration and Agenda for Action calling upon states to

      a.   Accord high priority to action against the commercial exploitation of children and allocate adequate resources to the effort

      b.   Promote stronger cooperation between states and all sectors of society and strengthen the role of families

      c.   Criminalize the commercial sexual exploitation of children

d. Condemn and penalize the offenders while ensuring that child victims are not penalized

e. Review and revise laws, policies, programs, and practices

f. Enforce laws, policies, and programs

2. Interpol has established a Standing Working Party (SWP) on Offenses against Minors that seeks to improve international cooperation in preventing and combating child pornography and other forms of child sexual exploitation.

G. Prostitution of juveniles

1. International rings and interstate crime operations traffic young girls to faraway places, promising them employment and money.

2. Runaway and homeless youths are recruited by pimps or engage in "survival sex."

3. Drug dealers get youths addicted, then force them to prostitute themselves to receive drugs or have a place to stay.

4. Some parents have advertised and prostituted their children over the Internet.

5. Often the trafficking of children precedes their involvement in prostitution.

H. Trafficking of children

1. Human trafficking often involves school-age children, particularly those not living with their parents, who are vulnerable to coerced labor exploitation, domestic servitude, or commercial sexual exploitation.

2. The average of entry into prostitution is 12 to 14 years of age.

XIV. Missing Children: Runaway or Abducted?

A. A special challenge in cases where a child is reported missing is to determine whether the child has run away or been abducted.

B. Runaway children

1. Many runaways are insecure, depressed, unhappy, and impulsive with low self-esteem. Typical runaways report conflict with parents; alienation from them; rejection and hostile control; lack of warmth, affection, and parental support.

2. Running away may compound their problems. Many runaways become streetwise and turn to drugs, crime, prostitution, or other illegal activities.

3. For 21 percent of the 1.7 million runaway/thrownaway youths, their episode involved physical or sexual abuse at home before leaving or fear of such abuse upon their return.

4. Other problems reported included parental drug and/or alcohol abuse, mental health problems within the family and domestic violence between the parents.

      5. Very few runaways are homeless and living on the street, and most do not go far.

C. Abducted children

      1. Abducted children are often kidnapped. Kidnapping is taking someone away by force, often for ransom, sometimes for sexual purposes and murder.

      2. The most frequent type of child abduction is parental abduction, often by a parent who has lost custody.

D. Investigating a missing child report

      1. First steps:

         a. Verify child is missing.

         b. Verify child's custody status.

         c. Conduct search of surrounding areas.

         d. Evaluate contents and appearance of child's room.

         e. Obtain photographs and videotapes of missing child.

         f. Enter the missing child into the NCIC Missing Persons File and report it to the NCMEC.

      2. Runaways

         a. Check agency records for recent contact with the child.

         b. Review school records and interview teachers, school personnel, and classmates; check contents of the school locker.

         c. Determine whether the child is endangered.

      3. Abductions

         a. Criminal charges against parents: Unlawful Flight to Avoid Prosecution Statute

         b. More complicated when suspect-parent leaves the country with the child.

         c. Seek assistance of national resources and specialized services, such as the AMBER Alert plan.

E. The AMBER Alert plan

      1. A voluntary partnership between law enforcement and broadcasters to activate an urgent bulletin in the most serious child abduction cases.

      2. Created in the Dallas–Fort Worth region in 1996 in response to the death of 9-year-old Amber Hagerman, who was abducted while riding her bicycle in Arlington, Texas, and then brutally murdered.

      3. All 50 states now have statewide AMBER Alert plans.

      4. The program has helped rescue more than 230 children nationwide.

F. Beyond AMBER alerts

      1. Law enforcement agencies should consider technologies to supplement the AMBER Alert program, such as e-mails to law

enforcement agencies, a call to a cell phone, a fax blast, an Internet pop-up window, or the A Child Is Missing system.

    a. Whatever system is used, however, it must be able to be implemented and accessed quickly, as time is of the essence in such cases.

    b. If an abductor is going to murder a child, 74 percent of the time he or she will do so within the first three hours.

  2. A child abduction response team (CART)

    a. The mission of a CART is to bring expert resources to child abduction cases quickly.

    b. Such a team typically consists of seasoned, experienced officers from around the region, each with a preplanned response related to that officer's field of expertise.

    c. Such teams might also include mounted patrol, ATVs, helicopters, and K-9s—whatever resources are readily available.

    d. A CART may also include a family coordinator, a media coordinator, a crime scene coordinator, a street patrol coordinator, an interview team coordinator, a research coordinator, a search coordinator, and a coordinator of other agencies involved.

G. Additional resources available

  1. The Missing and Exploited Children's Program provides training and technical assistance to law enforcement, and it conducts research.

  2. The Team HOPE helps families of missing children handle the day-to-day issues of coping by linking victim-parents with experienced and trained parent volunteers who have gone through the experience of having a missing child.

XV. Children as Witnesses in Court

A. Courts have altered some court procedures to accommodate children; these changes include the following:

  1. Some courts give preference to those cases by placing them ahead of other cases.

  2. Some courts permit videotaping child interviews.

  3. Courts are limiting privileges for repeated medical and psychological examinations of children.

  4. To reduce the number of times the child must face the accused, the courts are allowing testimony concerning observations of the child by another person who is not a witness, allowing the child to remain in another room during the trial and/or using videotape.

  5. Some courts remove the accused from the courtroom during the child's testimony.

XVI. Preventing Crimes against Children

    A. Parents should teach their children about sexual abuse.

    B. Parent should listen to their children.

    C. Children should be instructed to tell their parents when another adult asks them to keep a secret.

    D. Parents should understand that children do not usually tell tales about sexual abuse.

    E. Older children should be taught to tell their parents where they are going, etc.

    F. Children should be taught to stay with the group when they are at events.

    G. Children should be taught to lock the doors when they are home alone.

    H. Children should be taught that it is okay to sometimes lie.

    I. Parents should assist children in planning safe routes home from school.

    J. Babysitters should be selected carefully.

XVII. Summary

Chapter Questions

1. Child abuse can result in serious and permanent
   a. physical damage.
   b. mental damage.
   c. emotional damage.
   d. all of these.

2. Most reports of child abuse are made by
   a. third parties.
   b. the victim.
   c. the police.
   d. none of these.

3. Generally, it is better to interview the child
   a. in a large, impersonal space.
   b. with their parents.
   c. aggressively.
   d. in private, in a small, friendly space.

4. Evidence in child abuse cases includes
   a. the surroundings.
   b. home conditions.
   c. grades in school.
   d. both a and b.

5. MSBP stands for
   a. multiple sexual biographical partitions.
   b. major sexual bipolar provisions.
   c. multiphase sexual bipolar physical.
   d. Munchausen's syndrome by proxy

6. A *chicken hawk* is
   a. a pedophile
   b. a type of bird.
   c. a slang term for a young child.
   d. none of these.

7. A group of professionals from different law enforcement divisions who come together to prosecute a single case is referred to as a
   a. law enforcement task force.
   b. law enforcement network.
   c. law enforcement team.
   d. none of these.

8. Failure to properly care for a child because of inhumane living quarters, inadequate food, and inadequate love or attention is best described as what?
   a. mistreatment
   b. neglect
   c. abandonment
   d. physical abuse

9. Exploitation refers to
   a. taking unfair advantage of children or using them illegally
   b. the beating or whipping of children
   c. mental abuse of children
   d. emotional abuse of a child such as locking the child in a closet

10. Which of the following has been identified as the leading cause of death for children in the United States?
   a. traffic crashes
   b. exploitation
   c. abandonment
   d. child abuse

11. Kidnapping is taking someone away by force. True or False

12. Childhood abuse is not often associated with delinquency. True or False

13. In most child abuse cases, children tell the truth to the best of their ability. True or False

14. When interviewing children, investigators should be aggressive and use threats if necessary to get the truth. True or False

15. In cases of sexual assault, the child's description of the acts or experiences will probably not be normal for their age. True or False

16. Investigators should make use of the cognitive interview process with children. True or False

17. Pictures of injuries involving children should be taken quickly because children heal quickly. True or False

18. Venereal disease or other sexually transmitted diseases are an indicator of possible child sexual abuse. True or False

19. Child pornography is a highly developed and organized, multimillion-dollar industry producing and distributing millions of dollars of products. True or False

20. Computers are a good source of information when arresting an individual for child pornography. True or False

21. A _____ is the type of person that is most likely to be more dangerous to children, or even destroy a child.

22. _____ _____ is a brittle bone disease, which is a genetic disorder characterized by bones that break easily, often from little or no apparent cause. It may be mistaken for child abuse.

23. These juveniles may have had conflict with parents, alienation from them, rejection and hostile control, lack of warmth, affection and parental support, which leads them into being _____.

24. The drug production of _____has become a major factor in the severity of child abuse and neglect, with many children testing positive for toxic levels of chemicals in their bodies.

25. A child suffering from _____ syndrome has injuries that are self-induced or self-inflicted to seek attention or sympathy in an attempt to avoid something.

26. The National _____ Alert, a voluntary partnership between law enforcement and broadcasters, is a method to activate an urgent bulletin to alert the public in the most serious child abduction cases.

27. _____ is the failure to meet a child's basic needs, including housing, food, clothing, education, and access to medical care.

28. _____ abuse refers to causing fear or feelings of unworthiness in children by such means as locking them in closets, ignoring them, or constantly belittling them.

29. Physical and sexual abuse, regardless of the age of the victim, is also classified as a _____ crime.

30. Child abuse and _____ can result in serious and permanent physical, mental, and emotional damage, as well as future criminal behavior.

31. Describe sexual seduction, lewdness, and molestation.

32. What are three indicators that a child should be removed from the home?

33. What does the acronym SIDS stand for? What is its relation to SUID?

34. Identify the several types of child abuse that fall under the categories of maltreatment.

35. Name the numerous challenges that face investigators when investigating crimes against children.

Case Study

36. An officer has talked with a 16-year-old male who has informed him that a neighbor asked him to come over and then took pictures of him while he was nude. The youth was paid $50 for this activity. How should you, as the investigator, investigate this case?

_____

_____

_____

_____

_____

_____

_____

_____

_____

_____

_____

_____

_____

_____

Answer Key

1. d		11. True	
2. a		12. False	
3. d		13. True	
4. d		14. False	
5. d		15. True	
6. a		16. True	
7. b		17. True	
8. b		18. True	
9. a		19. True	
10. d		20. True	

21. misoped

22. osteogenesis imperfecta

23. runaways

24. methamphetamine

25. Munchausen

26. AMBER

27. Neglect

28. Emotional

29. violent

30. neglect

31. *Sexual seduction* means ordinary sexual intercourse, anal intercourse, cunnilingus, or fellatio committed by a nonminor with a consenting minor. *Lewdness* means touching a minor to arouse, appeal to, or gratify the perpetrator's sexual desires. *Molestation* is a broader term, referring to any act motivated by unnatural or abnormal sexual interest in minors that would reasonably be expected to disturb, irritate, or offend the victim.

32. The child's age or physical or mental condition makes the child incapable of self-protection, the home's physical environment poses an immediate threat to the child, the child needs immediate medical or psychiatric care and the parents refuse to get it, the parents cannot or will not provide for the child's basic needs, maltreatment in the home could permanently damage the child physically or emotionally, the parents may abandon the child.

33. The acronym SIDS stands for sudden infant death syndrome. It is a "diagnosis by exclusion" made when no other causes of death can be found, and is the diagnosis most often made in cases of sudden, unexplained infant death. Sudden unexplained infant death (SUID) cases may show visible signs of injury, the child may seem malnourished, siblings may show signs of injuries, there may be a pattern of injuries, the children are older.

34. Maltreatment categories typically include neglect, medical neglect, physical abuse, sexual abuse, and psychological maltreatment. Neglect refers to the failure to properly care for a child and can include not providing humane living quarters or adequate food and attention.

35. Challenges facing investigators include the need to protect the child from further harm, the possibility of parental involvement, the difficulty of interviewing children, credibility concerns, the need for collaborating with other agencies, and the perceived ambiguity of defining what child abuse is.

Case Study Answer

36. You need to be very familiar with the case before speaking with the neighbor. You will need to know if the parents are aware of this incident. The youth and the parents could tell you some things about the neighbor. You will want to have a good plan of action when you interview the neighbor. You should check to see what you can learn about the individual from criminal records and other civil records. You will want to try to develop the need for a search warrant before going to the house and will want to search the house for items related to the crime. This search may disclose other items that may cause you to enlarge the search warrant. Putting a "tail" on the suspect once you leave the search home may tell you some things about the individual. If use of a telephone is involved, you may want to put a tap on the telephone.

ROBBERY

OUTLINE

- Robbery: An Overview
- Classification
- Elements of the Crime: Robbery
- Responding to a Robbery in Progress Call
- Special Challenges in Investigation
- The Preliminary Investigation
- Proving the Elements of the Offense
- The Complete Investigation
- False Robbery Reports

Chapter 12
Robbery

By the end of this chapter, you should know how to define the terms and understand the application of the following concepts. Test your understanding of the chapter by verifying that you know this information. If you do not know it, review the chapter.

Can You Define?

bait money carjacking	dye pack robbery	Stockholm syndrome

Do you know?

- How robbery is defined?
- How robberies are classified?
- What home invaders are?
- What carjacking is?
- In what types of robbery the FBI and state officials become involved?
- What the elements of the crime of robbery are?
- What special challenges are posed by a robbery investigation?

- What factors to consider in responding to a robbery-in-progress call?
- How to prove each element of robbery?
- What descriptive information is needed to identify suspects and vehicles?
- What modus operandi information to obtain in a robbery case?
- What physical evidence can link a suspect with a robbery?

Chapter Outline

I. Robbery: An Overview

  A. Robbery data: view statistics with caution.

   1. According to the FBI Uniform Crime Reports, there were an estimated 417,122 robberies in the nation in 2006, a 7.2 percent increase from the 2005 estimate. However, the estimated number of offenses declined 20.3 percent in comparison with the data from 10 years ago.

   2. Data from the National Crime Victims Survey (NCVS) reports a much higher incidence of robberies—711,570 in 2006, at a rate of 2.9 per 1,000 households.

   3. Other facts about robbery reported in *Crime in the United States 2006* include

    a. Robbery accounted for 29.9 percent of all violent crimes in 2006.

    b. The clearance rate for robbery was 25.2 percent in 2006.

    c. By location type, most robberies (44.5 percent) were committed on streets or highways.

    d. The average dollar value of property stolen per robbery offense was $1,268.

    e. By location type, bank robbery had the highest average dollar value taken—$4,330 per offense.

    f. Losses estimated at $583 million were attributed to robberies during 2006.

    g. Firearms were used in 42.2 percent of robberies for which the UCR program received data.

   4. This crime poses a definite hazard to law enforcement officers: "According to the FBI, the number one reason why officers are killed and or assaulted while off duty is intervening in or being the victim of a robbery or robbery attempt" (Rayburn, 2007, p.56).

  B. Robbery is felonious taking of another's property, either directly from the person or in that person's presence, through force or intimidation.

  C. Characteristics of robberies:

   1. Most are committed by men.

   2. Committed by strangers rather than acquaintances.

   3. Committed with the use of stolen cars, stolen-motor-vehicle license plates, or both.

   4. Committed by two or more people working together.

   5. The offender lives within 100 miles of the robbery.

   6. Robberies committed by lone perpetrators tend to involve lone victims and are apt to be crimes of opportunity.

   7. Youths committing robberies tend to operate in groups and to use strong-arm tactics more frequently than do adults.

8. They take much less time than other crimes.

9. Less physical evidence is normally found after robberies than in other violent crimes.

10. Middle-aged and older people tend to be the victims.

11. Robbers are usually serial criminals and may commit 15 to 25 robberies before being apprehended.

II. Classification

A. Residential robberies

   1. May occur in hotel or motel rooms, garages or elevators, as well as private homes.

   2. One type of robber is the home invader. Home invaders are typically young Asian gang members who travel across the country robbing Asian families, especially Asian business owners.

B. Commercial robberies

   1. Convenience stores, loan companies, jewelry stores, liquor stores, gasoline or service stations, and bars are common targets.

   2. Drugstores may be targeted as a source of narcotics as well as cash.

   3. Stores with few employees on duty and poor visibility from the street are the most likely targets.

   4. Convenience stores that are robbed once are likely to be robbed again.

   5. About 8 percent of convenience stores account for more than 50 percent of convenience store robberies.

C. Street robberies

   1. Most frequently committed in public streets and sidewalks and in alleys and parking lots.

   2. Street robberies are frequently committed at night and in dimly lit areas.

   3. Typical scenarios include purse snatchings, strong-arm attacks at ATMs, and armed robbers demanding cash from people in parking lots.

   4. The crime is often characterized by its speed and surprise.

   5. Motives are often to obtain cash to pay for drugs.

   6. Victim is often unable to identify the suspect.

   7. Illegal immigrants are particularly vulnerable.

D. Vehicle–driver robberies

   1. Drivers of taxis, buses, delivery and messenger vehicles, armored vehicles, and personal cars are frequent targets.

      a. "Driving a taxi is one of the most dangerous professions" (Petrocelli, 2007a, p.22).

2. Armored-car robberies are usually planned by professional, well-armed robbers and involve large amounts of money.

   a. In 2006, according to the FBI, there were 37 armored carrier incidents with $4,158,127 in loot taken, most as cash. Thirty-five percent of the loot was recovered.

3. Drivers of personal cars are often approached at red lights or in parking lots in less-traveled areas.

E. Carjacking

   1. Carjacking is the taking of a motor vehicle by force or threat of force. It may be investigated by the FBI.

   2. The Anti-Car Theft Act (1992) made armed carjacking a federal offense.

   3. This category of robbery appeared late in 1990 and has increased substantially: "There are approximately 49,900 carjackings each year, with 8 out of 10 involving a weapon, usually a gun" (Jetmore, 2006, p.26).

   4. Carjackings often occur at gas stations, ATMs, car washes, parking lots, shopping centers, convenience stores, restaurants, train stations, and traffic control signals.

   5. Carjackers use many ruses to engage a victim. Some stage accidents. Others wait for their victims at workplace parking lots or residential driveways.

F. Bank robbery

   1. Bank robberies are within the jurisdiction of the FBI, the state, and the community in which the crime occurred and are jointly investigated.

   2. They may be committed by rank amateurs as well as habitual criminals. Amateurs are usually more dangerous because they are not as familiar with weapons and often are nervous and fearful.

   3. Robbers may appear to act alone inside the bank but most have a getaway car with lookouts posted nearby.

   4. The number of branch robberies has increased with the number of branch banks, many of which are housed in storefront offices and outlying shopping centers, thus providing quick entrance to and exit from the robbery scene.

   5. Deterrents:

      a. Adding clerks is not necessarily a deterrent, because a person with a gun has the advantage regardless of the number of clerks.

      b. Adding bulletproof glass around the cashier may increase the incidence of hostage taking. This problem has been reduced in some banks by enclosing and securing the bank's administrative areas.

    c.   Security cameras: new products have incorporated analytical tools like facial recognition and advanced video searching capabilities.

    d.   Bait money: U.S. currency with recorded serial numbers placed at each teller position.

    e.   Dye packs: bundle of currency containing a colored dye and tear gas.

6. Amateurs versus professionals

    a.   Amateurs:

       (1) Offenders: solitary offender, drug or alcohol use likely, no prior bank crime; lives nearby

       (2) Violence: note passed to teller or simple verbal demand, waits in line, no weapon

       (3) Robbery success: single teller window victimized, lower amounts stolen, higher percentage of money recovered, more failed robberies, short time from offense to case clearance, direct case clearance more likely

       (4) Robbery timing: targets banks when numerous customers are present, near closing, or on Friday

       (5) Target selection: previous robbery, heavy pedestrian traffic, parcels without barriers, parcels with egress obscured

       (6) Getaway: on foot or bicycle

    b.   Professionals:

       (1) Offender: multiple offenders with division of labor, shows evidence of planning, may be older, prior bank robbery convictions, travels further to rob banks

       (2) Violence: aggressive takeover, visible weapons, intimidation, physical or verbal threats

       (3) Defeat security: uses a disguise, disables surveillance cameras, demands that dye packs be left out, alarms not be activated, or police not be called

       (4) Robbery success: hits multiple teller windows, larger amounts stolen, lower percentage of money recovered, more successful robberies, fewer cases directly cleared, longer time from offense to case clearance

       (5) Robbery timing: when few customers are present, early in the week

       (6) Target selection: previous robbery, busy road near intersection, multidirectional traffic, corner locations, multiple vehicle exits

       (7) Getaway: via car

7. ATM robberies

      a.   Most ATM robberies are committed by a single armed offender acting against a lone victim.

      b.   Most ATM robberies occur at night.

      c.   Most ATM robberies involve the robbing of victims after they have made a withdrawal.

      d.   About 15 percent of victims are injured.

      e.   "The average loss is between $100 and $200" (Scott, 2006, p.4).

      f.   Best responses to reduce ATM robberies:

          (1) Ensuring adequate lighting at and around ATMs

          (2) Ensuring that the landscaping around ATMs allows for good visibility

          (3) Installing rearview mirrors on ATMs

          (4) Installing ATMs where there is a lot of natural surveillance

          (5) Installing ATMs in police stations

          (6) Relocating, closing, or limiting the hours of operation of ATMs at high-risk sites

          (7) Providing ATM users with safety tips

          (8) Installing and monitoring surveillance cameras at and around ATMs

          (9) Installing devices to allow victims to summon police during a robbery

III.   Elements of the Crime: Robbery

    A.   The wrongful taking of personal property

    B.   From the person or in the person's presence

    C.   Against the person's will by force or threat of force

IV.   Responding to a Robbery in Progress Call

    A.   Officers should anticipate the unexpected and assume the worst.

       1. Deployment may include a silent response and invisible deployment tactics.

       2. The possibility exists that the robbers have fled the scene, in which case it is important to notice vehicle traffic moving away from the scene.

    B.   Technology innovation: automatic license plate recognition (ALPR) systems

V.   Special Challenges in Investigation

    A.   The speed of robbery, its potential for violence and the taking of hostages, and the usual lack of evidence at the scene pose special challenges for investigators. Three major problems:

       1. Robberies are usually not reported until the offenders have left the scene.

       2. It is difficult to obtain good descriptions or positive identification from victims.

       3. The items taken, usually currency, are difficult to identify.

B. Response to a robbery-in-progress call:

       1. Proceed as rapidly as possible, but use extreme caution.

       2. Assume that the robber is at the scene, unless otherwise advised.

       3. Be prepared for gunfire.

       4. Look for and immobilize any getaway vehicle you discover.

       5. Avoid a hostage situation if possible.

       6. Make an immediate arrest if the suspect is at the scene.

C. Hostage situations

       1. Priorities in a hostage situation:

           a. Preserve life

           b. Apprehend the hostage taker

           c. Recover or protect property

       2. Direct assault should be considered only if there has already been a killing or if further negotiations would be useless.

       3. Hostage situations may last for less than an hour or for more than 40 hours; the average length is approximately 12 hours.

       4. There is usually no need to rush a hostage situation. Officers should

           a. Provide the opportunity for face-to-face contact with the hostage taker.

           b. Allow the negotiator to attempt to establish a trustful rapport.

           c. Permit mental, emotional, and physical fatigue to operate against a hostage taker.

           d. Increase the hostage taker's needs for food, water, sleep, and elimination.

           e. Increase the possibility of the hostage taker's reducing demands to reasonable compliance levels.

           f. Allow hostage-escape possibilities to occur. Provide for more rational thinking, in contrast to the emotionalism usually present during the initial stage of the crime.

           g. Lessen the hostage taker's anxiety and reduce his or her adrenalin flow, allowing more rational negotiations.

           h. Allow for important intelligence gathering concerning the hostage taker, hostages, layout, protection barriers, and needed police reinforcement.

5. The Stockholm syndrome occurs when hostages report that they have no ill feelings toward the hostage takers and, further, they feared the police more than they fear their captors.

VI. The Preliminary Investigation

A. Officers often arrive at the scene just after the suspect has left, when the victims are feeling vulnerable and fearful.

B. After taking care of emergencies, broadcast initial information about the suspect, the getaway vehicle and the direction of travel.

C. Robbery usually leaves victims and witnesses feeling vulnerable and fearful, making it difficult for them to give accurate descriptions and details of what occurred.

VII. Proving the Elements of the Offense

A. Know the elements of robbery in your jurisdiction.

B. Most states have three elements for the crime of robbery:

1. Was personal property wrongfully taken?

2. Was property taken from the person or the person's presence?

3. Against the person's will by force or the threat of force?

VIII. The Complete Investigation

A. Most robberies are solved through prompt actions by the victim, witnesses, and the police patrolling the immediate area or by police at checkpoints.

B. Identifying the suspect:

1. Disguises

2. Weapons

3. Vehicles

C. Establishing the modus operandi:

1. Type of robbery

2. Time (day and hour)

3. Method of attack (real or threatened)

4. Weapon

5. Number of robbers

6. Voice and words

7. Vehicle used

8. Peculiarities

9. Object sought

D. Physical evidence

1. Physical evidence that can connect a suspect with a robbery includes fingerprints, shoe prints, tire prints, restraining devices, discarded garments, fibers and hairs, a note, or the stolen property.

E. Mapping robbery

IX. False Robbery Reports

A. Investigators need to rule out the probability that a robbery report is false.

B. Indicators of a false report:

1. Unusual delay in reporting the offense
2. Amount of the loss not fitting the victim's apparent financial status
3. Lack of correspondence with the physical evidence
4. Improbably events
5. Exceptionally detailed or exceptionally vague description of the offender
6. Lack of cooperation

X. Summary

Robbery

Chapter Questions

1. Robbery is
   a. the felonious taking of property directly from a person.
   b. the felonious taking of property.
   c. the felonious taking of property with a weapon.
   d. the felonious taking of another's property, either directly from the person or in that person's presence, through force or intimidation.

2. Which of the below items is not characteristic of a robber?
   a. They are committed by strangers rather than acquaintances.
   b. The offender lives with a few miles (5–10) of the robbery.
   c. If committed by youths, robbery is more likely to be done in a group and using strong-arm tactics.
   d. Middle-age and older people tend to be the victims.

3. What are the four categories into which robberies are classified?
   a. residential, commercial, street, and personal.
   b. residential, commercial, street, and vehicle-driver.
   c. personal, commercial, street, and vehicle.
   d. none of these.

4. Which of the following is not one of the three general elements of robbery?
   a. the felonious taking of another's property
   b. either directly from the person or in that person's presence
   c. without the person's knowledge
   d. through force or intimidation

5. The element of being committed against a person's will by use of force or threat of force separates the act of robbery from
   a. burglary and larceny.
   b. all other crimes.
   c. theft.
   d. shoplifting.

6. The priorities at a hostage situation are to
   a. preserve life, recover property, and gain evidence for an arrest.
   b. preserve life, apprehend the hostage taker, and recover or protect property.
   c. preserve life, apprehend the hostage taker, and protect witnesses.
   d. none of these.

7. Physical evidence at the scene of a robbery might include
   a. fingerprints.
   b. shoe prints
   c. restraining devices.
   d. all of these.

8. False robbery reports may be characterized by
   a. unusual delay in reporting the offense.
   b. lack of correspondence with the physical evidence.
   c. improbable events.
   d. all of these.

9. Robbery is the felonious taking of another's property, either directly from the person or in that person's presence and
   a. through force or intimidation.
   b. with a weapon.
   c. with malice aforethought.
   d. where the value taken is more than $200.

10. The phenomenon that occurs when hostages report that they have no ill feelings toward the hostage takers and that they feared the police more than they feared their captors is defined as what?
    a. China syndrome
    b. Stockholm syndrome
    c. sympathetic response phenomenon
    d. good guy/bad guy syndrome

11. Most robbers carry a weapon or other threatening item or indicate to the victim that they are armed.   True or False

12. Robberies take much less time than other crimes.   True or False

13. Carjacking is a category of robbery that is related to taking a motor vehicle by force or threat of force and is part of vehicle-driver robberies.   True or False

14. To take something wrongfully, the robber must have no legal right to the property.   True or False

15. Robbery is considered to have been committed in the presence of another person even if the victim does not actually see the robber take the property.   True or False

16. The speed of robbery, its potential violence, the possible taking of hostages, and the usual lack of evidence at the scene do not pose special challenges for investigators.   True or False

17. The elapsed time between the commission of a robbery and the time the police are notified is usually longer than the actual police response time.   True or False

18. Officers responding to robberies should be careful of stereotyping suspects.   True or False

19. Officers should rush into a hostage taking because this can catch the hostage taker off guard.   True or False

20. The Stockholm syndrome refers to a situation where the hostages attack the hostage takers because they know they are about to be killed.   True or False

21. Most robbers are visibly armed with a weapon or dangerous device and make a(n) _____ demand of the victim.

22. The _____ investigates robberies of banks.

23. United States currency with the serial numbers recorded and placed at each teller position in a bank is referred to as _____ _____.

24. _____ _____ is a type of robbery that is usually associated with young Asian gang members.

25. One who takes a motor vehicle from the person or presence of another by force, violence or intimidation, has most likely committed _____.

26. One element that distinguishes professional versus amateur bank robbers is that professionals will flee the scene using a _____.

27. In 1992, Congress passed, and President Bush signed the Anti-_____ _____ Act making armed carjacking a federal offense.

28. Commercial robberies occur most frequently toward the end of the week between ____ P.M. and ____A.M.

29. The phenomenon that occurs when hostages report that they have no ill feelings toward the hostage takers and that they feared the police more than they feared their captors is defined as_____ syndrome.

30. The need for _____ is based on the principle that the main priority is to preserve life including the hostages, the hostage takers, the police, and innocent bystanders.

31. What are some items that a negotiator can offer to a hostage taker to reduce tension?

32. What are the elements of robbery?

33. How is the concept of an MO use to apprehend robbers?

34. Violence is not nearly as common in robberies as is believed by the general public. Statistically, the injury and death rates of victims involved in these crimes is small. Explain why.

35. Name several of the characteristics of robbery that would prove to be beneficial to an investigator.

Case Study

36. During the past two weeks, you have had several armed robberies (business robberies) in your jurisdiction. You have been assigned the case. There does not seem to be a pattern to the robberies based on any analysis. You do note that they all seem to occur during the evening rush hour and during cold weather. All but one occurred in a major travel corridor. What patterns should you look for and why?

_____

_____

_____

_____

_____

_____

_____

_____

_____

_____

_____

_____

_____

Answer Key

1. d		11. True	
2. b		12. True	
3. b		13. True	
4. c		14. True	
5. a		15. False	
6. b		16. False	
7. d		17. True	
8. d		18. True	
9. a		19. False	
10. b		20. False	

21. oral

22. FBI

23. bait money

24. Home invasion

25. carjacking

26. car

27. Car Theft

28. 6 P.M. and 4 A.M.

29. Stockholm

30. Negotiations

31. Negotiable items may include food and drink (but not alcohol), money, media access, and reduced penalties.

32. The wrongful taking of personal property, directly from another person or in the person's presence, against the person's will by force or threat of force.

33. The techniques or other characteristics of the robbery may be specific to the suspect, and he may have used them on previous occasions.

34. Theories surrounding low injury and death rates among robbery victims suggest that the reasons may be that the threat of force present, the use of force, or the presence of a weapon often reduces the likelihood of the victim resisting. Many victims comply with the demands of the perpetrator when presented with threatening statements, notes, or a visible weapon.

35. Common robbery characteristics include that they are usually committed by strangers, stolen cars or license plates are often used, they are often committed by two or more individuals, the offender often lives within 100 miles of the robbery, and they take much less time than other crimes. Additionally, much less evidence is customarily found in robberies than other crimes of violence, and youths involved in these types of crimes tend to operate in groups and are more apt to use strong-arm tactics than their adult counterparts.

Case Study Answer

36. A thorough, critical analysis based on solid knowledge of the MO will be necessary here. Computer technology or the crime analyst may help you develop hypotheses that can be tested by examining the data. The fact that the robberies have occurred during evening rush hour raises the possibility that the individual has a police scanner and waits until all or most of the cars are busy, that the person is riding a bicycle and can move quickly in traffic and blend in, or even that the person is committing robberies on the way home from work. The fact that the robberies coincide with cold weather might mean that the robber is able to wear a heavy coat at those times to hide his weapon of choice. What kinds of businesses exist in the travel corridor, and what, if anything, do the targets have in common? There may not be much of a pattern, or several contradicting patterns, which could indicate that two or three different individuals or groups are actually responsible. It is also possible that the robberies might be the work of someone recently released from prison who has committed similar robberies in the past, so you should search the records of such people for similar MOs. Finally, you may simply need to wait for more incidents so that you can gather enough information to complete an analysis.

BURGLARY

OUTLINE

- Burglary versus Robbery
- Classification
- Elements of the Crime: Burglary
- Establishing the Severity of the Burglary
- Elements of the Crime: Possession of Burglary Tools
- The Burglar
- Responding to a Burglary Call
- The Preliminary Investigation
- Determining Entry into Structures
- Determining Entry into Safes and Vaults
- Obtaining Physical Evidence
- Modus Operandi Factors
- Effective Case Management
- Recovering Stolen Property
- The Offense of Receiving Stolen Goods
- Preventing Burglary
- IACP/Choice Point Award for Excellence in Criminal Investigation

Chapter 13
Burglary

By the end of this chapter, you should know how to define the terms and understand the application of the following concepts. Test your understanding of the chapter by verifying that you know this information. If you do not know it, review the chapter.

Can You Define?

blowing a safe	dragging a safe	residential burglary
burglary	fence	routine-activity theory
burning a safe	hit-and-run burglary	safe
chopping a safe	peeling a safe	smash and grab
commercial burglary	presumptive evidence	target hardening
crime prevention through environmental design (CPTED)	pulling a safe	vault
	punching a safe	verified response policy

Do you know?

• What the basic difference between burglary and robbery is?	• What the most frequent means of entry to commit burglary is?
• What the two basic classifications of burglary are?	• How safes are broken into?
• What three elements are present in laws defining burglary?	• What physical evidence is often found at a burglary scene?
• What additional elements can be included in burglary?	• What modus operandi factors are important in burglary?
• What determines the severity of a burglary?	• Where to search for stolen property?
• What the elements of the crime of possession of burglary tools are?	• What the elements of the offense of receiving stolen goods are?
• How to proceed to a burglary scene and what to do on arrival?	• What measures may be taken to prevent burglary?

Chapter Outline

I. Burglary versus Robbery

    A. Burglary differs from robbery in that burglars are covert, seeking to remain unseen, whereas robbers confront their victims directly. Burglary is a crime against property; robbery is a crime against a person.

    B. Burglary is the unlawful entry of a structure to commit a crime.

    C. According to the FBI an estimated 2,183,746 burglary offenses occurred throughout the nation during 2006, an increase of 1.3 percent over 2005.

    D. The 10-year trend shows a decrease of 11.2 percent from 1997.

II. Classification

    A. Residential burglaries

        1. Burglaries occur in buildings, structures, or attachments that can be used as dwellings, even if unoccupied at the time.

            a. About two-thirds of all burglaries are residential burglaries (66.2 percent in 2006). Of these, 63.1 percent took place during the day.

        2. The routine-activity theory proposes that crime results from the simultaneous existence of three elements:

            a. The presence of likely or motivated offenders

            b. The presence of suitable targets

            c. An absence of guardians to prevent the crime

    B. Burglary at single-family house construction sites

        1. The two primary reasons for burglary at single-family house construction sites is the high cost of construction materials and lax builder practices.

        2. Amateur opportunists and professional thieves alike take advantage of unprotected construction sites.

    C. Commercial burglaries

        1. May involve churches, schools, barns, public buildings, shops, offices, stores, factories, warehouses, stables, ships, or railroad cars.

        2. In contrast to residential burglaries, most commercial burglaries take place after-hours, either at night (58.7 percent at night according to the FBI) or on weekends, whenever the establishment is closed.

III. Elements of the Crime: Burglary

    A. Entering a structure

    B. Without the consent of the person in possession

    C. With intent to commit a crime

    D. Additional elements may include

        1. Breaking into

2. The dwelling of another

3. During the nighttime

IV.   Establishing the Severity of the Burglary

A.   The severity of the burglary is established by determining

1.   The presence of dangerous devices in the burglar's possession.

2.   The value of the property stolen.

V.   Elements of the Crime: Possession of Burglary Tools

A.   Possessing any device, explosive, or other instrumentality

B.   With intent to use or permit their use to commit burglary

VI.   The Burglar

A.   Most amateur burglars are between the ages of 15 and 25: unskilled, steal radios, televisions, cash, and other portable property.

B.   Most professional burglars are 25 to 55 years of age: usually steal furs, jewelry, and more valuable items; have been trained by other professional burglars.

VII.   Responding to a Burglary Call

A.   Proceed to a burglary scene quietly. Be observant and cautious at the scene.

B.   Search the premises inside and outside for the burglar.

C.   False burglar alarms

1.   Data from the U.S. Justice Department indicates that 96 percent of all burglar alarm activations are false.

2.   Some law enforcement agencies have implemented a verified response policy, meaning that they will not respond to a burglary alarm unless criminal activity is first confirmed through either an onsite security officer or some method of electronic surveillance, such as closed-circuit television.

3.   An aggressive form of verified response is Enhanced Call Verification (ECV), which requires that a minimum of two phone calls be made from the alarm monitoring center, to assess whether user error activated the alarm.

4.   Another approach that departments are taking is to use an escalating series of fines and fees for police dispatch when the alarm turns out to be false.

5.   False alarms are a waste of time for responding officers, and, more important, they may cause officers to be caught off guard when a genuine alarm occurs.

VIII.   The Preliminary Investigation

A. The preliminary investigation is most critical.

B. Preliminary investigation of residential burglaries:
   1. Contact the resident(s).
   2. Establish points and methods of entry and exit.
   3. Collect and preserve evidence.
   4. Determine the type and amount of loss, with complete descriptions.
   5. Describe the MO.
   6. Check for recent callers such as friends of children, salespeople, and maintenance people.
   7. Canvass the neighborhood for witnesses, evidence, discarded stolen articles, and so on.

C. Preliminary investigation of commercial burglaries:
   1. Contact the owner.
   2. Protect the scene from intrusion by the owner, the public, and others.
   3. Establish the point and method of entry and exit.
   4. Locate, collect, and preserve possible evidence.
   5. Narrow the time frame of the crime.
   6. Determine the type and amount of loss.
   7. Determine who closed the establishment, who was present at the time of the crime, and who had keys to the establishment.
   8. Describe the MO.
   9. Identify employees' friends, maintenance people, and any possible disgruntled employees or customers.
   10. Rule out a faked or staged burglary for insurance purposes.

D. Fake burglaries: Check the owner's financial status.

IX. Determining Entry into Structures

A. Jimmying is the most common method of entry used in burglaries.

B. The hit-and-run burglary, also called "smash and grab," is most frequently committed by younger, inexperienced burglars.

C. Burglars use "code grabbers" to record and replicate the electronic signal emitted from an automatic garage door opener and use it to gain access to a house that way.

X. Determining Entry into Safes and Vaults

A. Safes and vaults are entered illegally by punching, peeling, chopping, pulling, blowing, and burning. Sometime burglars simply haul the safe away.
   1. Punching: dial is sheared from the safe door.
   2. Peeling: hole is drilled in a corner of the safe.

3. Chopping: heavy instrument is used to chop a hole in the bottom of the safe.

4. Pulling (also called dragging): a V plate is inserted over the dial then tightened until the dial and spindle are pulled out.

5. Blowing: hole drilled in the safe near the locking bar area or cotton is pushed into an area of the safe door crack and nitroglycerin is put on the cotton, which is then exploded.

6. Burning: a portable safecracking tool burns a hole into the safe.

B. Modern safes are more resistant to all these.

XI. Obtaining Physical Evidence

A. Physical evidence at a burglary scene includes fingerprints, footprints, tire prints, tools, tool marks, broken glass, paint chips, safe insulation, explosive residue, and personal possessions.

B. DNA is also becoming important in burglary investigations. If a burglar gets cut breaking into a structure, he or she may leave blood behind that can be analyzed for DNA, perhaps linking the burglary to others.

XII. Modus Operandi Factors

A. Important factors of the MO include the time, type of victim, type of premises, point and means of entry, type of property taken, and any peculiarities of the offense.

B. Check the MO with local files, talk to other officers, and inquire at other agencies within a 100-mile radius.

XIII. Effective Case Management

A. Because burglary is predominantly a serial crime, the serial burglar should be the primary target of the burglary unit.

B. Effective case management recognizes the mobility of burglars and makes assignments based on MO rather than geographical location.

C. The rise in narcotics and other prescription drug thefts from pharmacies has led to the creation of a new national database called Rx Pattern Analysis Tracking Robberies and Other Losses (RxPATROL).

XIV. Recovering Stolen Property

A. Stolen property is disposed of in many ways. Some burglars may sell items on the street, to pawn shops or to others, such as people who deal in stolen goods.

B. Technology innovation: JustStolen.net is a Web site where people can register the name, model, serial number, photos, and other details of their valued property.

XV. The Offense of Receiving Stolen Goods

A. The elements of the offense include

       1. Receiving, buying, or concealing stolen or illegally obtained goods.

       2. Knowing these goods to be stolen or otherwise illegally obtained.

    B. Sting operations: Police legally establish a fencing operation to catch individuals who purchase stolen goods for resale.

XVI. Preventing Burglary

    A. Premises that are burglarized are likely to be burglarized again.

    B. Homes without security systems are about three times more likely to be broke into than are homes with security systems.

    C. Target hardening, also known as crime prevention through environmental design (CPTED), involves altering the physical characteristics of property to make it less attractive to criminals.

    D. Methods that deter burglaries include

       1. Installing adequate locks, striker plates, and doorframes.

       2. Installing adequate indoor and outdoor lighting.

       3. Providing clearly visible addresses.

       4. Eliminating bushes or other obstructions to windows.

       5. Securing any skylights or air vents over 96 square inches.

       6. Installing burglarproof sidelight window glass beside doors.

       7. Installing a burglar alarm.

XVII. IACP/Choice Point Award for Excellence in Criminal Investigation

    A. First place for this IACP award was received by the Irvine (California) Police department for using intelligence-led policing, geographic profiling, crime forecasting, and new technology in DNA collection to arrest a serial offender responsible for a large number of residential burglaries.

XVIII. Summary

Chapter Questions

1. Burglary differs from robbery in that
   a. burglars are covert.
   b. robbers confront their victims.
   c. robbery is a crime against a person, and burglary is a crime against property.
   d. all of these.

2. The elements of the crime of burglary include which of these:
   a. entering a structure.
   b. without the consent of the person in possession.
   c. with the intent to commit a crime therein.
   d. all of these.

3. Most burglary laws increase a burglary's severity if the burglar possesses which of the following?
   a. burglary tools.
   b. explosives or a weapon.
   c. both burglary tools and explosives or a weapon.
   d. The possession of burglary tools, explosives, or weapons does not affect the severity of the burglary.

4. Most amateur burglars are between the ages of
   a. 14 and 18.
   b. 15 and 25.
   c. 26 and 35.
   d. none of these.

5. Most professional burglars are between the ages of
   a. 25 and 34.
   b. 25 and 49.
   c. 25 and 55.
   d. none of these.

6. The first two officers at the scene of a burglary should do which of the following?
   a. Enter the building.
   b. Wait for more officers.
   c. Place themselves at diagonally opposed corners of the building.
   d. None of these.

7. False alarms for burglary account for as much as
   a. 50% of alarms.
   b. 75% of alarms.
   c. 90% of alarms.
   d. 96% of alarms.

8. In cases of residential burglary, officers should do which of the following:
   a. contact the resident(s).
   b. determine the type and amount of loss, with complete descriptions.
   c. canvass the neighborhood first.
   d. both a and b.

9. Which is not a standard method used to enter a safe?
   a. punching
   b. peeling
   c. pounding
   d. pulling

10. Given that most burglars are convicted on circumstantial evidence, which of the following is true?
    a. Any physical evidence at the burglary scene is of the utmost importance.
    b. Officers should collect only the most critical evidence.
    c. Officers should determine if fingerprints are available before working to process the crime scene.
    d. None of these.

11. A residential burglary is the burglary of buildings, structures, or attachments that are used as or are suitable for dwellings, even though they may be unoccupied at the time of the burglary.   True or False

12. Some states classify vehicles, trailers, and railroad cars as structures for the purposes of burglary.   True or False

13. Because many people, especially mechanics and carpenters, possess tools that they might use in a burglary, circumstances must clearly show that they intended to use or allow their use in committing a crime for them to be convicted of possession of burglary tools.   True or False

14. Combination safe jobs, in which the safe is opened by the combination without the use of external force, are always the result of a dishonest employee selling the combination.   True or False

15. Burglary is a crime of planning and stealth, and most are well planned by the suspects.   True or False

16. Jimmying is the most common method of entry to commit burglary.   True or False

17. A hit-and-run burglary is the same as a smash and grab burglary.   True or False

18. DNA is not important in burglary investigation.   True or False

19. Many cities have established sting operations to catch individuals who purchase stolen goods for resale.   True or False

20. Research shows that premises that are burglarized are likely to be burglarized again.   True or False

21. According to *Crime in the United States, 2006,* of all the burglaries reported in 2006, law enforcement only cleared about _____ by arrest or exceptional means.

22. The common law definition of burglary that originated in 16th-century England required that the breaking and entering must be done during _____ hours.

23. Robbery is a crime against people, whereas burglary is a crime against _____.

24. _____ is the most common method of entry used to gain entry to a structure to commit a burglary.

25. The mere breaking and entering is _____ evidence that a crime is intended.

26. _____ and _____ burglary is a term that best describes a juvenile who smashes a store window with a brick to steal several watches on display and then flees the scene.

27. An individual who acts as a go-between who receives stolen goods for the purpose of resale is best referred to as a _____.

28. _____is the felonious taking of another's property, either directly from the person or in that person's presence, through force or intimidation.

29. Police should approach a burglary scene _____.

30. Burglaries are classified as either _____ or_____.

31. An MO is important to describe in the case of a burglary. Explain why.

32. Why is burglary considered a property crime?

33. Define residential and commercial burglaries and describe the differences regarding items taken and types of perpetrators.

34. Describe the routine-activity theory and how it relates to burglary.

35. Describe the two factors that influence the severity of a burglary.

Case Study

36. You have been assigned to investigate the arrest of a 16-year-old male who was apprehended when officers responding to a neighbor's call found the youth crawling out of a residential window. The officers believe that the youth was just leaving the scene when they arrested him. The youth had a small, portable radio and some cash on him at the time of the arrest. How should you investigate this case if you want to determine whether he has committed other burglaries?

_____

_____

_____

_____

_____

_____

_____

_____

_____

_____

_____

_____

_____

_____

_____

Answer Key

1. d	11. True
2. d	12. True
3. b	13. True
4. b	14. False
5. c	15. False
6. c	16. True
7. d	17. True
8. d	18. False
9. c	19. True
10. a	20. True

21. 13%

22. nighttime

23. property

24. Jimmying

25. presumptive

26. hit and run

27. fence

28. Robbery

29. quietly

30. residential or commercial

31. It allows investigators to link other burglaries to a suspect who may have been arrested in connection with only one burglary, as well as to determine how many different burglars are working in an area.

32. It involves the theft of property while no other person is present.

33. A residential burglary occurs in buildings, structures, or attachments that are suitable for dwellings. They do not need to be occupied at the time of burglary to comply with this definition. About two thirds of all burglaries are

residential in nature and are often committed by one or more juveniles or young adults who live in close proximity to the area. Items taken include cash and merchandise that can be easily fenced or converted to cash such as televisions, stereos, guns, and jewelry. A commercial burglary is one that involves a commercial establishment such as a school, church, warehouse, or service station. Commercial burglaries are often planned by casing the establishment in advance and commonly are committed by two or more people. Items taken can vary depending on the type of business and cash on hand.

34. Rather than focusing on the offender, the routine-activity theory shifts the focus towards the victim, time, and place. It proposes that crime results from the simultaneous existence of three elements: (1) the presence of likely or motivated offenders, (2) the presence of suitable targets, and (3) an absence of guardians to prevent the crime.

35. A burglary's severity is determined by (1) the presence of dangerous devices in the burglar's possession or (2) the value of the items taken. Most states increase the severity of a burglary statute if a weapon or explosive is involved in the commission of the offense or if they are stolen during the offense. Likewise, many statutes mention the monetary value or types of goods taken during a burglary which can enhance penalties.

Case Study Answer

36. As an investigator, you know that most burglars commit pattern crimes with a specific MO. You should look for all the cases of burglary in the same area with a similar MO. You will need to plan for this investigation by finding out which cases, if any, have patterns that can be linked to the MO of this youth. His fingerprints should be compared with any fingerprints that may have been left behind at other scenes. You should also find out whether the youth has a prior record of arrests for similar offenses, and what other contact he may have had with police. It might also be possible to determine whether he is known to local pawnshops or secondhand stores, and any items he has sold them previously, through cooperation with those businesses. Although the youth may break under interrogation and confess to other burglaries, this is unlikely without much preparation on your part. You should take care to assemble as much evidence as possible so you will be more effective in confronting him.

LARCENY/THEFT, FRAUD, AND WHITE-COLLAR CRIME

OUTLINE

- Larceny/Theft: An Overview
- Elements of the Crime
- Classification of Larceny/Theft
- Found Property
- The Preliminary Investigation
- Types of Larceny/Theft
- Proving the Elements of the Crime
- Fraud
- White-Collar Crime
- A Final Note about Jurisdiction

Chapter 14
Larceny/Theft, Fraud, and White-Collar Crime

By the end of this chapter, you should know how to define the terms and understand the application of the following concepts. Test your understanding of the chapter by verifying that you know this information. If you do not know it, review the chapter.

Can You Define?

burls	grand larceny	poaching
confidence game	holder	Ponzi scheme
corporate crime	identity theft	property
cramming	integration	property flipping
economic crime	jamming	short-con games
embezzlement	larceny/theft	shrinkage
flaggers	layering	slamming
floor-release limit	leakage	sliding
fluffing	long-con games	smurfing
forgery	money laundering	structuring
fraud	parallel proceedings	white-collar crime
goods	petty larceny	zero floor release
gouging	placement	

Do you know?

- How larceny differs from burglary and robbery?
- What the elements of larceny/theft are?
- What the two major categories of larceny are and how to determine them?
- What legally must be done with found property?
- What the common types of larceny are?
- Whether a shoplifter must leave the premises before being apprehended?

- When the FBI becomes involved in a larceny/theft investigation?
- What fraud is and how it differs from larceny/theft?
- What the common means of committing fraud are?
- What the common types of check fraud are?
- What the elements of the crime of larceny by debit or credit card are?
- What form of larceny/theft headed the FTC's top 10 consumer fraud complaints in 2004?

(continued)

(continued)

• What white-collar crime is and what offenses are often included in this crime category?	• What the main problems in prosecuting environmental crime are?
• What the nature of the FBI's two-pronged approach to investigating money laundering is?	• How the monetary loss value of certain thefts, frauds or other economic crimes influences which agency has jurisdiction over a criminal investigation?

Chapter Outline

I.   Larceny/Theft: An Overview

    A.   National statistics

        1.   Reported larceny/thefts exceed the combined total of all other Index crimes. Data from the FBI indicates that two-thirds of all property crimes in 2006 were larceny/thefts.

        2.   An estimated 6.6 million thefts occurred nationwide, a 2.6 percent decrease from 2005 and a 14.7 percent decrease from 1997. The Office for Victims of Crime's "Crime Clock" reports that one home is victimized by theft every 2.3 seconds.

        3.   The National Crime Victimization Survey (NCVS) reported 174,160 personal thefts (pick pocketing, purse snatching) in 2006, at a rate of 0.7 per 1,000 households, and 14,275,150 other thefts, at a rate of 121.0 per 1,000 households.

        4.   The average value of property stolen was $855 per offense, for an estimated $5.8 billion in lost property in 2006.

        5.   Nationwide, law enforcement cleared 17.4 percent of all reported larceny/thefts in 2006.

        6.   Typically, there must be either interstate involvement and/or a loss exceeding a minimum financial threshold of $250,000 for federal investigators to take the case.

    B.   Larceny/theft is the unlawful taking, carrying, leading, or driving away of property from the possession of another.

    C.   Like burglary, larceny is a crime against property, but it does not involve illegally entering a structure.

    D.   Larceny differs from robbery in that no force or threat of force is involved.

II.   Elements of the Crime

    A.   Felonious stealing, taking, carrying, leading, or driving away

    B.   The personal goods or property of another

        1.   *Goods* or *property* refers to all forms of tangible property, real or personal.

      2. *Another* refers to an individual, a government, a corporation, or an organization.

  C. Valued above (grand) or below (petty) a specific amount

  D. With intent to permanently deprive the owner of the property or goods

III. Classification of Larceny/Theft

  A. Grand larceny

    1. A felony

    2. Usually more than $100

  B. Petty larceny

    1. A misdemeanor

    2. Usually less than $100

IV. Found Property

  A. In most states keeping or selling property lost by the owner is a form of theft.

  B. Although the finder has possession of the property, it is not legal possession.

    1. Thieves apprehended with stolen property often claim to have found it—an invalid excuse.

    2. A reasonable effort must be made to find the owner of the property.

    3. If the owner is not located after reasonable attempts are made to do so and after a time specified by law, the finder of the property can legally retain possession of it.

V. The Preliminary Investigation

  A. Investigating larceny/theft is similar to investigating a burglary, except that in a larceny/theft even less physical evidence is available because no illegal or forcible entry occurred.

VI. Types of Larceny/Theft

  A. Common types of larceny are purse snatching, pocket picking, bicycle theft, theft from motor vehicles, theft of motor vehicle accessories, mail theft, theft from coin machines, theft from buildings, shoplifting, and jewelry theft.

  B. Pickpockets and purse snatchers

    1. Difficult to apprehend because the victim must identify the thief.

    2. Purse snatching may be a larceny/theft or a robbery depending on whether force is used.

  C. Bicycle theft

1. As bicycles have increased in popularity, so has bicycle theft. More than 1.5 million bicycles, worth an estimated $200 million, are stolen each year in the United States.

2. Almost 50 percent of all stolen bicycles are recovered every year by law enforcement, but only 5 percent are returned to their owners because most bikes are unregistered.

3. Bicycles are most frequently stolen from schoolyards, college campuses, sidewalk parking racks, driveways, and residential yards.

4. Juveniles are responsible for the majority of thefts, although some professional bike theft rings operate interstate, even exporting stolen bicycles out of the country.

5. In some bicycle thefts, the crime is grand larceny because of the high value of the stolen bike.

6. A single bike theft is best investigated by the patrol force. Determine the bicycle's value and have the owner sign a complaint. A juvenile apprehended for a single theft can be prosecuted, especially with a prior record of similar or other offenses.

7. Bike thefts are entered into the police computer system. Patrol officers are given a bike "hot sheet" similar to that for stolen vehicles and periodically check bike racks at parks, schools, and business areas against this sheet.

8. Bikes are sometimes reported stolen to defraud insurance companies.

9. Even if the bike is recovered, the owner has already collected its value, and there will seldom be a prosecution.

10. Large numbers of thefts in a short time may indicate an interstate ring has moved into the community.

D. Theft from motor vehicles

1. Though largely unreported, these thefts still account for at least one-third of all larcenies reported to police.

2. Thefts from cars usually involve a small amount of property value, but put a large strain on police resources.

E. Mail theft

1. Thieves may target mailboxes because many households receive government assistance checks and millions of people leave their bills, accompanied by checks, for pickup in their mailboxes.

2. Thieves known as flaggers go around neighborhoods targeting mailboxes with their flags up, searching for envelopes containing checks and other forms of payment. Thieves may also raid the large blue mailboxes.

F. Retail shrinkage: employee theft, shoplifting, and organized retail crime

1. *Shrinkage* refers to the unexplained or unauthorized loss of inventory, merchandise, cash, or any other asset from a retail establishment

because of employee theft, shoplifting, organized retail crime, administrative errors, and vendor fraud.

    a.   According to the *2006 National Retail Security Survey,* retail losses were $41.6 billion or 1.61 percent of sales, nearly unchanged from 1.60 in 2005.

    b.   According to the survey, almost half was due to employee theft, followed by shoplifting, administrative errors, and vendor fraud.

    c.   The survey also found that organized retail crime (ORC) was gaining more awareness within the retail industry.

    d.   Product categories that experienced the highest degrees of shrinkage were cards, gifts and novelties; specialty accessories; crafts and hobbies; and supermarket and grocery items.

2. Employee theft: Most any retail company's shrinkage is more generally due to internal employee theft rather than shoplifting by outsiders.

3. Shoplifting**,** also known as *boosting,* involves taking items from retail stores without paying for them.

    a.   It is usually committed by potential customers in the store during normal business hours.

    b.   It does *not* include thefts from warehouses, factories, or other retail outlets or thefts by employees.

    c.   Shoplifting is rising at many retail chains, and the prime cause is the sputtering economy. In the past, much of shoplifting was done to support a drug habit, but in the current economy, everyday items, such as groceries, are being stolen.

4. Elements of larceny by shoplifting

    a.   Intentionally taking or carrying away, transferring, stealing, concealing, or retaining possession of merchandise or altering the price of the merchandise

    b.   Without the consent of the merchant

    c.   With intent to permanently deprive the merchant of possession or of the full purchase price

    d.   Altering the price of an item is considered larceny.

    e.   It is usually not required that the person leave the premises with the stolen item before apprehension.

    f.   Shoplifting can be either petty or grand larceny, a misdemeanor or a felony, depending on the value of the property.

5. Organized Retail Crime (ORC)

    a.   Organized retail crime (ORC) refers to groups, gangs, and sometimes individuals who are engaged in illegally obtaining retail merchandise through both theft and fraud in substantial quantities as part of a commercial enterprise.

      b. ORC is a relatively low-risk, high-reward crime conducted by fairly sophisticated and skilled groups of criminals.

      c. The thefts usually involve specific small, high-priced items that have a high resale value on the black market.

      d. These groups might funnel money to terrorists.

      e. A web-based national database called the Law Enforcement Retail Partnership Network, or LERPnet, is a public-private partnership between the National Retail Federation, the Retail Industry Leaders Association and the FBI that will be used to analyze, track, and prevent activities by these criminal networks.

G. Jewelry theft

    1. According to the FBI, the jewelry industry loses more than $100 million each year to jewelry and gem theft.

    2. Most often stolen by sophisticated professional thieves, jewelry is also the target of armed robbers and burglars.

    3. Because jewel thieves operate interstate, the FBI becomes involved.

H. Art theft

    1. The FBI estimates losses as high as $6 billion annually.

    2. Art theft is an international problem. The FBI's National Stolen Art File (NSAF) provides a computerized index of stolen art and cultural property.

    3. Thefts of valuable art should be reported to the FBI and to the International Criminal Police Organization (INTERPOL).

I. Numismatic theft: coins, metals, and paper money

    1. Coin collections are typically stolen during commercial and residential burglaries.

    2. The increasing demand for copper and rising resale market prices have fueled copper thefts that cost industries across the country nearly $1 billion in 2006.

J. Agricultural theft

    1. Timber theft

    2. Cactus theft

    3. Livestock theft

    4. Farm equipment and chemicals

K. Fish and wildlife theft

    1. Poaching is the illegal taking or possession of fish, game, or other wildlife.

L. Cargo theft

    1. Increasing popularity of cargo theft: low risk (few thieves are apprehended, prosecuted, or incarcerated), and extremely profitable.

2. Leakage is the illegal or unauthorized removal of cargo from the supply chain (compare with shrinkage in retail industry).

3. Drivers may be hijacked en route or targeted at commercial truck stops.

4. Drivers may also be part of the theft crew itself.

5. Numerous challenges face cargo theft investigators:

    a. The lack of respect or seriousness historically given to the issue.

    b. The mobility of cargo thieves.

VII. Proving the Elements of the Crime

A. To prove the felonious stealing, taking, carrying, leading, or driving away of property, you must gather enough evidence to prove that the property is missing—not simply misplaced.

B. Intent to permanently deprive the owner of the property is shown by the suspect's selling, concealing, hiding, or pawning the property, or converting it to personal use.

C. Intent is proven by a motive of revenge, possession under circumstances of concealment, denial of possession where possession is proven, or flight from normal residence.

VIII. Fraud

A. Fraud is an intentional deception to cause a person to give up property or some lawful right.

1. Fraud differs from theft in that fraud uses deceit rather than stealth to obtain goods illegally.

2. If the value amount involved does not meet or exceed a minimum monetary threshold, the federal government may opt not to become involved in the case, leaving local jurisdictions to deal with many of these types of crimes.

B. Confidence games

1. A confidence game obtains money or property by a trick, device, or swindle that takes advantage of a victim's trust in the swindler.

2. Short-con games take the victims for whatever money they have with them at the time of the action.

3. Long-con games are usually for higher stakes.

4. Other scams

    a. Online auction sites are becoming used more frequently to perpetuate scams.

    b. Easy-credit scams

    c. Bogus prize offers

    d. Phony home repairs

    e. Travel scams

        f.   Cyber-scams

C.   Real estate and mortgage fraud

    1. Common mortgage fraud schemes include equity skimming, property flipping, air loans, foreclosure schemes, inflated appraisals, nominee loans/straw buyers, and silent seconds.

    2. Equity skimming schemes involve use of corporate shell companies, corporate identity theft, and use of bankruptcy/foreclosure to dupe homeowners and investors.

    3. Although property flipping per se is not illegal, it often involves mortgage fraud, which is illegal.

    4. Air loans involve a nonexistent property loan where there is usually no collateral.

    5. Foreclosure schemes involve perpetrators misleading homeowners at risk of foreclosure or already in foreclosure into believing they can save their homes in exchange for a transfer of the deed and up-front fees. The perpetrator then either remortgages the property or pockets the fees.

    6. Inflated appraisals involves an appraiser acting in collusion with a borrower and providing a misleading appraisal report to the lender.

    7. Nominee loans/straw buyers conceal the identity of the borrower through use of a nominee who allows the borrower to use the nominee's name and credit history to apply for a loan.

    8. In the silent second, the buyer of a property borrows the down payment from the seller through the issuance of a nondisclosed second mortgage. The primary lender believes the borrower has invested his own money as the down payment, when in fact, it is borrowed.

D.   Insurance fraud

    1. The most prevalent type of insurance fraud involves premium diversion by insurance agents and brokers, where customers' payments are pocketed for personal gain instead of being sent to the policy underwriter.

    2. Another type involves worker's compensation, in which the con operator collects a premium without providing any legitimate protection against claims.

E.   Health care fraud

F.   Mass marketing fraud

    1. Frauds that exploit mass-communication media, such as telemarketing, mass mailings, and the Internet.

    2. Although these fraud schemes take a variety of forms, they have in common use of false and/or deceptive representations to induce potential victims to make advance fee-type payments to fraud perpetrators.

3. Telemarketing fraud and other types of fraud using the telephone have proliferated, and the victims are predominantly the elderly.

4. Other telephone scams include

    a. Slamming

    b. Cramming

    c. Gouging

    d. Sliding

    e. Jamming

    f. Fluffing

G. Mail fraud: perpetuating scams through the mail.

H. Counterfeiting

1. INTERPOL's Counterfeits and Security Documents Branch (CSDB) has established programs that provide forensic support, operational assistance, and technical databases to help federal and local investigators in counterfeit currency cases.

2. Currency counterfeiting

3. Counterfeit identification documents: It is fairly easy for a perpetrator to make fake identification documents, a crime that can yield a large profit.

4. Commercial counterfeiting

    a. Trademark counterfeiting: the illegal production of cheap "knock-offs" of well-known pricier products, such as Rolex watches, Gucci handbags, or Mont Blanc fountain pens

    b. Copyright piracy: making for trade or sale unauthorized copies of copyrighted material, including print and sound media.

I. Check fraud

1. Deliberately issuing worthless checks

2. Forgery

3. The FBI maintains a National Fraudulent Check File to help track and identify professional check passers.

J. Debit and credit card fraud

1. Use of debit and credit cards, are referred to by the Department of Justice as *access devices.*

2. Elements of the crime of larceny by debit or credit card:

    a. Possessing a credit card obtained by theft or fraud

    b. By which services or goods are obtained

    c. Through unauthorized signing of the cardholder's name

3. Losses from debit and credit card fraud are in the billions annually, with U.S. businesses absorbing $3.2 billion in losses in 2007 from online credit card fraud alone, a figure that excludes fraudulent purchases made from retail stores.

4. Credit cards used for fraud are often obtained by people involved in other types of crime such as mugging, robbery, burglary, pickpocketing, purse snatching and prostitution.

5. Credit cards may also be obtained through fraudulent applications or by manufacturing counterfeit cards.

6. Some merchants may commit credit card fraud directly.

K. Identity theft

1. Identity theft, currently the fastest growing crime in the country:

   a. Unauthorized use or attempted use of existing credit cards

   b. Unauthorized use or attempted use of other existing accounts such as checking accounts

   c. Misuse of personal information to obtain new accounts or loans, or to commit other crimes

2. An estimated 9 million or more incidents each year, and approximately one in four people in the United States will fall victim to identity theft at some point in their lives.

3. Identity theft became a federal crime in the United States in 1998 with the passage of the Identity Theft Assumption and Deterrence Act. Most states have passed identity theft legislation, but the laws vary from state to state.

4. Growing use of the Internet has fueled a strong rise in identity theft. Also prevalent on college campuses.

5. Identity theft topped the list of consumer complaints made to the FTC in 2006, affecting more than 8 million Americans and totaling nearly $50 billion in losses.

6. Thieves steal identities through dumpster diving, skimming (using a special storage device when processing a card), completing a change of address form to divert billing statements to another location, "old-fashioned" stealing, and phishing.

   a. Phishing involves tricking consumers into replying to an e-mail or accessing a Web site that appears to be associated with a legitimate business but is actually a carefully concocted hoax intended to strip consumers of personal identifying information that can be used for criminal purposes.

   b. A Gartner survey showed that phishing attacks escalated in 2007 with more than $3 billion lost to these attacks.

   c. Debit cards were the financial instruments targeted most often by fraudsters.

7. Identity theft went to a new level when one company tried to steal $23 million by pretending to be another company in 2007.

8. Tools of the identity thief's trade: blank checks, laminating machines, laptop computers, typewriters, color scanners and copies, and skimming devices.

9. Collaborative efforts

    a. The President's Task Force on Identity Theft (established 2006): provides a coordinated approach among government agencies to combat identity theft.

    b. Law enforcement benefits by forming partnerships with the Federal Trade Commission (FTC), the National White Collar Crime Commission (NW3C), the Postal Inspection Service, the Secret Service, and the FBI.

IX. White-Collar Crime

A. White-collar crime, also called economic or corporate crime, involves illegal acts characterized by fraud, concealment, or a violation of trust and does not depend on the actual or threatened use of physical force or violence.

B. White-collar or economic crime includes (1) securities and commodities fraud; (2) insurance fraud; (3) health care and medical fraud; (4) telemarketing fraud; (5) credit card and check fraud; (6) consumer fraud, illegal competition and deceptive practices; (7) bankruptcy fraud; (8) computer-related fraud; (9) bank fraud, embezzlement, and pilferage; (10) bribes, kickbacks, and payoffs; (11) money laundering; (12) election law violations; (13) corruption of public officials; (14) copyright violations; (15) computer crimes; (16) environmental crimes; and (17) receiving stolen property.

C. Much white-collar crime is never reported because it involves top-level executives at organizations that do not want their reputations damaged.

D. Corporate fraud may include falsification of financial information, self-dealing by insiders such as insider trading and kickbacks, fraud in connection with an otherwise legitimately operated fund, and obstruction of justice designed to conceal such criminal conduct.

E. Money laundering

1. Converting illegally earned (dirty) cash to one or more alternative (clean) forms to conceal its illegal origin and true ownership.

2. Federal statutes prohibit money laundering.

3. The basic process of laundering money includes the following:

    a. Placement of the funds into the legitimate U.S. market

    b. Layering, where money is clean by moving it around through a series of elaborate transactions, often involving offshore bank accounts and international business companies

    c. Integration, where criminals repatriate their money through seemingly legitimate business transactions

F. Embezzlement

1. The fraudulent appropriation of property by a person to whom it has been entrusted.

2. Includes committing petty theft over time, "kiting" accounts receivable, overextending credit and cash returns, falsifying accounts payable records, and falsifying information put into computers.

3. Business, industries, banks and other financial institutions are victims.

4. Losses may be discovered by accident, by careful audit, by inspection of records or property, by the embezzler's abnormal behavior, by a sudden increase in the embezzler's standard of living, or by the embezzler's disappearance from employment.

5. Bank embezzlement is jointly investigated by the local police and the FBI.

G. Environmental crime

1. The most common environmental crimes prosecuted in the United States involve illegal waste disposal or dumping.

2. Hazardous wastes are the most frequently involved substances in such offenses.

3. Other substances often involved include used tires and waste oil.

4. Signs of possible environmental violations:

   a. Containers or drums that appear to be abandoned, especially if they are corroded or leaking

   b. Dead fish in streams or waterways, especially if the water appears to contain foreign substances (such as detergent, bleach, chemicals or has a strange color)

   c. Dead animals alongside a riverbank or in a field

   d. Discolored and/or stressed, dying plant life

   e. Foul smelling or oddly colored discharge on to the ground or into a stream or waterway

   f. Visible sheens on the ground or in the water

   g. Foul smelling or strange looking emissions into the air

   h. Stains around drains, sinks, toilets, or other wastewater outlets

5. Investigating possible environmental crimes

   a. Local law enforcement plays an important role in protecting the environment.

   b. Main problems in investigating are understanding the numerous laws regarding what constitutes environmental crime, that it is often considered a civil matter, and collaborating with civil regulatory agencies.

   c. Convictions and harsh penalties for crimes against the environment send a message to companies and individuals that local police actively monitor and enforce compliance with environmental laws

6. Trafficking in wildlife and organized crime

    a. An often-overlooked environmental crime is the international wildlife trade, estimated to be worth billions of dollars per year, including hundreds of millions of plant and animal specimens.

    b. Investigating wildlife crime may result in apprehending organized crime rings.

    c. Indicators that may reveal the involvement of organized crime in illicit wildlife trafficking: detailed planning, significant financial support, use or threat of violence, international management of shipments, sophisticated forgery and alteration of permits and certifications, well-armed participants with the latest weapons, and the opportunity for massive profits.

X. A Final Note about Jurisdiction

    A. Sometimes a single crime will violate local, state, and federal laws. Investigators must be aware that even though a crime may fall under federal jurisdiction, such as a theft of federally insured monies, that fact alone does not dictate whether another agency will assume responsibility for the investigation.

    B. Other factors, including the monetary value of the loss, will play a role in determining who is assigned the case.

    C. Jurisdictional issues are a reality in many cases involving theft, fraud, and other economic crimes.

    D. Investigators must be aware of monetary thresholds that must be surpassed for a case to elevate to a federal investigation.

XI. Summary

Chapter Questions

1. Which of the following is an element of larceny/theft?
   a. the felonious stealing, taking, carrying, leading, or driving away
   b. of another's personal goods or property, of value
   c. with the intent to permanently deprive the owner of the property or goods
   d. all of the above

2. In most states, taking found property with the intent to _____ is a crime.
   a. keep it or destroy it
   b. keep it or copy it
   c. keep it or sell it
   d. none of these

3. How much money do retailers lose each year to organized retail crime?
   a. 12 million dollars
   b. 30 billion dollars
   c. 5 million dollars
   d. 10 billion dollars

4. With reference to art theft, the abbreviation NSAF stands for:
   a. National Security Art File
   b. Nation Safety Art File
   c. National Scientific Art File
   d. National Stolen Art File

5. How many horses are stolen annually in the United States?
   a. Between 10,000 and 20,000
   b. Between 20,000 and 40,000
   c. Between 40,000 and 50,000
   d. More than 50,000

6. Confidence games involve
   a. locating the mark, selecting the game, conducting it, and then leaving the area as rapidly as possible.
   b. finding the mark, determining the game, winning the game, and then moving on to the next mark.
   c. separating the mark from the money.
   d. none of these.

7. Identify the two categories of larceny/theft.
   a. felony larceny; misdemeanor larceny
   b. grand larceny; small larceny
   c. grand larceny; petty larceny
   d. felony larceny; petty larceny

8. Although burglary and larceny are both crimes against property, they differ in one distinct way. Which of the following best describe this difference?
   a. Larceny does not involve the illegal entry into a structure.
   b. Larceny does not require that force be used.
   c. Larceny does not require that the threat of force be used.
   d. Larceny does not define the value of the items taken.

9. The unexplained or unauthorized loss of inventory, merchandise, or cash from a retail establishment resulting from employee theft or shoplifting is best described as
   a. insider theft.
   b. shrinkage.
   c. internally generated.
   d. corporate fraud.

10. More than 1.5 million bicycles are stolen each year in the United States. Although nearly _____ are recovered by the police, only _____ are returned to their owners because most bicycles are not registered.
    a. 90%; 20%
    b. 75%; 33%
    c. 50%; 5%
    d. 33%; 3%

11. Larceny/theft is just like burglary, without the breaking into a structure.

    True or False

12. In larceny/theft, the amount determines whether the offense is grand or petty larceny.

    True or False

13. Common types of larceny theft are purse snatching, pocket picking, theft from coin machines, shoplifting, bicycle theft, theft from motor vehicles, theft from buildings, theft of motor vehicle accessories, and jewelry theft.

    True or False

14. Pickpockets are difficult to apprehend because the victim must identify the thief.

    True or False

15. *Shrinkage* refers to the unexplained loss of inventory, merchandise, cash, or any other asset from a retail establishment.

    True or False

16. Businesses lose more due to employee theft than to shoplifting.

    True or False

17. *Boosting* is the same as shoplifting.

    True or False

18. Altering the price of an item is considered shoplifting.

    True or False

19. Just walking out of a store without paying is not shoplifting.

    True or False

20. Flaggers go around neighborhoods looking for mail boxes with their mail box flags up and steal envelops with checks in them.   True or False

21. *Goods* or *property* refers to all forms of _____ property, real or personal.

22. Because jewel thieves move jewels _____ , the FBI will get involved in these thefts.

23. Most people involved in credit card frauds are _____ in other types of crimes.

24. _____ is often the most difficult element to prove regarding the crime of larceny.

25. Obtaining money by trick, device, or swindle that takes advantage of a victim's trust in the swindler is best defined by _____ _____.

26. The _____ scheme is a pyramid-type fraud scheme involving the use of capital from new investors to pay off earlier investors, and requires an ever-expanding base of new investors to support the financial obligations of the "higher-ups."

27. An imitation Rolex watch or Gucci purse that is an illegal reproduction known as a "knock-off" falls under the category, _____ _____.

28. The crime of _____ _____ topped the list of consumer fraud-related complaints filed with the Federal Trade Commission in 2006.

29. The fraudulent appropriation of property by a person to whom it has been entrusted is known as _____.

30. Tricking consumers into replying to an electronic mail or accessing a Web site that appears to be associated with a legitimate business but is actually a hoax intended to gain personal information to be used for criminal purposes is best known as _____.

31. Name the basic elements of the crime of larceny/theft that are present in most state statutes.

32. Name several of the more common types of larceny that occur in society.

33. Describe the FBI's 2-prong approach to investigating money laundering.

34. Explain what a *flagger* is as it relates to mail theft fraud.

35. Describe what a confidence game is and the two basic approaches that are commonly used by con men when using them.

Case Study

36. There are several con artists (their actual number is indeterminate) circulating in your community. They are targeting both younger and older residents with a variety of con games. Patrol officers in your community have some information about their vehicles but are just one or two steps behind the con artists each time. The community has been alerted, but this does not seem to be stopping them. The group seems to move from community to community rather quickly and the larger metropolitan area beyond your community contains more than 20 communities with more than 800,000 people. What actions should you take at this time?

Answer Key

1. d	11. False
2. c	12. True
3. b	13. True
4. d	14. True
5. d	15. True
6. a	16. True
7. c	17. True
8. a	18. True
9. b	19. True
10. c	20. True

21. tangible

22. interstate

23. involved

24. Intent

25. confidence game

26. Ponzi

27. trademark counterfeiting

28. identity theft

29. embezzlement

30. phishing

31. The elements of the crime of larceny/theft include (1) the felonious stealing, taking, carrying, leading, or driving away, (2) of another's personal goods or property, (3) valued above (grand) or below (petty) a specified amount, (4) with the intent to permanently deprive the owner of the property or goods.

32. Common larceny types include purse snatching, pocket picking, theft from coin machines, shoplifting, bicycle theft, theft from motor vehicles, theft from buildings, theft of motor vehicle accessories, and jewelry thefts.

33. The FBI's two-pronged approach to investigating money laundering includes:
    - Prong 1: Investigating the underlying criminal activity. If there is no criminal activity, or specified unlawful activity that generates illicit proceeds, then there can be no money laundering.
    - Prong 2: A parallel financial investigation to uncover the financial infrastructure of the criminal organization. This involves following the money and discerning how it flows through an organization and what steps are taken to conceal, disguise or hide the proceeds.

34. Mailboxes are used to receive money from a variety of sources such as social security and other government assistance checks. On certain days of the month, thieves target mailboxes with their flags up searching for envelopes containing cash and checks. Additionally, many people send checks and credit card applications through the mail service from their homes. Thieves have been known to raid the large blue mailboxes used by people who may not trust sending their mail from home.

35. A confidence game obtains money or property by a trick, device, or swindle that takes advantage of a victim's trust in the swindler. The short-con game takes the victim for whatever money they have with them at the time of the transaction. The long-con game is for much higher stakes and allows the victim to "win" some money early on to initially gain their confidence to scam the victim out of thousands of dollars in the end.

Case Study Answer

36. This case is difficult and will need to involve a metropolitan-wide response. A metropolitan-wide meeting of all law enforcement agencies should be held and a plan developed to go after the suspects. This will take some time and the involvement of some representatives of the target groups. There will need to be much coordination of the services and intelligence among the law enforcement agencies involved with the investigation. The approach needs to involve getting information out to the public, sharing crime prevention tips with the targeted groups, and sharing information among agencies. The patrol officers will need to be briefed on the information known about the con artists, including their physical descriptions, intelligence, and type of cons used. One characteristic of this group of criminals is that they are targeting both young and old. This may indicate something about the group that may assist with finding the criminals or approaching the community.

MOTOR VEHICLE THEFT

OUTLINE

- Motor Vehicle Identification
- Classification of Motor Vehicle Theft
- Elements of the Crime
- Motor Vehicle Embezzlement
- The Preliminary Investigation
- Insurance Fraud
- Cooperating Agencies in Motor Vehicle Theft
- Recognizing a Stolen Motor Vehicle or an Unauthorized Driver
- Recovering an Abandoned or Stolen Motor Vehicle
- Combating Motor Vehicle Theft
- Preventing Auto Theft
- Thefts of Trucks, Construction Vehicles, Aircraft and Other Motorized Vehicles

Chapter 15
Motor Vehicle Theft

By the end of this chapter, you should know how to define the terms and understand the application of the following concepts. Test your understanding of the chapter by verifying that you know this information. If you do not know it, review the chapter.

Can You Define?

chop shop Dyer Act	motor vehicle telematic technology	vehicle identification number (VIN)

Do you know?

• What a VIN is and why it is important? • What the five major categories of motor vehicle theft are? • What the elements of the crime of unauthorized use of a motor vehicle are? • What types of vehicles are considered "motor vehicles"? • What embezzlement of a motor vehicle is?	• How the Dyer Act assists in motor vehicle theft investigation? • Why false reports of auto theft are sometimes made? • What two agencies can help investigate motor vehicle theft? • How to improve effectiveness in recognizing stolen vehicles? • How to help prevent motor vehicle theft?

Chapter Outline

I. Motor Vehicle Identification

   A. The vehicle identification number (VIN) is the primary nonduplicated, serialized number assigned by a manufacturer to each vehicle made. This number is critical in motor vehicle theft investigation because it identifies the specific vehicle in question.

   B. The VIN of a vehicle is the automotive equivalent of human DNA.

   C. VINs for vehicles manufactured between 1958 and 1970 may have 11 numbers and letters or fewer, while all automobiles manufactured in North America since 1971 contain a series of 17 numbers and letters. For example, for the number **1F1CY62X1YK555888**,

      1. **1** = Nation of origin
      2. **F** = Manufacturer symbol
      3. **1** = Make
      4. **C** = Restraint
      5. **Y** = Car line
      6. **62** = Body type
      7. **X** = Engine symbol
      8. **1** = Check digit
      9. **Y** = Model year
      10. **K** = Assembly plant
      11. **555888** = sequential production number

II. Classification of Motor Vehicle Theft

   A. Motor vehicle theft is classified based on the motive of the offender:

   B. Joyriding

      1. Joyrider is generally a younger person who steals for thrills and excitement.
      2. Stolen vehicles are often found where young people congregate.

   C. Transportation

      1. Can involve joyrider, but more apt to involve a transient, a hitchhiker, or a runaway.
      2. A vehicle stolen for transportation is kept longer than one stolen for joyriding.

   D. Commission of another crime

      1. Automobiles are used in most serious crimes.
      2. A stolen motor vehicle driven by a criminal is 150 to 200 times more likely to be in an accident than is a vehicle driven by a noncriminal.

   E. Stripping for parts and accessories

      1. Airbag theft

      2. Stealing for chop shops

  F. Reselling

      1. Committed by professional thieves who take an unattended vehicle, with or without the keys, and drive it away.

      2. Car is altered by repainting, changing seat covers, repairing existing damage, altering the engine number.

      3. Many stolen cars are exported for resale in other countries, most commonly Central and South America.

III. Elements of the Crime

  A. Unauthorized use of a motor vehicle

      1. Most car thieves are prosecuted for unauthorized use rather than theft because proof that the thief intended to permanently deprive the owner of the vehicle is often difficult to establish.

      2. The elements of the crime include

        a. Intentionally taking or driving

        b. A motor vehicle

        c. Without the consent of the owner or the owner's authorized agent

IV. Motor Vehicle Embezzlement

  A. Motor vehicle embezzlement exists if the person who took the vehicle initially had consent and then exceeded the terms of that consent.

  B. Interstate transportation:

      1. The Dyer Act made interstate transportation of a stolen vehicle a federal crime and allowed for federal help in prosecuting such cases.

      2. Amended in 1945 to include aircraft: now the Interstate Transportation of Stolen Motor Vehicles Act.

      3. Elements of the crime of interstate transportation:

        a. The motor vehicle was stolen.

        b. It was transported in interstate or foreign commerce.

        c. The person transporting or caused it to be transported knew it was stolen.

        d. The person receiving, concealing, selling, or bartering it knew it was stolen.

      4. The crime may be prosecuted in any state through which the vehicle passed.

      5. Intent is not required.

V. The Preliminary Investigation

  A. When a motor vehicle theft is reported, initial information obtained by police includes the time, date, and location of the theft; the make, model, and color of the vehicle; the state of issue of the license plate; the license plate number; the direction of travel; a description of any suspect; and the complainant's present location.

B. False motor vehicle theft reports are often filed when a car has been taken by a family member or misplaced in a parking lot, when the driver wants to cover up for an accident or crime committed with the vehicle, or when the driver wants to provide an alibi for being late for some commitment.

C. Recovered vehicles must be examined for usable latent prints and other physical evidence.

D. Common tools and methods: Investigators must be familiar with the tools and methods commonly used to commit vehicle theft, including car openers, rake and pick guns, tryout keys, impact tools, keyway decoders, modified vise grips, tubular pick locks, modified screwdrivers, and hot wiring.

VI. Insurance Fraud

A. Vehicle insurance fraud is a major economic crime that affects every premium payer through increased insurance rates.

B. Vehicle cloning

1. Vehicle cloning is a growing crime affecting consumers who purchase used vehicles.

2. Criminals apply counterfeit labels, plates, stickers, and titles to these stolen cars, making them appear legitimate.

3. High-end luxury cars are the usual targets of cloning.

4. Conservative U.S. vehicle cloning profits are estimated to exceed more than $12 million annually, with an average net of $30,000 per cloned vehicle.

5. Compounding the cloning problem is the fact that many cloned vehicles are used for illegal operations.

VII. Cooperating Agencies in Motor Vehicle Theft

A. State departments of motor vehicles

B. The FBI's National Crime Information Center (NCIC)

C. The National Insurance Crime Bureau (NICB)

VIII. Recognizing a Stolen Motor Vehicle or an Unauthorized Driver

A. Keep a list of stolen vehicles or a "hot sheet" in your car.

B. Develop a checking system to rapidly determine whether a suspicious vehicle is stolen.

C. Learn the common characteristics of stolen vehicles and car thieves.

1. Potential car thieves on foot usually appear nervous.

2. Drivers of a stolen vehicle tend to make sudden jerks or stops, drive without lights or excessively fast or slow, wear gloves in hot weather, attempt to avoid or outrun a squad car.

3. Juveniles account for some 16 percent of stolen vehicles, so it makes sense to take a second glance at stature and youthful appearances of drivers"

D. Take time to check suspicious person and vehicles.

1. One license plate when two are required, or two when one is required.

2. Double or triple plates with one on top of the other.

3. Old set of plates with new screws, wired-on plates, altered numbers, dirty plates on a clean car or clean plates on a dirty car, differing front and rear plate numbers, plates bent to conceal a number, upside-down or hanging plates, and homemade cardboard plates are all suspicious.

E. Learn how to question suspicious drivers and occupants.

F. *Parked cars* may have been stolen if debris under the car indicates it has been in the same place for a long time.

G. Fridays and Saturdays are the busiest car theft days.

IX. Recovering an Abandoned or Stolen Motor Vehicle

A. Most stolen vehicles are recovered, most of them within 48 hours.

B. If you suspect the vehicle was used in another crime, take it to a garage or lock and seal it with evidence tape, then notify proper authorities.

C. Technology is facilitating the recovery of stolen vehicles.

X. Combating Motor Vehicle Theft

A. Methods

1. Sting operations

2. Providing officers with auto theft training

3. Coordinating efforts across jurisdictional lines

4. Instituting anti–car theft campaigns

5. Increasing penalties for stealing vehicles

B. License plates

1. New technology includes automatic license plate recognition (ALPR) systems.

C. Routine activities and motor vehicle theft

1. Bait cars can be enhanced using telematic technology, which transfers data between a remote vehicle and a host computer.

2. Most interceptions take place within about 2 minutes and most arrests within 4.

D. Border-area auto theft

1. According to the NICB, many of the top metropolitan areas for vehicle theft are in or near ports or the Mexican or Canadian borders.

2. There is no international border for this highly mobile crime.

E. Theft of patrol cars

1. Police vehicles are also vulnerable to thieves.

2. Technology answers: break-light kill switch, secure-idle system.

XI. Preventing Auto Theft

A. Common sense

B. Visible and audible warning devices

C. Immobilizing devices

D. Tracing devices

XII. Thefts of Trucks, Construction Vehicles, Aircraft and Other Motorized Vehicles

A. Trucks and trailers

B. Construction vehicles and equipment

1. The National Equipment Register (NER)

a. 24/7 access to specialist NER operators who will offer expert advice on equipment identification, PIN locations, and other identification techniques.

b. 24/7 searches of the NER database online via a toll-free number (866-FIND-PIN).

c. 24/7 access to millions of ownership records through NER operators.

d. Additional online investigation tools such as PIN location information.

e. Local and national training programs.

2. Transport

a. Equipment being transported late at night or on weekends or holidays.

b. Hauled equipment that is being moved in a hurry and therefore lacks the proper tie-downs, over-width/over-weight signs, or lights.

c. Equipment being hauled on trucks not designed to haul such equipment.

d. Equipment being hauled with buckets in the up position or booms not lowered.

e. New equipment on old transport.

f. The labels/markings on a piece of equipment do not match those of the unit carrying or hauling it.

3. Use and location

        a.   Equipment in an unsecured location that has not been moved for some time.

        b.   The type of equipment does not suit the location or use.

   4. Equipment and markings

        a.   Equipment with missing PIN plates.

        b.   Equipment that has been entirely repainted or that has decals removed or painted over.

        c.   Manufacturer decals or model number stickers do not match the piece of equipment to which they are affixed.

        d.   A commercially manufactured trailer with registration plates reflecting a homemade trailer (certain states only).

   5. Price: Equipment that is being offered, or has been purchased, at a price well below market value.

C. Recreational vehicles

D. Motorized boats and jet skis

E. Snowmobiles

F. Motorcycles, motor scooters, and mopeds

G. Aircraft

   1. Aircraft identification consists of a highly visible *N* identification number painted on the fuselage.

   2. After the September 11, 2001, attacks, security of aircraft has become more of a priority.

XIII. Summary

Chapter Questions

1. Motor vehicle thefts are classified in which of the following categories?
   a. theft, use in another crime, taking parts of a car
   b. joyriding, transportation, commission of another crime, stripping for parts and accessories, reselling for profit
   c. cars, trucks, construction equipment, recreational equipment
   d. none of these

2. A chop shop is
   a. a business that repairs body damage on cars.
   b. a business that takes stolen cars apart to sell the parts for a profit.
   c. neither a nor b.
   d. both a and b.

3. The elements of motor vehicle theft are
   a. intentionally taking or driving a motor vehicle without the consent of the owner or the owner's authorized agent.
   b. taking a motor vehicle from the owner with the intent to sell or remove the vehicle.
   c. taking an automobile with the intent to sell the automobile.
   d. None of these.

4. The elements of interstate transportation of a motor vehicle are
   a. a stolen vehicle was transported to another state and sold.
   b. the motor vehicle was stolen, it was transported in interstate or foreign commerce, the person transporting or causing it to be transported knew it was stolen, and the person receiving, concealing, selling, or bartering it knew it was stolen.
   c. an automobile was sold in a state other than the state in which it was stolen.
   d. none of these.

5. Vehicle cloning is
   a. manufacturing an unauthorized reproduction of a type of vehicle (typically in a foreign country) and selling the reproductions under the pretense that they are the actual type of vehicle from which they have been copied.
   b. a crime in which stolen vehicles assume the identity of legally owned, or "non-stolen," vehicles of a similar make and model.
   c. using a VIN from another vehicle.
   d. none of these.

6. NCIC stands for
   a. National Criminal Information Commission.
   b. National Cooperative Information Commission.
   c. National Crime Information Center.
   d. none of these.

7. A bait car is
   a. a car that the police use for patrol.
   b. a car that is used to attract people so that the officers can get their fingerprints off the car.
   c. a vehicle that is selected and placed in a high-crime area where the police then wait for it to be stolen in order to catch the thieves.
   d. none of these.

8. BATIC stands for
   a. Border Auto Theft Identification Center.
   b. Border Auto Theft Information Center.
   c. Bureau Auto Theft Identification Center.
   d. none of these.

9. AOPA stands for
   a. Aircraft Operators and Pilots Association.
   b. Aircraft Owners and Pilots Academy.
   c. Aircraft Owners and Pilots Association.
   d. none of these.

10. The largest majority of vehicle thefts fall under which of the following categories?
    a. Transportation
    b. Joyriding
    c. Stripping for parts and accessories
    d. Reselling for profit

11. In addition to identifying a specific vehicle, each of the numbers in a VIN contains information about that vehicle.   True or False

12. A stolen vehicle, driven by the thief, is not more likely to be involved in a motor vehicle crash.   True or False

13. There is a large market for the selling of stolen airbags.   True or False

14. A motor vehicle includes self-propelled devices for moving people or property or pulling implements, whether operated on land, or in the air.   True or False

15. Motor vehicle embezzlement exists if the person who took the vehicle initially had consent and then exceeded the terms of the consent.   True or False

16. The Dyer Act made vehicle theft a federal crime.   True or False

17. In cases of possible motor vehicle theft, officers should check to see if the vehicle might have been reclaimed by a loan company.   True or False

18. One method of improving an officer's ability to find stolen motor vehicles is developing a checking system to rapidly determine whether a suspicious vehicle is stolen.   True or False

19. One characteristic of a stolen vehicle is having one license plate when two are required.   True or False

20. Most motor vehicle thefts are local problems involving a locally stolen and recovered vehicle.   True or False

21. Setting up a _____ operation is one method of combating motor vehicle theft.

22. A younger person who steals for thrills and excitement is known as a _____.

23. The National Insurance Crime Bureau (NICB) reports that _____ are one of the primary accessories being stripped from cars today to be resold on the black market.

24. A business or body shop that illegally disassembles stolen autos and steals the parts for resale is best known as a _____ _____.

25. _____ is the process of applying counterfeit labels, plates, stickers, and titles to stolen vehicles to make them appear legitimate.

26. Numerous motor vehicle thefts could be prevented by effective educational campaigns and installing _____ devices in vehicles during manufacture.

27. The_____ is the primary nonduplicated, serialized number assigned by a manufacturer to each vehicle made.

28. Motor vehicle thefts are often classified by the thief's_____, recognizing that it is impossible to determine the motive for thefts that end in the vehicle's being abandoned.

29. Most car thieves are prosecuted not for auto theft but for _____ use of a motor vehicle.

30. Prosecution for auto theft requires proof that the thief intended to _____ deprive the owner of the vehicle, which is often difficult or impossible to establish.

31. Explain what a vehicle identification number (VIN) is and its importance in regard to the investigation of motor vehicle thefts.

32. Explain and briefly define the various classifications of motor vehicle theft based on the motive of the offender.

33. Explain the difference between owner and true owner concerning a motor vehicle.

34. Explain the various ways that an officer may improve his chances of spotting a stolen vehicle.

35. Explain telematic technology and its application to motor vehicle theft.

Case Study

36. Officers report that one body shop in town has been open almost 24 hours a day lately, and that many cars with out-of-town license plates have been parked in front of the shop during the night and are then gone in the morning. They have seen individuals drop off cars as late as 3:00 A.M. When officers make contact with the workers, they have been met with hostility and resistance. What would you do as an auto theft investigator?

_____

_____

_____

_____

_____

_____

_____

_____

_____

_____

Answer Key

1. b	11. True
2. b	12. False
3. a	13. True
4. b	14. True
5. b	15. True
6. c	16. False
7. c	17. True
8. b	18. True
9. c	19. True
10. b	20. True

21. sting

22. joyrider

23. airbags

24. chop shop

25. Cloning

26. antitheft

27. VIN

28. motive or purpose

29. unauthorized

30. permanently

31. With millions of cars on our nation's roadways, an identification process is invaluable. VIN numbers are the primary, nonduplicated, serialized numbers assigned to a specific vehicle by the manufacturer. The number identifies the specific vehicle in question and is used to identify key body parts, frame, and engine components. The series of numbers represent the model, year, manufacturer, car line, country of origin, and assembly plant.

32. Joyriding, transportation, commission of another crime, stripping parts and accessories, and reselling for profit are the most common types of vehicle

thefts. Juveniles usually commit joyriding strictly for the purpose of thrills and excitement. Transportation usually involves an individual that steals a vehicle strictly to have transportation from one point to another. A vehicle is also routinely stolen to be used in the commission of another crime such as a getaway car. Vehicles are also stolen solely for the purpose of being stripped of valuable parts that can be resold to unscrupulous dealers. Reselling for profit involves the theft of a vehicle to be resold intact after the VIN has been altered.

33. Legitimate ownership of a motor vehicle exists when the vehicle is in the factory being made, when it is being sold by an authorized dealership, or when a private person or company owns it. The true owner may be a lending agency or bank that actually retains the title of the car.

34. The following information may prove beneficial to improving the chances of spotting a stolen vehicle: (1) Keep a current list of stolen vehicles in your car. (2) Develop a checking system to determine if a suspicious vehicle is stolen. (3) Learn the common characteristics of stolen vehicles and their drivers. (4) Take time to check out and question suspicious vehicles and their drivers. (5) Learn how to question suspicious drivers and occupants.

35. Telematic technology involves the use of a bait car and transceivers and receivers for the tracing and recovery of stolen motor vehicles. Internet, wireless technology, and global positioning systems allow officers to track and follow a stolen vehicle. Many systems allow the officer to remotely kill the engine and automatically lock the doors of the stolen vehicle, preventing an avenue of escape for the suspect.

Case Study Answer

36. Although the possibility that this case involves a chop shop seems somewhat obvious, be sure to safeguard against jumping to an incorrect conclusion. Thus, you need to get some additional information, possibly even stake out the business day and night. Having patrol stop a car that seems to be driving toward the business some early morning to determine if the car is stolen might be a good approach. If you take this approach, you will need to make certain that the officer has probable cause to stop the vehicle. Additionally, if the car has been recently stolen, it may not have been reported. You may be incorrect in your "assumption" or guess as to what the business is up to and thus you need to use care as to how long you detain the stopped car. If you know of a pattern of the types of vehicles being stolen, that will add to your probable cause in the future. One approach might be to find out the owner of the vehicle and call the owner at home to see if he or she knows that the car is being driven. You will want to develop the grounds for a search warrant and then search the business.

ARSON, BOMBS AND EXPLOSIVES

OUTLINE

- Classification of Fires
- Elements of the Crime
- Classification of Arson
- The Model Arson Law
- The Arsonist
- Police and Fire Department Cooperation
- Other Sources of Assistance in Investigating Arson
- Special Challenges in Investigation
- Responding to the Scene
- The Preliminary Investigation
- Search Warrants and Fire Investigations
- Investigating Vehicle Arson
- Prosecuting Arsonists
- Preventing Arson
- Investigating Bombings and Explosions
- Responding to a Bomb Threat
- Investigating Bomb Explosions

Chapter 16
Arson, Bombs and Explosives

By the end of this chapter, you should know how to define the terms and understand the application of the following concepts. Test your understanding of the chapter by verifying that you know this information. If you do not know it, review the chapter.

Can You Define?

accelerants	crazing	line of demarcation
administrative warrant	depth of char	simple arson
aggravated arson	disrupters	spalling
alligatoring	fire triangle	strikers
arson	igniters	trailer
burn indicators		

Do you know?

• How fires are classified?	• What common burn indicators are?
• What presumption is made when investigating fires?	• How to determine a fire's point of origin?
• What the elements of arson are?	• How fires normally burn?
• What constitutes aggravated arson? simple arson?	• What factors indicate the likelihood of arson?
• What degrees of arson the Model Arson Law establishes?	• When an administrative warrant is issued? a criminal warrant?
• Who is responsible for detecting arson? investigating arson?	• When a warrant is needed for investigating a fire scene and what the precedent case is?
• What special challenges exist in investigating arson?	• What to check when investigating suspected arson of a vehicle?
• What the fire triangle is and why it is important in arson investigations?	• What to pay special attention to when investigating explosions and bombings?
• What accelerants are and which are most commonly used in arson?	
• What common igniters are used in arson?	

Chapter Outline

I.   Classification of Fires

    A.   Natural

    B.   Accidental

    C.   Criminal (arson)

    D.   Suspicious

    E.   Of unknown origin

    F.   Fires are presumed natural or accidental unless proven otherwise.

II.   Elements of the Crime

    A.   Willful, malicious burning of a building or property

        1.   *Willful* means "intentional."

        2.   *Malicious* denotes a vindictive desire to harm others.

        3.   *Burning* is the prime element in the corpus delicti.

    B.   Of another or of one's own to defraud

    C.   Or causing to be burned, or aiding, counseling, or procuring such burning.

        1.   A person who hires a professional (a "torch") to commit arson is also guilty of the crime. Seek evidence connecting this person with the actual arsonist.

III. Classification of Arson

    A.   Aggravated arson

        1.   Intentionally destroying or damaging a dwelling or other property by means of fire or explosives.

        2.   Creating an imminent danger to life or great bodily harm, which risk was known or reasonably foreseeable to the suspect.

    B.   Simple arson: Intentional destruction by fire or explosives that does not create imminent danger to life or risk of great bodily harm.

    C.   Attempted arson

        1.   Elements include the intent to set a fire and some preparation to commit the crime.

        2.   The intent is normally specific, and the act must be overt.

    D.   Setting negligent fires: Causing a fire to burn or to get out of control through culpable negligence.

IV.   The Model Arson Law

    A.   First-degree: burning of dwellings

    B.   Second-degree: burning of buildings other than dwellings

    C.   Third-degree: burning of other property

    D.   Fourth degree: attempting to burn building or property

V. The Arsonist

    A. The typical adult male arsonist has been reared in a broken or unstable home, has an extensive criminal history, is below average intelligence, lacks marital ties, is socially maladjusted or a loner, is unemployed or working in an unskilled position, and is intoxicated at the time he sets the fire.

    B. Female arsonists usually burn their own property, rarely that of an employer, neighbor, or associate. Often self-destructive, mentally defective, older, lonely, and unhappy.

    C. Juvenile firesetting

        1. According to the FBI's UCR, the majority of those arrested for arson are white males and more than half are under age 18, a higher rate of juvenile involvement than any other Index crime.

        2. *Fireplay* conveys a low level of intent to inflict harm and an absence of malice; rather it involves curiosity and fascination.

        3. *Firesetting* is "decidedly different" and involves malice and intent to inflict harm

        4. Juvenile firesetters are often divided into four categories:

            a. Curiosity/experimental

            b. Troubled/crisis

            c. Delinquent/criminal

            d. Pathological/emotionally disturbed

    D. Motivation

        1. Revenge, spite, and jealousy

        2. Vandalism and malicious mischief

        3. Crime concealment and diversionary tactics

        4. Profit and insurance fraud

        5. Intimidation and extortion

        6. Psychiatric afflictions, pyromania, alcoholism, and mental retardation

VI. Police and Fire Department Cooperation

    A. In many jurisdictions, arson is a joint investigation, with the fire department determining origin and cause, and the law enforcement agency handling the criminal investigation.

    B. Fire department expertise

        1. Expertise: Determining cause and nature of fires

        2. Role: Detecting arson

    C. Police department expertise

        1. Expertise: Investigating crimes

        2. Role: Apprehending criminals

    D. Coordinating efforts

       1. Need for joint command/coordination

       2. Cross training between fire and police

VII.   Other Sources of Assistance in Investigating Arson

    A. Bureau of Alcohol, Tobacco, Firearms and Explosives (ATF)

    B. News media

    C. Insurance companies

    D. Local arson task forces

       1. Detecting arson

       2. Reducing the number of arsons and deliberately set fires

       3. Developing a preventive program

    E. Importance of the dispatcher

       1. Emergency dispatchers are often a fire investigator's first link to solving what may turn out to be a difficult fire investigation.

       2. Often and without realizing it, the person answering the 911 call for help may be speaking to the person responsible for starting the fire.

VIII. Special Challenges in Investigation

    A. Coordinating efforts with the fire department and others

    B. Determining whether a crime has in fact been committed

    C. Finding physical evidence, most of which is destroyed by the fire

    D. Finding witnesses

    E. Determining whether the victim is a suspect

IX.   Responding to the Scene

    A. Responders should note the following at the scene of a fire:

       1. The presence, location, and conditions of victims and witnesses

       2. Vehicles leaving the scene, bystanders, unusual activities near the scene

       3. Flame and smoke conditions

       4. The type of occupancy, use, and condition of the structure

       5. Conditions surrounding the scene

       6. Weather conditions

       7. Fire-suppression techniques used, including ventilation, forcible entry, and utility shutoff measures

       8. Status of fire alarms, security alarms, and sprinklers

X.   The Preliminary Investigation

    A. The fire triangle

       1. Air

       2. Fuel

3. Heat
B. Arson indicators
   1. Accelerants
      a. Evidence of accelerants, substances that promote combustion, especially gasoline, is a primary form of physical evidence at an arson scene.
      b. Look for residues of liquid fire accelerants on floors, carpets, and soil because the liquid accelerants run to the lowest level.
      c. Olfactory *detection,* the sensitivity of the human nose to gasoline vapor, is ineffective if the odor is masked by another strong odor, such as that of burned debris.
      d. *Catalytic combustion detectors* are the most common type of flammable vapor detector used by arson investigators. Commonly known as a *sniffer,* a *combustible gas indicator,* an *explosimeter,* or a *vapor detector.*
   2. Igniters: matches; candles; cigars; cigarettes; cigarette lighters; electrical, mechanical, and chemical devices; and explosives.
   3. Burn indicators
      a. Alligatoring: checking of charred wood that gives it the appearance of alligator skin. Large, rolling blisters indicate rapid, intense heat. Small, flat alligatoring indicates slow, less intense heat.
      b. Crazing: formation of irregular cracks in glass caused by rapid, intense heat, possibly caused by a fire accelerant.
      c. Depth of char: how deeply wood is burned, indicates the length of burn and the fire's point of origin. Use a ruler to measure depth of char.
      d. Line of demarcation: a boundary between charred and uncharred material. A puddle-shaped line of demarcation on floors or rugs can indicate use of a liquid fire accelerant. In a cross section of wood, a sharp, distinct line of demarcation indicates a rapid, intense fire.
      e. Spalling: the breaking off of surface pieces of concrete or brick due to intense heat. Brown stains around the spall indicate use of an accelerant.
   4. Point of origin: established by finding the area with the deepest char, alligatoring, and usually the greatest destruction. More than one point of origin indicates arson.
   5. Burning pattern
      a. Fires normally burn upward, not outward. They are drawn toward ventilation and follow fuel paths.
      b. Given adequate ventilation, a fire will burn upward. If a door or window is open, it will be drawn toward that opening.

      c.   If the arsonist places a path of flammable liquid, the fire will follow that path, known as a trailer. The char marks will follow the trailer's path.

    6. Appearance of collapsed walls.

    7. Smoke color:

      a.   Blue smoke results from burning alcohol.

      b.   White smoke from burning vegetable compounds, hay, or phosphorous.

      c.   Yellow or brownish yellow smoke from film, nitric acid, sulfur, hydrochloric acid, or smokeless gunpowder.

      d.   Black smoke from petroleum or petroleum products.

C. Summary of arson indicators:

    1. More than one point of origin

    2. Deviation from normal burning patterns

    3. Evidence of trailers

    4. Evidence of accelerants

    5. Odors or smoke of a color associated with substances not normally present at the scene

    6. Signs that an abnormal amount of air, fuel, or heat was present

    7. Evidence of incendiary igniters at the point of origin

D. Photographing and videotaping an arson fire

    1. Pictures of a fire in progress show the smoke's color and its origination as well as the size of the fire at different points and times.

    2. Pictures taken of people at the fire scene might reveal the presence of a known arsonist or show a person who repeatedly appears in photos taken at fires and is therefore an arson suspect.

    3. After the fire, take enough pictures to show the entire scene in detail.

E. Physical evidence

    1. Preserving evidence is a major problem because much of the evidence is very fragile.

    2. An important step in an arson investigation is identifying potential accelerants at a fire scene.

F. Using K-9s in arson investigations:

    1. Can detect accelerants at fire scenes

    2. Search a crowd for possible suspect

    3. Search a suspect's clothing and vehicle for accelerants

    4. Search areas for accelerant containers

G. Evidence on a suspect

H. Observing unusual circumstances

I. Interviewing the victims, witnesses, and firefighters

XI.   Search Warrants and Fire Investigations

    A.   Entry to fight a fire requires no warrant. Once in the building, fire officials may remain a reasonable time to investigate the cause of the blaze.

        1.   After this time, an administrative warrant is needed, as established in *Michigan v. Tyler* (1978).

    B.   Administrative warrant: Issued when it is necessary for a government agent to search the premises to determine the fire's cause and origin.

        1.   The scope of the search must be limited to determining the cause and origin.

        2.   If evidence of a crime/arson is discovered, a criminal warrant is required to continue the search.

    C.   Criminal warrant: issued on probable cause when the premises yield evidence of a crime.

    D.   The Court established guidelines for arson investigators in *Michigan v. Clifford* (1984).

    E.   In *Coolidge v. New Hampshire* (1971), the Court held that evidence of criminal activity discovered during a search with a valid administrative warrant may be seized under the plain-view doctrine.

    F.   Guidelines on the current legal status of searches conducted during fire investigations include the following:

        1.   Warrants are not required when an authorized individual consents to the search.

        2.   Warrants are not required when investigators enter under "exigent circumstances," such as while firefighters are extinguishing the blaze or conducting overhaul.

        3.   Warrants are required if the premises are subject to a "reasonable expectation of privacy."

        4.   Evidence of a crime discovered during an administrative search may be seized if in plain view.

        5.   Once evidence of arson is discovered, the fire's cause and origin are assumed to be known. A criminal warrant is required to continue the search.

        6.   When in doubt, obtain a warrant.

XII.   Investigating Vehicle Arson

    A.   Look for evidence of accelerants. A quart to a half-gallon of flammable liquid is required to cause a major vehicle fire.

    B.   Determine whether the vehicle was insured.

XIII.   Prosecuting Arsonists

    A.   Some studies indicate that considerably more than 90 percent of arsonists go unpunished, probably because arson is most often committed without the benefit of witnesses.

B. Most arson cases involve only circumstantial evidence.

C. Prosecutors may choose not to prosecute such cases.

XIV. Preventing Arson

    A. Six key risk factors for arson:

        1. Abandoned properties

        2. Negative-equity properties

        3. Properties whose gas and/or electric were shut off

        4. Sites of prior-year fires

        5. Gang locales

        6. Known drug hot spots

XV. Investigating Bombings and Explosions

    A. Most explosive incidents in this country fall into one of five classes:

        1. Juvenile/experimentation

        2. Recovered military ordnance/commercial explosives

        3. Emotionally disturbed persons

        4. Criminal actions

        5. Terrorist or extremist activity

    B. Common types of bombs (referred to as improvised explosive devices [IEDs] or homemade):

        1. Dry ice

        2. Mailbox

        3. Car bomb

        4. Nail bomb

        5. Pipe bomb

    C. Terrorists have long used cellular phones to trigger IEDs.

    D. Other remote control devices are also used to trigger IEDs.

    E. A homemade explosive known as "TATP," triacetone triperoxide, is a liquid explosive. These devices should not be underestimated.

    F. Car bombs: vehicle-born improvised explosive device (VBIED), or the "car bomb"

XVI. Responding to a Bomb Threat

    A. Searchers must pay attention to unattended bags, boxes, or briefcases.

    B. If a bomb is found:

        1. Do not touch the device.

        2. Clear an area of at least 300 feet around the area.

        3. All radios should be turned off.

        4. Ensure that a secondary explosive device is not in the area.

5. Ensure that the scene has been secured.
6. Ensure that the chain of custody is initiated for evidence that may have been previously collected.
7. Establish procedures to document personnel entering and exiting the scene.
8. Establish and document procedures for evidence collection, control, and chain of custody.

C. Using K-9s to detect explosives
D. Using stationary technology in detecting explosives: Airports and cargo terminals use X-ray and computed axial tomography (CAT) equipment to scan large numbers of items and people.
E. Using robots: can be equipped with disrupters, devices that use gunpowder to fire a jet of water or a projectile at a particular component of an explosive to make it safe.

XVII. Investigating Bomb Explosions

A. When investigating explosions and bombings, pay special attention to fragments of the explosive device as well as to power present at the scene.
B. Determine motive.
C. Raising awareness.
D. Importance of the team approach.

XVIII. Summary

Chapter Questions

1. The elements of the crime of arson include
   a. malicious burning of a building or property of another with the intent to destroy the building.
   b. willful, malicious burning of a building or property of another or of one's own to defraud, or causing to be burned or aiding, counseling or procuring such burning.
   c. setting a fire to a building that is not your own, for profit.
   d. two or more conspirators.

2. The purpose of the law enforcement officer in arson investigations is to
   a. assume control of the investigation.
   b. provide protection for the fire officer.
   c. provide resources for the fire department.
   d. work cooperatively with the fire officer to handle the criminal part of the investigation.

3. Private insurance investigators
   a. interfere with law enforcement and fire investigators and should be kept away.
   b. are supportive, but not helpful.
   c. can assist fire and police efforts in investigating fire losses.
   d. are forbidden to enter or assist without a warrant.

4. The fire triangle consists of the three elements necessary for a substance to burn. They are
   a. oxygen, fire, and heat.
   b. fuel, heat, and warmth.
   c. wood, warmth, and fire.
   d. air, fuel, and heat.

5. Alligatoring is the
   a. checking of charred wood that gives it the appearance of alligator skin.
   b. the formation of irregular cracks in glass due to rapid, intense heat.
   c. an indication of how deeply the wood is burned.
   d. subterranean cracking of the floorboards.

6. Crazing is
   a. checking of charred wood that gives it the appearance of alligator skin.
   b. the formation of irregular cracks in glass due to rapid, intense heat.
   c. an indication of how deeply the wood is burned.
   d. a series of concentric spirals in burned glass.

7. What is the breaking off of surface pieces of concrete or brick due to intense heat?
   a. crazing
   b. spalling
   c. decomposition
   d. starring

8. Blue smoke results from the burning of
   a. alcohol.
   b. vegetable compounds.
   c. film, nitric acid, sulfur, hydrochloric acid, or smokeless gunpowder.
   d. petroleum or petroleum products.

9. Black smoke results from the burning of:
   a. alcohol.
   b. vegetable compounds.
   c. film, nitric acid, sulfur, hydrochloric acid, or smokeless gunpowder.
   d. petroleum or petroleum products.

10. The Model Arson Law divides arson into several categories. Which of the following is not one of them?
   a. first-degree: burning of dwellings
   b. second-degree: burning of buildings other than dwellings
   c. third-degree: burning of other property
   d. aggravated arson: including injury or death

11. Attempted arson has the same elements as arson, but without the success.   True or False

12. Female arsonists usually burn their own property, rarely that of an employer, neighbor or associate.   True or False

13. ATF is responsible for alcohol, tobacco, firearms, and explosive investigations.   True or False

14. Per the Model Arson Law, third-degree is burning of property including dwellings.   True or False

15. Crime concealment and diversionary tactics motivate criminals to set fires to conceal their crimes.   True or False

16. Arson investigations are usually joint investigations involving both law enforcement and fire officers.   True or False

17. If a bomb is found, the most important rule in handling suspect packages is to not touch the package.   True or False

18. It is sometimes difficult to determine whether the victim is a suspect in arson cases.

True or False

19. Evidence of accelerants (substances that promote combustion) is a primary form of physical evidence at an arson scene.

True or False

20. Brown stains around the spalling indicate use of an accelerant.

True or False

21. Juvenile firesetters are often divided into four categories: curiosity/experimental, delinquent/criminal, pathological/emotionally disturbed, and _____ firesetters.

22. Juvenile _____ is often a first major outward sign of usually more deeply rooted problems and is a risk factor associated with delinquency, although usually not identified as one of them.

23. Profit and _____ fraud are frequent motives for arson.

24. Police or firefighters who intentionally set fires to receive attention and praise at having "played the hero," are referred to as _____

25. Intimidation, extortion, and_____ are motives of striking workers and employers to apply pressure during a labor action and arson may be one of the methods that is used.

26. _____ start fires because of an irresistible urge or passion for fire. Some derive sexual satisfaction from watching fires.

27. The professional _____—the arsonist for hire—is extremely difficult to identify because such individuals have no apparent link to the fire.

28. On January 24, 2003, the Bureau of Alcohol, Tobacco and Firearms became part of the Department of Justice under the Homeland Security bill and had its name expanded to the Bureau of Alcohol, Tobacco, Firearms and _____ to reflect the new focus on bomb-related crime and terrorism.

29. _____ investigators have the additional advantage of being able to enter the fire scene without a warrant in their efforts to examine the damage and to determine the cause of the fire.

30. Evidence of _____, substances that promote combustion, especially gasoline, is a primary form of physical evidence at an arson scene.

31. Where would you look for evidence of accelerants at an arson scene?

32. Which is more effective in detecting accelerants? One's own olfactory senses (smell) or other means?

33. Describe some of the most common burn indicators at arson scenes and what they may tell the investigator?

34. What are some of the challenges to investigating a fire scene with regard to the physical evidence?

35. Describe the warrant process for investigating crimes involving fires.

Case Study

36. A large, three-story building in the middle of downtown exploded following a fire. A pedestrian walking by smelled smoke, and by the time he called 911, the building had become fully engulfed in flames. He said the smoke was black in color. As the fire trucks were pulling up to the front of the building, it exploded, and three firefighters were killed. The time from the pedestrian smelling smoke to the building being fully engaged was about 45 seconds, based on the time of the 911 call. While the pedestrian was on the telephone, he yelled that flames were coming out of the top floor of the three-story building. The explosion seemed to come from the first floor of the building. The firefighters were killed when building material fell on them or was exploded through their bodies. Based on the available information, the arson investigators believe that this was a case of arson. What actions should you take as the arson investigator for the police department?

_____

_____

_____

_____

_____

_____

_____

_____

Answer Key

1. b		11. True
2. d		12. True
3. c		13. True
4. d		14. False
5. a		15. True
6. b		16. True
7. b		17. True
8. a		18. True
9. d		19. True
10. d		20. True

21. troubled/crisis

22. firesetting

23. insurance

24. strikers

25. sabotage

26. Pyromaniacs

27. torch

28. Explosives

29. Insurance

30. accelerants

31. Look for residues of liquid fire accelerants on floors, carpets, and soil because the liquid accelerants run to the lowest level. In addition, these areas often have the lowest temperatures during the fire and may not have enough oxygen to support complete combustion of the accelerant. Accelerants may seep through porous or cracked floors to underlying soil that has excellent retention properties for flammable liquids. Accelerants can also be found on the clothes and shoes of the suspect if apprehended. You can also identify

fire accelerants at the scene either by your own sense of smell or by using portable equipment that detects residues of flammable liquids.

32. *Olfactory detection,* the sensitivity of the human nose to gasoline vapor, is ineffective if the odor is masked by another strong odor, such as that of burned debris. Moreover, it is often inconvenient or impossible to sniff for accelerant odors along floors or in recessed areas.

    Catalytic combustion detectors are the most common type of flammable vapor detector used by arson investigators. Commonly known as a *sniffer,* a *combustible gas indicator,* an *explosimeter,* or a *vapor detector,* this detector is portable, moderately priced, and fairly simple to operate. Basically, vapor samples are pumped over a heated, platinum-plated wire coil that causes any combustible gas present to oxidize. The heat from the oxidation raises the coil's electrical resistance, and this change is measured electrically.

33. Burn indicators are visible evidence of the effects of heating or partial burning. They indicate various aspects of a fire such as rate of development, temperature, duration, time of occurrence, presence of flammable liquids, and points of origin. Interpreting burn indicators is a primary means of determining the causes of fires.

    Common burn indicators include alligatoring, crazing, the depth of char, lines of demarcation, sagged furniture springs, and spalling.

34. Preserving evidence is a major problem because much of the evidence is very fragile. Use disposable cellulose sponges to sop up accelerants for transfer to a container. Use hypodermic or cooking syringes to suck up accelerants between boards or crevices. Sift ashes to detect small objects such as the timing device from an igniter.

    Incendiary evidence at the point of origin can be part of a candle, an empty flammable liquid container, excessive amounts of unburned newspaper folded together, or a number of unburned matches.

    Paper exposed to high temperatures and sufficient air burns with little ash to examine. However, with a limited supply of air, only partial combustion occurs, leaving charred paper evidence that can be collected for laboratory examination. Paper in a fireplace or stove may be only partially burned, even if the building was totally consumed. These papers may provide a motive for the arson. If the paper is not destroyed, a laboratory may be able to recover any messages on it.

35. The U.S. Supreme Court requires a two-step warrant process for investigating fires involving crimes. The initial search may require an *administrative warrant* for searching the premises for cause of fire and origin determination *and* a *criminal warrant* when evidence of a crime is discovered. Both require probable cause for issuance.

An administrative warrant is issued when it is necessary for a government agent to search the premises to determine the fire's cause and origin. A criminal warrant is issued on probable cause when the premises yield evidence of a crime.

Case Study Answer

36. This case is clearly very complex and highly critical. The most important steps right now are to conduct a background investigation and locate witnesses. The fire department member of the team will be best equipped to determine if there are reasons to suspect that the fire is arson. The building's ownership and its insurance status are both critical pieces of information, as well as whether the building was occupied by businesses or used for private dwelling, and what kind of flammable materials might have been inside it. Black smoke indicates a source of petroleum or petroleum products.

   The person who called 911 should be thoroughly examined, not only to obtain information about the type of smoke and the pattern in which the fire spread, but also to determine whether he is a suspect. The explosion is a different issue, and an expert should be brought in to examine the occurrence and determine whether it was an accidental or planned result of the fire.

COMPUTER CRIME

OUTLINE

- The Scope and Cost of the Problem
- Terminology and Definitions
- Classification and Types of Computer Crimes
- Special Challenges in Investigation
- The Preliminary Investigation
- Forensic Examination of Computer Evidence
- Legal Considerations in Collecting and Analyzing Computer Evidence
- Follow-Up Investigation
- Security of the Police Department's Computers
- Legislation
- The Investigative Team
- Resources Available
- Preventing Computer Crime

Chapter 17
Computer Crime

By the end of this chapter, you should know how to define the terms and understand the application of the following concepts. Test your understanding of the chapter by verifying that you know this information. If you do not know it, review the chapter.

Can You Define?

adware	firewall	piracy
biometrics	hacker	port scanning
computer crime	hacktivism	sniffing
computer virus	hardware disabler	spam
cracker	imaging	spoofing
cybercrime	Internet Protocol (IP)	spyware
cyberspace	address	steganography
cybertechnology	ISP	trashing
cyberterrorism	keystroke logging	Trojan horse
data remanence	logic bomb	URL
denial of service	malware	virtual reality
domain name	pharming	worm
e-crime	phreaking	zombie
encryption		

Do you know?

- What two key characteristics of computer crime are?
- How computer crime can be categorized?
- What special challenges are presented by computer-related crimes?
- What a common protocol for processing a crime scene involving electronic evidence is?
- What a basic tenet is for first responders at a computer crime scene?

- How an investigator with a search warrant should execute it in a computer crime investigation?
- What form electronic evidence and other computer crime evidence may take?
- What precautions to take when handling computer disks?
- How electronic evidence should be stored?
- Whether "deleted" data are really deleted?

(continued)

(continued)

• Whether most cybercrimes against businesses are committed by insiders or outsiders? • How cybercriminals may be categorized?	• What motivates the different types of cybercriminals? • What approach is often required in investigating computer crime? • How computer crimes can be prevented?

Chapter Outline

I.   The Scope and Cost of the Problem

    A.   The current crime tool is a personal computer linked to the Internet.

        1.   Cybercrime has significant economic impacts and threatens U.S. national security interests.

        2.   According to the Federal Trade Commission (FTC), that annually, nearly 9 million people are victims of identity theft, many of whom had information stolen from cyberspace.

        3.   Computers are pervasive in the home, workplace, and school. At the end of 2006, CTIA–The Wireless Association reported 233 million U.S. wireless subscribers, more than 76 percent of the total U.S. population.

    B.   The IC3 2007 Internet Crime Report

        1.   Internet Crime Complaint Center (IC3) is a partnership between the FBI and the National White Collar Crime Center (NW3C) designed to serve as a clearinghouse for cybercrime data for law enforcement and regulatory agencies at the federal, state, and local levels.

        2.   The IC3 received 206,884 complaints in 2007, leading to a reported dollar loss of nearly $240 million, an all-time high.

        3.   Among the 2007 top ten complaint categories, Internet auction fraud was by far the most reported offense, comprising 35.7 percent of referred crime complaints.

        4.   In addition, nondelivery of merchandise or payment represented 24.9 percent of complaints.

        5.   The top scams of 2007: scams involving pets, checks, spam, and online dating sites. Of the top ten countries reporting, the United States ranked first at 63.2 percent, followed by the United Kingdom at 15.3 percent.

    C.   The 2007 E-Crime Watch Survey

        1.   This survey is conducted jointly by the U.S. Secret Service, Carnegie Mellon University Software Engineering Institute's CERT® Program, and Microsoft Corporation.

        2.   The fourth annual survey reported that 57 percent of participants said they are increasingly concerned about the potential effects

of e-crime, and 49 percent reported experiencing an increase in e-crime during 2006 compared with the prior year.

3. The top e-crimes perpetrated by outsiders were

    a. Virus, worms, or other malicious code (experienced by 74 percent of respondents).

    b. Unauthorized access to/use of information, systems, or networks (experienced by 55 percent).

    c. Illegal generation of spam e-mail (experienced by 53 percent).

    d. Spyware (not including adware—experienced by 52 percent).

    e. Denial of service attacks (experienced by 49 percent).

    f. Fraud (experienced by 46 percent).

    g. Phishing (experienced by 48 percent).

4. The survey found that the most effective technologies were

    a. Stateful firewalls, maintaining its position as #1 at 82 percent).

    b. Access controls (79 percent).

    c. Electronic access controls (78 percent).

    d. Application layer firewalls (72 percent).

    e. Host-based antivirus (70 percent).

D. The 2007 CSI Computer Crime and Security Survey

1. Since 1995, the Computer Security Institute (CSI), with the help of the FBI, has conducted annual surveys of computer security practitioners in corporations, financial and medical institutions, universities, and government agencies throughout the nation to analyze and assess the current state of computer network security.

2. The average annual loss shot up to $350,424, from $168,000 the previous year. Not since the 2004 report have average losses been this high.

3. Almost one-fifth (18 percent) of those respondents who suffered one or more kinds of security incident further said they'd suffered a "targeted attack," defined as a malware attack aimed exclusively at their organization or at organizations within a small subset of the general population.

4. Financial fraud overtook virus attacks as the source of the greatest financial losses. Virus losses, which had been the leading cause of loss for seven straight years, fell to second place. Another significant cause of loss was system penetration by outsiders.

5. Insider abuse of network access or e-mail (such as trafficking in pornography or pirated software) edged out virus incidents as the most prevalent security problem, with 59 and 52 percent of respondents reporting each respectively.

6. When asked generally whether they'd suffered a security incident, 46 percent said yes, down from 53 percent last year and 56 percent the year before.

7. The percentage of organizations reporting computer intrusions to law enforcement continued upward after reversing a multi-year decline over the past two years, standing now at 29 percent as compared with 25 percent in last year's report.

II. Terminology and Definitions

    A. Major definitions include

       1. Cybercrime—a criminal act that can only be carried out using cybertechnology and can only take place in the cyberspace.

       2. Cybertechnology—the spectrum of computing and information/communication technologies, from individual computers to computer networks to the Internet.

       3. Cyberspace—an intangible, virtual world existing in the network connections between two or more computers.

       4. E-crime—any criminal violation in which a computer or electronic form or media is used in the commission of that crime.

    B. Other terms: adware, browser, byte, digital evidence, disk drive, electronic device, electronic evidence, encryption, firewall, floppy disk, gigabyte (GB), hacktivism, imaging, keystroke, logging, kilobyte (KB), logic bomb, malware, megabyte (MB), network, phreaking, piracy, port scanning, script, sniffing, spyware, trashing, Trojan horse, URL, virtual reality, zombie

    C. The net versus the Web:

       1. The Internet is a network of networks.

       2. The Web is an abstract (imaginary) space of information. On the Net, you find computers; on the Web, you find information.

       3. Deciphering e-mail and Web addresses

          a. A domain name is the unique name of a computer system on the Internet that distinguishes it from all other online systems. A domain name is *not* the same as a Web address, although many people incorrectly refer to it as such.

          b. A Web address or Uniform Resource Locator (URL) has several more elements. For example: URL: http://www.amz456.com

          c. Scheme name: http (*https* typically denotes a secure Web site)—this part means an http request is being made to the host server

    D. Live chat and instant messaging (IM).

       1. Allow two or more people to "talk" online in real time.

       2. Internet Relay Chat (IRC) environment offers worldwide communication.

       3. Investigators should be familiar with the types of crimes that may involve computers.

III.　Classification and Types of Computer Crimes

  A.　Computer as target

    1.　Hacking/hacker/cracker

      a.　Act of gaining unauthorized access to a computer system.

      b.　Many investigative agencies refer to these people simply as "intruders" or "attackers" instead of hackers or crackers.

    2.　Viruses: Programs that attack, attach themselves to and become part of other executable programs.

    3.　Worms: Self-contained programs that travel from machine to machine across network connections, often clogging networks and information systems as they spread.

    4.　Denial-of-service attacks: Disrupt or degrade a computer or network's Internet connection or e-mail service, thus interrupting the regular flow of data.

    5.　Extortion: Cybercriminals may attempt to extort large sums of money from companies by threatening to or actually damaging the company's computers, network, or Web presence.

  B.　Computer as tool

    1.　Fraud

    2.　Re-shipper schemes

    3.　Spam

      a.　Unsolicited bulk e-mail messages, similar to junk mail and commonly commercial. Lesser known by its formal designation as unsolicited commercial e-mail (UCE), spam is most often perceived by recipients as an annoyance and nothing more.

      b.　Sometimes, however, spam is distributed on such a massive scale, with such malicious or contentious content, or with intent to defraud, that the spamming becomes criminal.

      c.　Chain letters calling for a payment to participate may be construed as pyramid schemes, which are illegal in most states.

      d.　Spam that leaves no question as to its illegality is that intended to phish, commit identity theft, or otherwise extract sensitive information from a computer user with the ultimate goal of using such information to engage in criminal activity.

    4.　Spoofing

      a.　Often considered synonymous with phishing, is acquiring unauthorized access to a computer or network through a message using an IP address that appears to be from a trusted host, in an attempt to commit identity theft.

    5.　Pharming is a cybercrime that is catching even the most cautious, experienced Internet users off guard. Pharming involves hijacking a domain name to redirect online traffic away from a legitimate Web site toward a fake site, such as a bogus bank Web site. Even if a computer user types in the correct domain name of a legitimate site, if that site has been pharmed, the user will be unknowingly taken to the fraudulent site, where they may unwittingly reveal account numbers, passwords, and other sensitive personal information that can be used for identity theft or other criminal endeavors.

6. Theft of intellectual property
7. Online child pornography and child sexual abuse
8. Cyberterrorism

IV. Special Challenges in Investigation

A. Law enforcement's ability to identify coordinated threats is directly tied to the amount of reporting that takes place.

B. Nonreporting of computer crimes

1. Law enforcement's ability to identify coordinated threats is directly tied to the amount of reporting that takes place.

2. Victims of computer-related crimes are often unaware that a crime has been committed or have a reason for not reporting the crime to authorities.

   a. The *2007 E-Crime Watch Survey* found that most e-crimes are handled internally without involving legal action or law enforcement (67 percent for insiders, 66 percent for outsiders).

   b. Reasons included the damage level was insufficient to warrant prosecution (40 percent), a lack of evidence (34 percent), or the individuals responsible could not be identified (28 percent).

   c. The *CSI Survey* reports that the most common reason for not reporting e-crimes to law enforcement was a fear that negative publicity would hurt the organization's stock or image (26 percent), followed by a belief that law enforcement would be unable to help.

C. Lack of investigator training

D. Need for specialists and teamwork

E. The fragility of the evidence

F. Jurisdictional issues

1. The global reach of the Internet poses challenge in computer crime cases by introducing jurisdictional complications on top of an already complex area of criminal investigation.

2. The traditional concept of jurisdiction focuses almost exclusively on the territorial aspect of "where did the act take place?"

3. Traditional territorial boundaries are often complicated in cybercrime cases, as the location of the acts must take into account the location of the defendant and where the material originated (was uploaded from), any servers this information passed through, the location of

computers where material was downloaded, and the location of any effects this material may have set in motion.

4. It is necessary to determine whether the act is illegal in all of the countries involved.

5. Virtual child pornography, illegal in Canada and the European Union, was declared illegal in the United States under the Child Pornography Prevention Act (CPPA) of 1996. However, the Supreme Court ruled in *Ashcroft v. Free Speech Coalition* (2002) that the portion of the CPPA prohibiting the production or distribution of such virtual pornography was overly broad and an unconstitutional infringement on the First Amendment right to freedom of speech.

6. A computer crime investigation may also involved domestic jurisdictional issues, between state and federal levels of jurisdiction as well as between states.

V. The Preliminary Investigation

A. Securing and evaluating the scene

1. Recommended steps:

   a. Remove all individuals from the immediate area from which evidence is to be collected.

   b. At this point in the investigation, do not alter the condition of any electronic device: If it is on, leave it on. If it is off, leave it off.

   c. Protect perishable data on pagers, caller ID boxes, cell phones, and so on, physically and electronically, always keeping in mind that devices containing perishable data should be immediately secured and documented (photographed).

   d. Identify any communications lines (telephone, LAN/Ethernet connections) attached to devices such as modems and caller ID boxes. Document, label, and disconnect each line from the wall rather than the device, if possible. Communication via such lines must be severed to prevent remote access to data on the computers.

   e. *Do not touch* the keyboard, mouse, diskettes, CDs, or any other computer equipment or electronic devices (evidence) at this stage.

2. A basic tenet for first responders at computer crime scenes is to observe the ON/OFF rule: If it's on, leave it on. If it's off, leave it off.

B. Preliminary interviews

1. The NIJ recommends the following information be obtained in the preliminary interviews:

   a. Names of all users of the computers and devices

   b. All computer and Internet user information

   c. All login names and user account names

      d.   Purpose and uses of computers and devices

      e.   All passwords

      f.   Any automated applications in use

      g.   Types of Internet access

      h.   Any offsite storage

      i.   Internet service provider

      j.   Installed software documentation

      k.   All e-mail accounts

      l.   Security provisions in use

      m. Web mail account information

      n.   Data access restrictions in place

      o.   All instant message screen names

      p.   All destructive devices or software in use

      q.   MySpace, Facebook, or other online social networking Web site account information

2. The investigator should attempt to assess the skill levels of the computer users involved because proficient users may conceal or destroy evidence by employing sophisticated techniques such as encryption.

3. Before evidence can be collected, determine if it is necessary to obtain a warrant, because having a search warrant generally decreases the amount of resistance investigators face at the scene and increases the odds of successful prosecution should the case go to court.

C. Obtaining a search warrant

1. Searches may be conducted by consent.

2. If the suspect is unknown, this is not desirable because it could alert the person who committed the crime. In such cases, a search warrant must be obtained.

3. Privacy issues surrounding some or all of the information contained in the digital evidence desired may pose a legal technicality. If the organization involved is the victim of the crime, its management normally grants permission.

4. If the organization is not the victim, it may be necessary to obtain permission from individuals named in the evidentiary file, which could be an enormous task.

5. It may be better to take the evidence to a court and obtain court permission if possible.

6. Investigators may have both a consent search form and a search warrant, thus avoiding the possibility of destruction of evidence.

7. Consent is better than a search warrant because it avoids the usual attack by the defense in search warrant cases.

D. Recognizing evidence—traditional and digital
   1. Cybercrime evidence:
      a. Latent like fingerprints or DNA evidence.
      b. Crosses jurisdictional borders quickly and easily.
      c. Fragile and easily altered, damaged or destroyed.
      d. Can be time-sensitive.
   2. Investigators should remember that digital evidence may also contain physical evidence such as DNA, fingerprints, or serology.

E. Documenting digital evidence
   1. Observe and document the physical scene.
   2. Document the condition and location of the computer system.
   3. Identify and document related electronic components that will not be collected.
   4. Photograph the entire scene with 360-degree coverage if possible.
   5. Photograph the front and back of the computer, the monitor screen and other peripheral components connected to the computer.
   6. Check and identify status of computers at the scene.
   7. Indicators of a computer network:
      a. Presence of multiple computer systems
      b. Presence of cables and connectors running between computers or central devices such as hubs
      c. Information provided by those on the scene or by informants

F. Collecting physical and digital evidence
   1. Investigators assigned to cybercrimes or other computer-related crimes must have ready certain tools and equipment commonly required in cases involving electronic evidence.
      a. Digital evidence is often contained on disks, CDs, hard drives, or any number of peripheral electronic devices.
      b. Avoid contact with recording surfaces of computer tapes and disks.
      c. Other nonelectronic evidence that may prove valuable to the investigation includes material found in the vicinity of the suspect computer system, such as handwritten notes, Post-It notes with passwords written on them, blank pads of paper with the indentations from previous pages torn off, hardware and software manuals, calendars, and photographs.
      d. Investigators should be aware that the chain-of-custody issues regarding data are additional to the chain-of-custody issues regarding the physical item.
   2. Collecting evidence from cyberspace
      a. Most, if not all cyber crimes leave some type of cyber trail or e-print evidence.

b. If an investigator knows a suspect user's screen name, it can be linked to an identifiable IP address, which can provide such information as the suspect's billing address and log-in records, which can in turn lead to the location of the computer used, such as in a private residence, a public library, or an Internet cafe.

c. After the desired target information is culled from the general ISP data records, the investigator needs a search warrant to delve further into a particular user's account information.

d. Understanding how to decipher e-mail headers is a necessary skill for cyberinvestigators.

3. Mobile evidence

a. Evidence on a mobile or cell phone system may be found on the communication equipment (the phone itself), the subscriber identity module (SIM), a fixed base station, switching network, the operation/maintenance system for the network, and the customer management system.

b. It may also be possible to retrieve deleted items.

c. Call data records (CDRs) obtained from the network service provider are also very valuable as evidence, for they can reveal the location of the mobile phone user every time a call is sent or received.

d. Because of its digital nature, mobile evidence must be handled carefully, yet few standards have been widely implemented regarding how best to collect such evidence.

G. Packaging, transporting, and storing digital evidence.

1. Before electronic evidence is packaged, it must be properly documented, labeled, marked, photographed, video recorded or sketched, and inventoried.

2. All connections and connected devices should be labeled for easy reconfiguration of the system later.

3. All digital evidence should be packed in antistatic packaging and in a way that will prevent it from being bent, scratched, or otherwise deformed.

4. When transporting computer evidence, investigators should keep digital evidence away from magnetic fields such as those produced by radio transmitters, speaker magnets, and magnetic mount emergency lights.

5. Store electronic evidence in a secure area away from temperature and humidity extremes and protected from magnetic sources, moisture, dust, and other harmful particles or contaminants.

6. Do not use plastic bags.

H. Crime-specific investigations

1. *Investigations Involving the Internet and Computer Networks* (2007) provides in-depth explanations of investigations involving e-mail;

Web sites; instant message services and Chat Rooms; file sharing networks, network intrusion/denial of service; and bulletin boards, message boards, and newsgroups.

2. *Electronic Crime Scene Investigation* (2008) contains detailed discussions of electronic crime and digital evidence considerations by crime category: child abuse or exploitation; computer intrusion; counterfeiting; death investigation; domestic violence, threats, and extortion; e-mail threats, harassment, and stalking; gaming; identity theft; narcotics; online or economic fraud; prostitution; software piracy/ telecommunication fraud; and terrorism. For those interested in these in-depth discussions, search the Internet by their titles.

VI. Forensic Examination of Computer Evidence

A. Computer forensics carries the potential to benefit nearly every type of criminal investigation.

B. Data analysis and recovery.

1. Data recovery is a computer forensic technique that requires an extensive knowledge of computer technology and storage devices and an understanding of the laws of search and seizure and the rules of evidence.

2. Data remanence refers to the residual physical representation of data that have been erased.

3. A qualified computer forensic analyst may be able to recover evidence of the copying of documents, whether to another computer on the network or to some removable storage device such as a diskette; the printing of documents; the dates and times specific documents were created, accessed, or modified; the type and amount of use a particular computer has had; Internet searches run from a computer; and more.

VII. Legal Considerations in Collecting and Analyzing Computer Evidence

A. The Privacy Protection Act's (PPA) prohibition on use of a search warrant does not apply in the following circumstances (*Investigations Involving the Internet*):

1. Materials searched for or seized are contraband, fruits, or instrumentalities of the crime.

2. There is reason to believe that the immediate seizure of such materials is necessary to prevent death or serious bodily injury.

3. Probable cause exists to believe that the person possessing the materials has committed or is committing a criminal offense to which the materials relate.

B. The NIJ also cautions first responders seizing electronic devices that improper access of data stored within may violate provisions of certain federal laws, including the Electronic Communications Privacy Act.

C. An evolving area of legal wrangling concerns copyright laws and investigative agencies that seize computers that have an operating system installed on them, as most do. Operating systems, which are copyright protected, may not be copied without the author's, or in this case the software company's, expressed permission.

VIII. Follow-Up Investigation

    A. Developing suspects

        1. Most cybercrimes against businesses are committed by "outsiders."

            a. The *2007 E-Crime Watch Survey* reports that of the 74 percent of businesses who were victims of virus, worms, or other malicious code, 46 percent were infiltrated by outsiders compared with 18 percent victimized by insiders.

            b. Of the 55 percent who reported being victims of unauthorized access to/use of information, systems, or networks, 30 percent fell victim to outsiders compared with 25 percent victimization by insiders.

            c. Of the 53 percent of businesses victimized by illegal generation of spam, 38 percent of the cases were committed by outsiders compared to 6 percent by insiders.

        2. Cybercriminal categories:

            a. Crackers/hackers

            b. Vandals

            c. Thieves

        3. Organization level:

            a. Most computer criminals commit their criminal acts alone.

            b. A smaller percentage of cybercriminals will exist in organized groups.

        4. In 2007, perpetrators were predominantly male (75.8 percent) and half resided in one of the following states: California, Florida, New York, Texas, Illinois, Pennsylvania, and Georgia.

            a. Most reported perpetrators were from the United States.

            b. A significant number of perpetrators also were located in the United Kingdom, Nigeria, Canada, Romania, and Italy.

            c. Most perpetrators were in contact with the complainant through either e-mail or via the web.

    B. Organized cybercrime groups

        1. A few hacker groups have been observed to have a Mafia-like hierarchy.

        2. Particularly challenging are cases involving cybergangs that operate in countries with weak hacking laws and lax enforcement, such as Russia, eastern European countries, and China.

3. An effective tactic being used to apprehend organized cybercrime networks is undercover investigation and surveillance.

C. Undercover investigation and surveillance

1. Covert investigation including ongoing surveillance operations is a method being used to gather evidence against cybercrime gangs.

2. Undercover tactics are also commonly used in cases of online child pornography and sexual exploitation.

IX. Security of the Police Department Computers

A. Law enforcement officers should not overlook the possibility that their own computers may be accessed by criminals.

B. Any computer attached to a phone line is accessible by unauthorized people outside the department, even thousands of miles away on a different continent.

C. Ensuring the security of an agency's network should be a top priority.

X. Legislation

A. Since the advent of the Internet, online pornography, real and virtual child pornography, organized crime, narcoterrorism, and global terrorism, legislation efforts have been challenged to keep up with security safeguards.

B. The USA PATRIOT Act (2001) consists of more than 150 sections, many of which pertain to electronic communications and other areas of cybercrime investigation

C. The PATRIOT Act also changed key features of existing National Security Letter (NSL) protocol.

1. NSLs are a type of subpoena issued in foreign counterintelligence and international terrorism investigations to obtain records under the statutory authority of the Electronic Communications Privacy Act (telephone and ISP records), the Right to Financial Privacy Act (financial institution records), and the Fair Credit Reporting Act (records from credit bureaus).

2. The act expanded signature authority for NSLs to increase the efficiency and effectiveness of processing such subpoenas.

D. Other federal statutes relevant to computer-related crimes include patent laws, espionage and sabotage laws, trade secret laws, the Copyright Act of 1976, and the Financial Privacy Act of 1978.

E. Phishing schemes are likely to violate not only various existing state statutes on fraud and identity theft but also several federal criminal laws.

F. Transmission of computer viruses and worms may be prosecuted under the federal provisions of the computer fraud and abuse statute relating to damage to computer systems and files.

XI. The Investigative Team

A. Investigating computer crimes often requires a team approach.

B. The investigative team is responsible for assigning all team personnel according to the specialties, including securing outside specialists if necessary; securing the crime scene area; obtaining search warrant applications; determining the specific hardware and software involved; searching for, obtaining, marking, preserving, and storing evidence; obtaining necessary disks, printouts, and other records; and preparing information for investigative reports.

C. Law enforcement agencies and private nonprofits such as the National Center for Missing and Exploited Children (NCMEC) are increasingly relying on computer crimes units and experts to answer questions.

D. To assist in combating increasing computer crimes, government and private businesses are developing computer crime teams similar to the FBI's kidnapping crime teams and the arson investigation specialist teams of the Bureau of Alcohol, Tobacco, Firearms and Explosives.

E. The FBI's Computer Analysis Response Team (CART) helps state and local law enforcement as well as federal agents.

XII. Resources Available

A. Police agencies in many states are forming cooperative groups and providing training seminars on investigating computer crimes.

B. The U.S. Department of Justice (DOJ) has developed the National Cybercrime Training Partnership (NCTP) to develop and promote a long-range strategy for high-tech police work, including interagency and interjurisdictional cooperation, information networking and technical training; to garner public and political understanding of the problem and generate support for solutions; and to serve as a proactive force to focus the momentum of the entire law enforcement community to ensure that proposed solutions are fully implemented.

C. The IC3 provides to cybercrime victims a convenient, user-friendly reporting mechanism that notifies authorities of suspected violations.

D. The Electronic Crimes Task Forces (ECTFs) network brings together federal, state, and local law enforcement, as well as prosecutors, private industry, and academia to prevent, detect, mitigate, and provide aggressive investigation of attacks on the nation's financial and critical infrastructures.

E. The Computer Crime and Intellectual Property Section of the DOJ maintains a web resource for law enforcement (www.cybercrime.gov) to prevent, detect, investigate, and prosecute cybercrime.

F. Other resources include the Computer Crime Research Center and the Electronic Evidence Information Center.

G. Perverted justice—citizen sleuths: An Internet-based organization whose volunteers pose as young kids, then trawl the Internet for predators

H.   The CyberAngels Cyber Crime Unit (CCU) is devoted to assisting victims of cybercrime.

XIII.   Preventing Computer Crime

   A.   Methods of prevention:
      1.   Educating top management and employees.
      2.   Instituting internal security precautions.
      3.   Obtaining ongoing commitment from management to protect against computer crime.
      4.   The National Center for Missing and Exploited Children, the Internet Crimes against Children Task Force, and the Boys and Girls Clubs of America have created an Internet safety and awareness program called NetSmartz.
      5.   The National Crime Prevention Council and others have joined forces to teach millions of consumers how to identify, report, and protect themselves against cyber crime.
      6.   The FBI and the U.S. Secret Service have collaborated to produce guidelines on how businesses should plan for and respond to attacks on information systems, including viruses, hacks, and other breaches.
      7.   The U.S. Secret Service contends that law enforcement must take a proactive approach to cyberthreats and that prevention coupled with aggressive proactive investigations deliver the best outcome in the fight against cybercrime.

   B.   National strategy to secure cyberspace:
      1.   Besides individuals and companies, the entire U.S. population faces risk of victimization by cybercriminals because of our increasing reliance on information technology and the role computers play in many aspects of our daily lives.
      2.   Cyberattacks on any part of this infrastructure could lead to tremendous loss of revenue and intellectual property and to loss of life.

XIV.   Summary

Chapter Questions

1. Cyber crime is a
   a. local problem.
   b. transnational problem.
   c. federal problem.
   d. minor problem when related to street crime and the losses it causes to the public.

2. IC3 stands for
   a. Internet Computer Three.
   b. International Computer Classification Corporation.
   c. Internet Crime Complaint Center.
   d. none of these.

3. NW3C stands for
   a. North West Computer Crime Center.
   b. National White Collar Crime Center.
   c. New West Crime Center Corporation.
   d. none of these.

4. A logic bomb
   a. secretly attaches another program to a company's computer system.
   b. enters into a computer and destroys programs.
   c. destroys software.
   d. none of these.

5. Port scanning is
   a. looking for access into a computer.
   b. scanning for a portable computer that is using a wireless connection to the Internet.
   c. scanning for radio signals.
   d. scanning for ports of entry into a harbor.

6. A zombie is
   a. a computer program.
   b. an old computer.
   c. a computer used by hackers to copy other computer programs.
   d. a computer that has been taken over by another computer.

7. Computer-related crimes are divided into all but one of the following categories. Which is not used?
   a. computer as a target
   b. computer as a tool
   c. computer as incidental to the crime
   d. computer as a weapon

8. A computer virus is intended to do which of the following?
   a. replace or destroy data on the computer's hard drive
   b. leave a "back door" open to later effect a DoS
   c. copy code words and transfer bank accounts
   d. both a and b

9. A method of getting someone to voluntarily provide personal information so that the information can be used illegally is called:
   a. pharming
   b. phishing
   c. phantasm
   d. fizzing

10. Theft of intellectual property
    a. involves the theft of ideas, not property.
    b. is hacking into a computer and stealing individual programs, but not ideas.
    c. involves the pirating of proprietary information and copyrighted material.
    d. none of these.

11. Cybercrime is generally defined as criminal activity that can only be carried out using cybertechnology, and can only take place in the cyber realm.   True or False

12. A byte is the amount of space needed to store one word.   True or False

13. A search warrant is not needed to search a computer as long as it is connected to the World Wide Web because in that case there is no expectation of privacy.   True or False

14. When removing a computer, the investigator should just unplug the computer from the wall.   True or False

15. There are no organized cybercrime groups, only individuals committing cybercrime.   True or False

16. Virus attacks rank as the most common crime against a computer.   True or False

17. Malware, short for "malicious software" is developed to cause harm to computers.   True or False

18. A cracker is a hacker who cracks software protection and removes it in order to maliciously intrude into a computer or network to cause damage.   True or False

19. Worms are more powerful and destructive than a virus.   True or False

20. Materials searched for or seized are contraband, fruits, or
    instrumentalities of the crime.   True or False

21. _____ is exploiting the telephone system's vulnerabilities
    to acquire free access and usage in a dial-up Internet provider system.

22. Monitoring data traveling along a network is called _____.

23. _____ is unsolicited bulk e-mail messages, similar to junk mail
    and commonly commercial.

24. Chain letters calling for a payment to participate may be construed as
    _____ .

25. _____ , often considered synonymous with phishing, is
    acquiring unauthorized access to a computer or network through a message
    using an IP address that appears to be from a trusted host, in an attempt to
    commit identity theft.

26. Another challenge facing investigators assigned to computer crimes is that
    often they have not been adequately _____ or equipped to
    investigate these felonies.

27. Recognizing the need for a more unified global approach to
    handling cybercrime, the Council of Europe formed a Convention on
    _____ on November 23, 2001.

28. Investigators should remember that digital evidence may also contain
    physical evidence such as DNA, fingerprints, or _____ .

29. Officers should have radio _____-shielding material such
    as faraday isolation bags or aluminum foil to wrap cell phones, smart phones,
    and other mobile communication devices after they have been seized,
    thereby preventing the phones from receiving a call, text message, or other
    communications signal that may alter the evidence.

30. A _____ _____ is a device designed to ensure a
    self-destruct sequence of any potential evidence.

31. One of the special challenges of investigating cybercrime is that victims
    choose not to report the crimes. What are two of the reasons for this?

32. What are some of the major differences between traditional evidence and computer crimes?

33. What did the Supreme Court say in *Ashcroft v. Free Speech Coalition* (2002) regarding child pornography issues? This was in response to virtual child pornography, illegal in Canada and the European Union, being also declared illegal in the United States under the Child Pornography Prevention Act (CPPA) of 1996.

34. Clarify some of the jurisdictional challenges to prosecuting cybercrimes.

35. Explain the concept of data remanence in a computer investigation.

Case Study

36. A small computer software firm has reported that one of their employees sold one of the software programs that they were developing to another firm. The employee had been passed over for a promotion and seems to have been upset and unhappy. After purchasing the software, the second firm determined that it was stolen and contacted the CEO of the victim firm. The police department was called, and you have been assigned the case. What would you do? Think about the possible avenues of investigation depending on whether you determine that the suspect used a company computer at work or his own computer at home to hack into the company's primary computer and to obtain information or programs or to destroy what is on the computer.

_____

_____

_____

_____

_____

_____

_____

_____

_____

_____

_____

_____

_____

Answer key

1.	b	11.	True
2.	c	12.	False
3.	b	13.	False
4.	a	14.	False
5.	a	15.	False
6.	d	16.	True
7.	d	17.	True
8.	d	18.	True
9.	b	19.	True
10.	c	20.	True

21. Phreaking

22. sniffing

23. Spam

24. pyramid schemes

25. Spoofing

26. trained

27. Cybercrime

28. serology

29. frequency

30. hardware disabler

31. The *2007 E-Crime Watch Survey* found that most e-crimes are handled internally without involving legal action or law enforcement (67 percent for insiders, 66 percent for outsiders). When asked why they had not referred these e-crimes for legal action, respondents echoed last year's finding that either the damage level was insufficient to warrant prosecution (40 percent), there was a lack of evidence (34 percent), or they could not identify the individuals responsible (28 percent).

The *CSI Survey* reports that the most common reason for not reporting e-crimes to law enforcement was a fear that negative publicity would hurt the organization's stock or image (26 percent), followed by a belief that law enforcement would be unable to help (22 percent), competitors would use the incident to their advantage (14 percent), a civil remedy was sought (7 percent), the victim company was unaware of a law enforcement interest (5 percent), and other reasons (2 percent).

32. The biggest difference between traditional evidence and computer evidence is the fragility of the latter. As stressed in *Forensic Examination of Digital Evidence: A Guide for Law Enforcement* (2004), "Digital evidence, by its very nature, is fragile and can be altered, damaged, or destroyed by improper handling or examination. For these reasons special precautions should be taken to preserve this type of evidence. Failure to do so may render it unusable or lead to an inaccurate conclusion." Much the same way an officer responding to a more traditional crime may contaminate the scene by inadvertently altering the environment, an officer responding to a computer crime may destroy digital evidence simply by turning a computer or other device on or off at the wrong time.

33. The Supreme Court ruled in *Ashcroft v. Free Speech Coalition* (2002) that the portion of the CPPA prohibiting the production or distribution of such virtual pornography was overly broad and an unconstitutional infringement on the First Amendment right to freedom of speech.

34. Another piece of the jurisdiction puzzle—one the courts have yet to reach consensus on—centers on whether cybercrime necessarily falls under federal jurisdiction because of the commerce clause and what is commonly referred to as *the nexus requirement*. Disagreement exists between the various courts regarding when a nexus, or link, exists regarding the interstate commerce clause to justify federal jurisdiction. Some courts have ruled that cybercrime automatically comes under federal jurisdiction because the Internet falls under the commerce clause as an instrumentality of interstate commerce, just as do common carriers, phone services, and so forth (*United States v. Sutcliffe*, 2007). Other courts, however, have held that digital content does not automatically come under federal jurisdiction simply because it was transmitted across the Internet and that judicial notice is required, similar to showing that a gun traveled in interstate commerce, for the case to elevate to federal jurisdiction (*United States v. Shaefer*, 2007).

35. Data remanence refers to the residual physical representation of data that have been erased. In addition to recovering deleted material, a qualified computer forensic analyst may be able to recover evidence of the copying of documents, whether to another computer on the network or to some removable storage device such as a diskette; the printing of documents; the dates and times specific documents were created, accessed, or modified; the type and amount of use a particular computer has had; Internet searches run from a computer; and more.

Case Study Answer

36. The case may appear simple, in that a suspect has already been developed who is both linked to the sale of the software and possesses a likely motive. The complexity of the case is that you are dealing with a victim and a witness firm that know much more about the nature of the crime than you do. You will have a difficult time relying on the victim firm and the witness firm for all of the needed expertise, and should not do so in any case. Additionally, you will probably need knowledge of computers. Gather all the information you can and then seek assistance with the technology. You are going to need some expertise that may be outside of your agency. This depends on what resources you have internally in your agency. The issue here is the theft of organizational or business property. It is neither the theft of computers nor the theft of something using a computer. Some would refer to this as intellectual property. It is possible that the person who is a suspect downloaded the program to his computer, or that he gained access to the work computer and downloaded the program from home. This information is important in that it may lead to some alternative places to search. The expert you bring into the investigation may be useful when meeting with the district attorney and presenting the case.

A DUAL THREAT

Drug-Related Crime and Organized Crime

OUTLINE

- The Threat of Drugs
- Seriousness and Extent of the Drug Problem
- Legal Definitions
- Identification and Classification of Controlled Drugs
- Investigating Illegal Possession or Use of Controlled Substances
- Investigating Illegal Sale and Distribution of Controlled Substances
- Clandestine Drug Laboratories
- Indoor Marijuana Growing Operations
- Investigative Aids
- Agency Cooperation
- Drug Asset Forfeitures

- Preventing Problems with Illegal Drugs: Community Partnerships
- The National Drug Control Strategy
- Organized Crime: An Overview
- Applicable Laws against Organized Crime
- Major Activities of Organized Crime
- The Threat of Specific Organized Crime Groups
- Organized Crime and Corruption
- The Police Response
- Agencies Cooperating in Investigating Organized Crime
- Methods to Combat Organized Crime
- The Decline of Organized Crime?

Chapter 18
A Dual Threat: Drug-Related Crime and Organized Crime

By the end of this chapter, you should know how to define the terms and understand the application of the following concepts. Test your understanding of the chapter by verifying that you know this information. If you do not know it, review the chapter.

Can You Define?

analogs	drug addict	OTC drugs
bookmaking	Ecstasy	pharming
capital flight	excited delirium	raves
club drugs	flashroll	reverse buy
cook	hallucinogen	robotripping
crack	loan-sharking	sinsemilla
crank	MDMA	skittling
criminal enterprise	mules	sting
depressant	narcotic	tweaker
designer drugs	organized crime	victimless crime

Do you know?

- What act made it illegal to sell or use certain narcotics and dangerous drugs?
- When it is illegal to use or sell narcotics or dangerous drugs and what physical evidence can prove these offenses?
- How drugs are commonly classified?
- What drugs are most commonly observed on the street, in the possession of users and seized in drug raids, and what the most frequent drug arrest is?
- What the major legal evidence in prosecuting drug use and possession is?
- What the major legal evidence in drug sale and distribution is?
- When an on-sight arrest can be made for a drug buy?

- What precautions to take in undercover drug buys and how to avoid a charge of entrapment?
- What hazards exist in raiding a clandestine drug laboratory?
- What agency provides unified leadership in combating illegal drug activities and what its primary emphasis is?
- What the key to reducing drug abuse is?
- What the distinctive characteristics of organized crime are? its major activities?
- What organized crime activities are specifically made crimes by law?
- What the investigator's primary role in dealing with the organized crime problem is?
- What agencies cooperate in investigating organized crime?

Chapter Outline:

I.   The Threat of Drugs

    A.   Cocaine was common by the 1880s.

    B.   By the early 1900s, the situation was so bad, President Theodore Roosevelt pressed for antidrug legislation.

    C.   In 1914, the federal government passed the Harrison Narcotics Act, which made the sale or use of certain drugs illegal.

    D.   In 1937, under President Franklin Delano Roosevelt, marijuana became the last drug to be banned.

    E.   After the 1960s and the Vietnam War, the drug "culture" had been created.

    F.   The 1980s saw a turnaround in drug use: "Just say no to drugs."

II.   Seriousness and Extent of the Drug Problem

    A.   Today, more than 19 million Americans 12 and older, use illegal drugs on a monthly basis.

    B.   The trafficking and abuse of illicit drugs are a great burden on citizens, private businesses, financial institutions, public health systems, and law enforcement agencies in the United States.

    C.   The most striking evidence of the impact of drug trafficking and abuse on U.S. society is the thousands of drug-related deaths (overdoses, homicides, accidents, or other fatal incidents) that occur each year.

    D.   An increasing threat is posed by drug trafficking organizations (DTOs), complex entities with highly defined command-and-control structures that produce, transport, or distribute large quantities of one or more illicit drugs.

    E.   Especially disturbing is the violence connected with the Mexican drug cartels, with drug violence from Mexico spilling into the United States, the brutality giving rise to formidable new problems for both countries

    F.   Although the drug problems remains a serious issues, encouraging data are found in *Monitoring the Future 2007* (MTF).

    G.   The United Nations Office on Drugs and Crime (UNODC) found that U.S. production of and markets for illicit drugs continue to decrease, reflecting both increased law enforcement efforts and a large shift of drug production from South America to Mexico.

III.   Legal Definitions

    A.   It is illegal to possess or use narcotics or dangerous drugs without a prescription and to sell or distribute them without a license.

    B.   Laws generally categorize drugs into five schedules of controlled substances, arranged by the degree of danger associated with the drug, with Schedule I drugs being the most dangerous.

C. The laws also establish prohibited acts concerning the controlled substances and assign penalties in ratio to the drug's danger.

D. Specific laws vary by state. For example, possessing a small amount of marijuana is a felony in some states, a misdemeanor in others, and not a crime at all in a few states.

IV. Identification and Classification of Controlled Drugs

A. The sale of prescription drugs, the fastest-growing category of drugs being abused, has skyrocketed since 1990.

B. Identification via field testing can be tricky.

1. Several brands of self-contained, single-use test kits are available that reduce the likelihood of user error and require very small samples.

2. Officers must understand that field testing cannot be used to *establish* probable cause, only *confirm* it.

C. Drugs can be classified as depressants, stimulants, narcotics, hallucinogens, cannabis, or inhalants.

1. Stimulants and depressants are controlled under the Drug Abuse Control Amendments to the Federal Food, Drug and Cosmetic Act (U.S. Code Title 21).

2. The most commonly observed drugs on the street, in possession of users and seized in drug raids are cocaine, codeine, crack, heroin, marijuana, morphine, and opium. Arrest for possession or use of marijuana is the most frequent drug arrest.

3. There are five federal schedules of controlled substances, ranging from Schedule I, high abuse tendency, high likelihood of addiction, to Schedule V, low abuse tendency, low chance of addiction.

D. Powder cocaine and crack

1. Crack is much less expensive than cocaine and has 10 times the impact on the user.

2. For the past two decades, the cocaine supply in the United States has been controlled by the Colombian Medellin and Cali mafias. The U.S.–Mexico border is the primary point of entry for cocaine into the United States,

E. Heroin

1. Commonly abused narcotic, synthesized from morphine, and as much as 10 times more powerful in its effects.

2. Physically addictive and relatively expensive.

F. Marijuana

1. The most widely available and most commonly used illicit drug in the United States, with 14.6 million current users.

2. Some users lace marijuana with other substances, including PCP, cocaine, and even embalming fluid, or formaldehyde.

3. Mexican commercial-grade marijuana is the most common variety.

4. Large quantities of marijuana are being grown hydroponically indoors, often in abandoned barns or other buildings in rural areas.

G. Methamphetamine (crank)

1. Methamphetamine is now firmly entrenched as a major U.S. drug problem that is only getting bigger.

2. Meth abuse is a particular problem in rural communities, where most meth production occurs, because of the lack of resources available to address addiction and its side effects such as crime and child abuse.

3. A chemical additive, GloTell, can identify those who handle anhydrous ammonia fertilizer, a common ingredient in producing methamphetamine.

H. Club drugs, often found at "raves"

1. Ecstasy: 3,4-Methylenedioxymethylamphetamine (MDMA)

2. Rohypnol

3. GHB: Gamma-hydroxybutyric acid

4. Ketamine

5. LSD (Acid)

6. 2C-B or Nexus

I. Prescription drugs

1. Prescription drug abuse has become a nationwide epidemic.

2. Pain relievers—such as Vicodin, Percodan, Percocet, and OxyContin—top the list of abused prescription drugs.

3. Other commonly abused prescription drugs include tranquilizers such as Xanax and Valium, stimulants, and Viagra.

4. Marijuana, the illicit drug that has previously and pervasively been the most popular drug with teens, has lately taken a backseat to the nonmedical use of pain relievers.

5. Pharmacy thefts are increasing nationwide to feed the growing demand for prescription drugs.

6. Law enforcement officers spend a significant amount of time investigating cases involving prescription fraud, many of which also involve insurance, Medicare or Medicaid fraud.

J. Inhalants: use has increased during the past few years

K. Khat (pronounced "cot"), a natural narcotic whose primary psychoactive ingredients are chemically similar to amphetamines, is a relative newcomer to the U.S. drug scene but is well known in eastern African and southern Middle Eastern countries, some of which consider it a legitimate and quite profitable export.

L. Over-the-counter (OTC) drugs

1. Drinking bottles of cough syrup, such as Robitussin DM, to get high is called robotripping.

2. Skittling, so named because the pills resemble small, red pieces of Skittles candy, is ingesting high doses of Coricidin Cough and Cold ("Triple C") tablets.

3. Pharming is rifling through the family medicine cabinet for pills, both OTC and prescription, combining everything in a bowl, scooping out and ingesting a handful, and waiting to see what happens.

4. Because these drugs are legal, law enforcement requires a more proactive approach to the problem, such as educating youths and their parents and networking with professional organizations.

M. Other narcotics and drugs

1. Designer drugs are created by adding to or omitting something from an existing drug.

2. In many instances, the primary drug is not illegal. The illicit drugs are called analogs of the drug from which they are created—for example, meperidine analog or mescaline analog.

V. Investigating Illegal Possession or Use of Controlled Substances

A. Recognizing the drug addict: drug-recognition experts

1. Congress has defined a drug addict as "any person who habitually uses any habit-forming narcotic drug so as to endanger the public morals, health, safety or welfare, or who is or has been so far addicted to the use of habit-forming narcotic drugs as to have lost the power of self-control with reference to the addiction."

2. Drug addiction is a progressive disease.

3. Drug Evaluation Classification (DEC) programs, more commonly known as Drug Recognition Expert (DRE) programs, have demonstrated international success in detecting and deterring drug-impaired driving.

B. Physical evidence of possession or use of controlled substances:

1. Actual drugs or controlled substances

2. Apparatus or paraphernalia

3. Suspect's appearance and behavior

4. Urine and blood tests

C. In-custody deaths

1. Excited delirium

2. According to one study, 53 percent of the people who die suddenly while in police custody have used illicit substances proximal to their collapse.

VI. Investigating Illegal Sale and Distribution of Controlled Substances

A. The actual transfer of drugs from the seller to the buyer is the major legal evidence in prosecuting drug-sale cases.

B. Drug users often become sellers to support their habits. Many such individuals, called *mules*, sell or transport drugs for a regular dealer in return for being assured of a personal drug supply.

C. Challenges concern the wide variety of drugs, the difficulty faced when trying to identify them under street conditions, and the special types of searches often required to locate minute amounts of drugs that may be hidden ingeniously.

D. Confidential informants
   1. Crucial to many law enforcement investigations, especially in the field of narcotics investigations.
   2. Can provide specific information that is not available from other sources.
   3. Often criminals themselves.
   4. Often vital to making on-site arrests.

E. On-sight arrests
   1. Officers observing an apparent drug buy can make a warrantless arrest based on probable cause.
   2. Probable cause is established through knowledge of the suspect's criminal record, by observing other people making contact with the suspect and finding drugs on them, by knowing the suspect's past relationships with other drug users or sellers, and through observing actions of the suspect that indicate a drug buy.

F. Surveillance
   1. Some common indicators of residential drug trafficking are
      a. A high volume of foot or vehicle traffic to and from a residence at late or unusual hours.
      b. Periodic visitors who stay at the residence for very brief periods.
      c. Altered property to maximize privacy.
   2. Surveillance officers must have patience because many planned drug buys necessitate a long period of surveillance before the actual sale, or bust, is made.

G. Undercover assignments
   1. Undercover investigations are used more routinely in drug cases than perhaps any other type of criminal investigation.
   2. Planned buys
      a. Usually involve working an undercover agent into a group selling or buying drugs or having an informant make the buy.
      b. Usually police officers of the investigating agency (in large cities) or of cooperative agencies on the same level of government in

an exchange operation or a mutual-aid agreement that provides an exchange of narcotics officers.

    c.   Undercover drug buys are carefully planned, witnessed, and conducted so that no charge of entrapment can be made.

    d.   Make two or more buys to avoid the charge of entrapment.

3. Stings/reverse buys

    a.   Complex operation organized and implemented by undercover agents to apprehend drug dealers and buyers and to deter other users from making drug purchases at a certain location.

    b.   Labor intensive, complex and require officers to be well trained.

H. Narcotics raids

1. Another method used to apprehend narcotics dealers.

2. Surveillance frequently provides enough information for obtaining a no-knock search or arrest warrant.

3. The raid itself must be carried out forcefully and swiftly because drugs can easily be destroyed in seconds.

4. Narcotics raids are often dangerous.

I. Drug paraphernalia stores

1. "Head shops" sell products that help the end user ingest drugs, such as pipes, syringes, and so on.

2. "Cut or vial stores," in contrast, sell adulterants, diluents and other "office supplies" used by drug organizations in measuring, separating, chemically altering and packaging mass quantities of drugs.

J. Online drug dealers

1. Club drugs, prescription narcotics and ultra-pure forms of DXM, an ingredient found in OTC cough medication, can all be purchased online and shipped directly to the user's home—transactions that are extremely difficult for law enforcement to detect.

2. Online drug dealers commonly try to disguise their activities by posting their available products as some type of legitimate substance.

VII.   Clandestine Drug Laboratories

A. Clandestine drug laboratories present physical, chemical, and toxic hazards to law enforcement officers engaged in raids on the premises.

B. The production of meth involves ingredients such as strong acids and bases, flammable solvents, and very explosive and poisonous chemicals.

C. Identifying a clandestine (clan) lab

1. From the outside:

    a.   Strong chemical odors

    b.   Blacked out or boarded up windows

       c.   Hoses sticking out through windows and doors

       d.   Dead vegetation from dumped chemical wastes

       e.   Exhaust fans running constantly

       f.   Disturbed ground or dead vegetation

       g.   Excessive traffic

   2. On the inside:

       a.   Coffee grinders with white residue

       b.   Coffee filters with red stains

       c.   Large quantities of acetone, antifreeze, camping fuel, drain cleaner, lithium batteries, matches, plastic baggies, cold tablets or cough syrup containing the ingredient pseudoephedrine

       d.   An abundance of mixing containers such as Pyrex glassware, crock pots, and other large pots

       e.   Strips of bed linen or cloth for filtering liquid drug mixtures

       f.   General clutter, disarray, and filthy living conditions

  D. Entering a clandestine drug lab

   1. Only properly trained and certified personnel should proceed onto the site.

   2. Personnel entering a suspected meth lab should have a self-contained breathing apparatus and complete skin protection.

   3. The entry team faces the possibility of armed resistance as well as booby traps.

   4. Autonomous robotics can enhance officers' safety in investigating a suspected meth lab and be an important force multiplier.

   5. The assessment team deals with immediate hazards.

   6. The processing team identifies and collects evidence.

  E. Cleanup of clandestine drug labs

   1. Estimates suggest that for every pound of meth produced, as much as five pounds of waste are created.

   2. Such trash requires special handling and disposal, often at great expense.

   3. The Comprehensive Methamphetamine Control Act (MCA) of 1996 allows the courts to order a defendant convicted of manufacturing methamphetamine to pay the cost of cleanup of the lab.

VIII. Indoor Marijuana Growing Operations

  A. Indoor growing operations are often indicated by an excessive use of electricity (stolen or legally acquired).

  B. If such a residence is identified, police may observe the type and amount of traffic to and from the house and, based on the combination of information involving electricity use and traffic, obtain a search warrant.

C. Many grow operations steal electricity by diverting power from a main supply line.

D. Inherent dangers associated with the high-energy needs of these indoor grow operations include the risk of electrocution, explosion and fire risks, and upper respiratory infections caused by mold that thrives in these high-humidity environments.

IX. Investigative Aids

A. National Drug Pointer Index (NDPIX): A national database on drug trafficking.

B. Canines are an effective force multiplier.

C. Special high-accuracy laser rangefinder developed for the U.S. Customs Service can find secret compartments that might contain drugs.

D. Flying "drones" for aerial surveillance

X. Agency cooperation

A. The federal drug enforcement administration (DEA) provides unified leadership in attacking narcotics trafficking and drug abuse.

B. The DEA emphasis is on stopping the flow of drugs at their foreign sources, disrupting illicit domestic commerce at the highest levels of distribution and helping state and local police prevent the entry of illegal drugs into their communities.

XI. Drug Asset Forfeitures

A. The Federal Comprehensive Crime Control Act of 1983 initiated procedures for asset forfeitures as a result of drug arrests.

1. The U.S. Congress gave final approval to the Civil Asset Forfeiture Reform Act of 2000, which lowered the burden of proof from "clear and convincing" to "a preponderance of the evidence."

2. The act also reduced the statute of limitations from 11 years to 5 years for a property owner to make a claim on the property.

B. Assets used may be seized by the investigating agencies.

C. Confiscating drug dealers' cash and property has been effective in reducing drug trafficking.

D. Confiscated funds may be used only in police department antidrug efforts.

XII. Preventing Problems with Illegal Drugs: Community Partnerships

A. Tremendous national, state, and local efforts are being directed to meeting the challenges of drug use and abuse in the United States.

1. National drug czar

2. Federal funding through state agencies

3. Operation Weed and Seed—a national initiative

4. Local initiatives

5. State laws restricting sales of OTC drugs

B. Strategic crime-control partnerships with a range of third parties are more effective at disrupting drug problems than law-enforcement-only approaches.

XIII. The National Drug Control Strategy

A. Drug arrests have nearly tripled since 1980, when the federal drug policy shifted to arresting and incarcerating users.

B. Approximately 1.7 million people were arrested on drug charges in 2004, about 700,000 of them for marijuana use.

C. The key to reducing drug abuse is prevention coupled with treatment.

D. *National Drug Control Strategy 2007*:

1. Stop drug use before it starts: education and community action.

2. Heal America's drug users: getting treatment resources where they are needed.

3. Disrupt the market: attacking the economic basis of the drug trade.

XIV. Organized Crime: An Overview

A. Characteristics of organized crime:

1. Definite organization and control

2. High-profit and continued-profit crimes

3. Singular control through force and threats

4. Protection through corruption

B. Other characteristics not as frequently mentioned in definitions of organized crime include restricted membership, nonideological, specialization, and code of secrecy.

C. Organized crime functions through many forms of corruption and intimidation to create a *singular control* over specific goods and services that ultimately results in a monopoly.

D. Organized crime flourishes most where protection from interference and prosecution exist.

E. Organized crime

1. Is not a single entity controlled by one superpower.

2. Does not exist only in metropolitan areas.

3. Is involved in virtually every area where profits are to be made, including legitimate businesses.

4. Citizens are not isolated from organized crime.

XV. Applicable Laws against Organized Crime

A. Acts that make it permissible to use circumstantial rather than direct evidence to enforce conspiracy violations: 1946 Hobbs Anti-Racketeering Act, the 1968 Omnibus Crime Control and Safe Streets Act, the RICO Act of 1970, and the Organized Crime Control Act of 1970.

B. Title 18 U.S. Code, Section 1962 makes it a prosecutable conspiracy to

　　1. Acquire any enterprise with money obtained from illegal activity.

　　2. Acquire, maintain, or control any enterprise by illegal means.

　　3. Use any enterprise to conduct illegal activity.

XVI. Major Activities of Organized Crime

A. Organized crime is heavily involved in the so-called victimless crimes of gambling, drugs, pornography and prostitution, as well as fraud, loan-sharking, money laundering and infiltration of legitimate businesses.

B. Federal crimes prosecutable under the RICO statute include bribery, sports bribery, counterfeiting, embezzlement of union funds, mail fraud, wire fraud, money laundering, obstruction of justice, murder for hire, drug trafficking, prostitution, sexual exploitation of children, alien smuggling, trafficking in counterfeit goods, theft from interstate shipment and interstate transportation of stolen property.

C. State crimes chargeable under RICO include murder, kidnapping, gambling, arson, robbery, bribery, extortion, and drug offenses.

D. Organized crime bosses manipulate the business economy to their benefit. Such crimes as labor racketeering, unwelcome infiltration of unions, fencing stolen property, gambling, loan-sharking, drug trafficking, employment of illegal aliens, and white-collar crimes of all types can signal syndicate involvement.

E. Victimless crimes: an illegal activity in which all involved are willing participants.

　　1. Gambling

　　　　a. Bookmaking

　　　　b. Soliciting and accepting bets on any type of sporting event—the most prevalent gambling operation

　　2. Drugs

　　3. Pornography

　　4. Prostitution

F. Loan-sharking: lending money at exorbitant interest rates

G. Money-laundering and the infiltration of legitimate businesses

XVII. The Threat of Specific Organized Crime Groups

A. Italian organized crime (IOC)

　　1. Four separate groups: the Sicilian Mafia; the Neapolitan Camorra; the 'Ndrangheta, or Calabrian Mafia; and Sacra Corona Unita, or "United Sacred Crown"

   2. La Costra Nostra (LCN)
      a. Nationwide alliance of criminals with both familial and conspiratorial connections.
      b. Rooted in Italian organized crime, but an Americanized version of the "old school" mafias from Italy, separate and distinct from the other IOC groups.
      c. Estimated membership 1,100 nationwide, with the vast majority (roughly 80 percent) operating in the New York metropolitan area.
      d. Five crime families make up New York City's LCN: Bonanno, Colombo, Genovese, Gambino, Lucchese.

B. Asian organized crime (AOC)
   1. Involved in murder, kidnapping, extortion, prostitution, pornography, loan-sharking, gambling, money laundering, alien smuggling, trafficking in heroin and methamphetamine, counterfeiting of computer and clothing products and various protection schemes.
   2. Often well run and hard to crack; use very fluid, mobile global networks of criminal associates.
   3. Asian criminal enterprises are classified as either traditional, such as the Yakuza and Triads, or nontraditional, such as ethnic Asian street gangs.
   4. Japanese organized crime is sometimes known as Boryokudan but is more commonly known as the Yakuza. A gyangu (Japanese gangster) is a member of the Yakuza (organized crime family) and is affiliated with the Yamaguchi-gumi (Japan's largest organized crime family) as a boryokudan (used primarily for muscle).
   5. Triads are the oldest of the Chinese organized crime (COC) groups and engage in a wide range of criminal activities, including money laundering, drug trafficking, gambling, extortion, prostitution, loan-sharking, pornography, alien smuggling, and numerous protection schemes.
   6. Vietnamese organized crime is generally one of two kinds: roving or local.
      a. Roving bands travel from community to community, have a propensity for violence, have no permanent leaders or group loyalty, lack language and job skills, and have no family in the United States.
      b. Local groups tend to band together in a certain area of a specific community, have a charismatic leader, have a propensity for violence, and tend to engage in extortion, illegal gambling, and robbery.

C. Latino organized crime
   1. Include Cubans, Colombians, Mexicans, and Dominicans.

2. Heavily involved in drug trafficking.

3. Because of Mexico's proximity to the United States, its organized crime groups are becoming an increasing threat to the United States and are among the fastest growing gangs in the country.

D. African organized crime

1. An emerging criminal threat facing law enforcement agencies worldwide and known to be operating in at least 80 other countries,

2. African criminal enterprises have proliferated in the United States since the 1980s.

3. Although some groups comprise members originating in Ghana and Liberia, by far the predominant nationality in African organized crime is Nigerian.

E. Russian organized crime (aka: Russian Mafia)

1. Since the collapse of the Soviet Union, Russian organized crime has gone international and poses a great threat to and challenge for U.S. justice.

2. The FBI refers to these groups as Eurasian Organized Crime (EOC).

3. Tend to be well educated.

4. Focus on a wide range of frauds and scams, including insurance scams, securities and investment fraud, fuel oil scams, and credit card scams.

5. Other activities: contract murders, kidnappings, business arson transnational money laundering, traffic in women and children, traffic in such hazardous commodities as weapons and nuclear material smuggled out of their homeland.

6. EOC consists of hundreds of groups, all acting independently, with no formal hierarchy.

7. Most members are already hardened criminals, have military experience, and are highly educated.

XVIII. Organized Crime and Corruption

A. One of the greatest threats posed by organized crime is the corruption it engenders throughout the entire legal system.

XIX. The Police Response

A. The daily observations of local law enforcement officers provide vital information for investigating organized crimes.

B. Report in writing all information pertaining to such activities, either immediately, if the activity involves an imminent meeting, or when time permits

XX. Agencies Cooperating in Investigating Organized Crime

A. Organized crime strike forces coordinate all federal organized crime activities and work closely with state, county, and municipal law enforcement agencies.

B. Other agencies that play important roles in investigating organized crime:

1. FBI: often has a member on the strike forces
2. Postal Inspection Service: in charge of mail fraud, embezzlements and other crimes involving material distributed through the mails
3. U.S. Secret Service: investigates government checks and bonds as well as foreign securities
4. Department of Labor: investigates organized crime activities related to labor practices and pension funds
5. Securities and Exchange Commission: investigates organized crime activities in the purchase of securities
6. Internal Revenue Service: investigates violations of income tax laws

XXI. Methods to Combat Organized Crime

A. The enterprise theory of investigation (ET) is a combined organized crime/drug strategy used by the FBI that focuses investigations and prosecutions on entire criminal enterprises rather than on individuals.

B. Investigative aids

1. Electronic surveillance
2. Pen registers
   a. Pen registers record the numbers dialed from a telephone by monitoring the electrical impulses of the numbers dialed.
   b. These do not constitute a search under the meaning of the Fourth Amendment (*Smith v. Maryland,* 1979).
   c. Several state courts, however, have held that using a pen register *is* a search under the respective state statutes and that a warrant supported by probable cause *is* needed.
3. The same situation exists for trap-and-trace devices, which reveal the telephone number of the source of all incoming calls to a particular number. Their use may or may not require a warrant, depending on the specific state.
4. Regional Information Sharing System (RISS), a multijurisdictional intelligence sharing system comprising nearly 5,000 local, state, and federal agencies, helps investigators identify, target, and remove criminal conspiracies and activities that reach across jurisdictional boundaries.

C. Asset forfeiture

XXII. The Decline of Organized Crime?

A. It can be difficult to determine whether criminal events are the work of organized crime or of gangs.

B. Following the 9/11 terrorist attacks, many of the law enforcement resources previously allocated to organized crime investigations have been redirected toward counterterrorism efforts, allowing a resurgence in organized crime activity throughout the country.

XXIII. Summary

Chapter Questions

1. Drugs are classified as
   a. depressants, stimulants, narcotics, hallucinogens, cannabis, or inhalants.
   b. depressants, prescription drugs, narcotics, or inhalants.
   c. bad drugs and good drugs.
   d. legal drugs and illegal drugs.

2. OxyContin is
   a. a pain medication derived from cannabis.
   b. a general depressant.
   c. a pain medication derived from opium with heroin-like effects.
   d. a hallucinogenic drug.

3. With reference to drugs, OTC stands for
   a. Office of Trading Control.
   b. Official Technological Commission.
   c. Operation Traffic Control.
   d. over-the-counter.

4. Mescaline and peyote are
   a. narcotics.
   b. depressants.
   c. stimulants.
   d. hallucinogens.

5. If not properly managed, these people can render a law enforcement investigation useless, destroy an agency's credibility, and even endanger officers' live. Yet, they are often vital to making on-site arrests.
   a. dispatchers
   b. reporting parties
   c. informants
   d. nosey neighbors

6. Physical examination for a drug suspect can include all but which of the following field tests?
   a. an eye examination
   b. an improved walk-and-turn test
   c. the Rhomberg Standing Balance test
   d. the drop and run test

7. This device allows officers to inexpensively conduct sobriety checks in the field. This lightweight, handheld binocular-type instrument measures absolute pupil dynamics to presumptively detect alcohol, drugs, inhalants, or fatigue in a suspect.
   a. breathalyzer
   b. P.A.S. device
   c. pupilometer
   d. electrolysis meter

8. Drinking bottles of cough syrup, such as Robitussin DM, to get high is called
   a. robotripping
   b. skittling
   c. pharming
   d. needling

9. OTC drugs taken in excessive quantities for their psychoactive effects fall into three general categories: uppers, downers, and all-arounders. Which of the following is an incorrect statement?
   a. The most popular upper is pseudoephedrine, a main ingredient in nasal decongestants such as Sudafed.
   b. Benadryl Allergy formula is the top downer choice.
   c. DXM, often purchased over the Internet, has been linked to numerous overdose deaths.
   d. DXM, often purchased over the Internet, has been cleared of any links to numerous overdose deaths.

10. This drug, whose primary psychoactive ingredients are chemically similar to amphetamines, is a natural narcotic and is a relative newcomer to the United States drug scene. It is well known in eastern African and southern Middle Eastern countries.
    a. hashish
    b. khat
    c. sinsemilla
    d. peyote

11. It is illegal to possess or use most narcotics and many dangerous drugs, as defined by the FBI, and to sell or distribute them without a license.   True or False

12. The sale of prescription drugs has skyrocketed since 1990.   True or False

13. Heroin is synthesized from morphine and is as much as 10 times more powerful in its effects.   True or False

14. Methamphetamine is a highly addictive synthetic stimulant that looks like cocaine but is made from toxic chemicals, such as drain cleaner, paint thinner, and other easily obtained over the counter products, including cold medication products containing pseudoephedrine.   True or False

15. Ecstasy is the common term for 3,4-Methylenedioxymethylamphetamine.   True or False

16. LSD is derived from lysergic acid, a fungus that grows on corn.   True or False

17. Ketamine can produce delirium, impaired motor function, high blood pressure, depression, and potentially fatal respiratory problems.   True or False

18. A pupilometer allows officers to inexpensively conduct sobriety checks in the field.   True or False

19. A sting is a reverse buy.   True or False

20. "Head shops" sell products that help the end user ingest drugs.   True or False

21. _____ is produced by making cocaine with baking soda and water.

22. Rohypnol is one of the _____ drugs.

23. _____ is the most widely available and most commonly used illicit drug in the United States.

24. At the beginning of the twentieth century, _____ was the drug of choice, said to cure everything from indigestion to toothaches. It was even added to flavor soft drinks such as Coca-Cola.

25. In 1914, the federal government passed the _____ Narcotics Act, which made the sale or use of certain drugs illegal.

26. According to *Monitoring the Future 2007* (MTF), the University of Michigan's Institute for Social Research report, use of nearly all types of drugs has _____ from 2001 to 2007.

27. Eighth, tenth and twelfth graders across the country are continuing to show a gradual _____ in the proportions reporting use of illicit drugs.

28. A chemical additive, GloTell, can identify those who handle anhydrous ammonia fertilizer, a common ingredient in producing methamphetamine. GloTell leaves bright _____ stains on the skin and clothes of anyone who comes in contact with the fertilizer and is detectable with blacklight for as long as 72 hours after exposure. The additive also impedes the production process of meth by making the drug very difficult to dry.

29. At low dosage, _____ impairs attention, learning ability, and memory. At higher doses, it can produce delirium, impaired motor function, high blood pressure, depression, and potentially fatal respiratory problems

30. Although many drugs have shown steady or declining numbers of users over the past few years, _____ use has increased.

31. What are some of the key characteristics of organized crime?

32. How has drug asset forfeiture helped in the war on drugs? What does it allow the police to do?

33. What may investigators find when outside and, later, inside a suspected clandestine methamphetamine lab?

34. What challenges are the 21st-century narcotics investigators likely to face?

35. What did the Supreme Court say about whether or not a warrant was needed for a canine "sniff" in a public area, versus at the door of an apartment or home?

Case Study

36. You are an investigator for the sheriff's department in the small western community where you grew up. You have been assigned to work with the DEA concerning the growth and sale of marijuana in your community. It seems that the DEA has been monitoring the use of electricity and water by some of the residents in the area and has found a large increase in the use of electricity by three farmers. You are not aware of any changes in any farming practices or other reasons that might explain this sudden increase. You have known the farmers for all of your life, and do know that they have been having financial difficulties in the past several years. However, they have been paying their bills on time lately, though you have not noted any increased farming activity. What background research could you complete to assist the DEA with this investigation? How would you proceed?

_____

_____

_____

_____

_____

_____

_____

_____

_____

_____

_____

_____

Answer Key

1. a	11. True
2. c	12. True
3. d	13. True
4. d	14. True
5. c	15. True
6. d	16. False
7. c	17. True
8. a	18. True
9. d	19. True
10. b	20. True

21. Crack

22. club

23. Marijuana

24. Cocaine

25. Harrison

26. decreased

27. decrease

28. pink

29. ketamine

30. inhalant

31. Distinctive characteristics of organized crime include
    - Definite organization and control.
    - High-profit and continued-profit crimes.
    - Singular control through force and threats.
    - Protection through corruption.

Other characteristics not as frequently mentioned in definitions of organized crime include restricted membership, nonideological, specialization, and code of secrecy.

32. Asset forfeiture is a tool that allows agencies investigating various types of crimes, including drug trafficking, to seize items used in or acquired through committing that crime. The Federal Comprehensive Crime Control Act of 1984 initiated procedures for asset forfeitures as a result of drug arrests. The U.S. Congress gave final approval to the Civil Asset Forfeiture Reform Act of 2000, which lowered the burden of proof from "clear and convincing" to "a preponderance of the evidence." The act also reduced the statute of limitations from 11 years to 5 years for a property owner to make a claim on the property. Confiscating drug dealers' cash and property has been effective in reducing drug trafficking and is providing local, state, and federal law enforcement agencies with assets they need for their fight against drugs. Asset forfeiture laws provide for the confiscation of cash and other property in possession of a drug dealer at the time of the arrest. Seized vehicles, boats, or airplanes may be used directly by the agency or sold at auction to generate funds. Monetary assets may be used to purchase police equipment, to hire additional law enforcement personnel, or to provide training in drug investigation.

33. From the outside of a structure, investigators may observe blacked out or boarded up windows, hoses sticking out through windows and doors, dead vegetation from dumped chemical wastes, and strong chemical odors, all of which may indicate a clan lab is operating inside. Inside a structure indicators of a clan lab include coffee grinders with white residue; coffee filters with red stains; large quantities of acetone, antifreeze, camping fuel, drain cleaner, lithium batteries, matches, plastic baggies, cold tablets or cough syrup containing the ingredient pseudoephedrine; an abundance of mixing containers such as Pyrex glassware, crock pots, and other large pots; strips of bed linen or cloth for filtering liquid drug mixtures; and general clutter, disarray, and filthy living conditions.

34. More of a move from the street corner into cyberspace. Club drugs, prescription narcotics, and ultra-pure forms of DXM, an ingredient found in OTC cough medication, can all be purchased online and shipped directly to the user's home—transactions that are extremely difficult for law enforcement to detect. Online drug dealers commonly try to disguise their activities by posting their available products as some type of legitimate substance.

35. The Supreme Court has ruled that a canine sniff in a public area or during a lawful traffic stop is not a Fourth Amendment "search." However, use of a narcotics-detection dog to sniff at the door of an apartment or a home has been ruled a search within the meaning of the Fourth Amendment and therefore requires a warrant.

Case Study Answer

36. The indicators of what is happening are fairly strong here. However, you lack any evidence other than conjecture. The increase in marijuana coming from the community, the increase in use of electricity (a possible indicator of indoor growth of plants, or hydroponics), and the fact that farmers who were formerly in debt are now able to pay their bills on time, add up to little other than suspicion. You will need much more than that to obtain a warrant. You also face a problem common to law enforcement (and specifically drug enforcement) in smaller communities. Everyone in the community knows who you are and what you do for a living, so your ability to operate clandestinely is limited. Once you have obtained all the information that your position allows you to, you might recommend that the DEA send some undercover agents to the community or find some informants. You may be able to provide support to the agents and to assist with finding informants. With enough patience, background work, and continued monitoring, it may be possible to advance the case beyond conjecture, to conduct planned buys or a sting operation, or to secure a warrant. In preparing for this case, you should focus on the long-term, on cooperation between agencies, and on sharing information and resources.

CRIMINAL ACTIVITIES OF GANGS AND OTHER DANGEROUS GROUPS

OUTLINE

- The Threat of Gangs: An Overview
- Gangs Defined
- Extent of Gangs
- Why People Join Gangs
- Types of Gangs
- Gangs, Organized Crime and Terrorism
- Gang Culture, Membership and Organization
- Gang Activities
- Recognizing a Gang Problem
- Identifying Gang Members
- Investigating Illegal Gang Activity
- Approaches to the Gang Problem
- Collaborative Efforts: Gang Task Forces
- Prosecuting Gang-Related Crimes
- Federal Efforts to Combat the Gang Problem
- Bias and Hate Crime: An Overview
- Motivation for Hate Crime
- Hate Groups
- The Police Response
- Efforts to Combat Bias and Hate Crimes
- Ritualistic Crime: An Overview
- Terminology and Symbols of Cults
- The Nature of Ritualistic Crimes
- Who Commits Ritualistic Crime?
- Investigating Ritualistic Crimes
- Special Challenges in Ritualistic Crime Investigations

Chapter 19
Criminal Activities of Gangs and Other Dangerous Groups

By the end of this chapter, you should know how to define the terms and understand the application of the following concepts. Test your understanding of the chapter by verifying that you know this information. If you do not know it, review the chapter.

Can You Define?

Antichrist	Hand of Glory	predatory gangs
Beelzebub	hate crime	pulling levers
bias crime	hate incidents	ritual
Black Mass	hedonistic/social gangs	ritualistic crime
Bloods	incantation	sabbat
coven	instrumental gangs	scavenger gangs
Crips	magick	serious delinquent
cult	moniker	gangs
cultural gangs	occult	street gang
drug gangs	organized/corporate	swarming
gang	gangs	territorial gangs
graffiti	party gangs	turf

Do you know?

- Whether the gang problem is increasing or decreasing?
- How criminologists have categorized street gangs?
- What types of crimes gangs typically engage in?
- What the first step in dealing with a gang problem is?
- How to identify gang members?
- What kinds of records to keep on gangs?
- What special challenges are involved in investigating illegal activities of gangs?
- What strategies have been used to combat a gang problem?

- What two defense strategies are commonly used by gang members' lawyers in court?
- What the primary motivation for bias or hate crimes is and who is most frequently targeted?
- What a cult is? How better to refer to cults?
- What a ritualistic crime is?
- What may be involved in ritualistic crime?
- What are indicators of ritualistic crimes?
- What special challenges are involved in investigating ritualistic crimes?

Chapter Outline

I.   The Threat of Gangs: An Overview

    A.   Belonging to a gang is not illegal in the United States.

    B.   However, many activities that gangs engage in are illegal.

II.   Gangs Defined

    A.   No single definition exists to describe a gang.

    B.   A gang is a group of individuals with a recognized name and symbols who form an allegiance for a common purpose and engage in continuous unlawful activity.

    C.   A definition commonly accepted by law enforcement is that a gang is any group gathering continuously to commit antisocial behavior.

III.   Extent of Gangs

    A.   The number of gangs and gang members in the United States has decreased over the last few years, but gang-related crime is still a major concern to law enforcement.

    B.   Gang migration: As society in general has become more mobile, gangs and gang members have also increased their mobility, contributing to gang migration.

IV.   Why People Join Gangs

    A.   Material reasons

    B.   Recreation

    C.   A place of refuge and camouflage

    D.   Physical protection

    E.   Resistance against parents or society

    F.   Lack of commitment to community

V.   Types of Gangs

    A.   Criminologists have classified gangs as cultural or instrumental.

        1.   Cultural gangs: neighborhood-centered, exist independently of criminal activity.

        2.   Instrumental gangs: formed by the express purposes of criminal activity, primarily drug trafficking.

    B.   Major types of gangs, according to researchers:

        1.   Hedonistic/social

        2.   Party

        3.   Predatory

        4.   Scavenger

        5.   Serious delinquent

      6. Territorial gangs

      7. Organized/corporate

      8. Drug

C. Girl gangs

    1. Although the number of female gangs is increasing, gangs are still predominately male.

    2. Three types of female gang involvement are

      a. Membership in an independent gang

      b. Membership in a male gang as a coed

      c. Membership in a female auxiliary of a male gang

D. Ethnic gangs

    1. Based on race and ethnicity

    2. Trends:

      a. Hispanic gang membership is on the rise.

      b. Migration of California-style gang culture remains a particular threat.

      c. Indian Country is increasingly reporting escalating levels of gang activity.

    3. Mara Salvatrucha 13 (MS 13)

      a. Considered by many gang experts to be America's most dangerous gang.

      b. Estimated to have 10,000 members operating in 42 states.

      c. Active in smuggling people, drugs, and money across the border.

    4. Native American gangs

      a. Relatively new phenomenon

      b. Poses an increasing threat to tribal reservations

E. Hybrid gangs

    1. Members are generally young and particularly profit driven.

    2. Singularly focused on making money from drugs, robbery, and prostitution.

F. Outlaw motorcycle gangs

    1. Major gangs are Hell's Angels, Bandidos, Outlaws, and Pagans

    2. Primary source of income is drug trafficking, but also involved in murder, assault, kidnapping, prostitution, moneylaundering, weapons trafficking, intimidation, extortion, arson, and smuggling.

G. Prison gangs: Prison provides a prime recruiting opportunity for some gangs.

VI.   Gangs, Organized Crime and Terrorism

A.   Gangs are associating with organized crime entities, such as Mexican drug organizations, Asian criminal groups and Russian organized crime groups.

B.   Few gangs have been found to associate with domestic terrorist organizations.

C.   The susceptibility of gang members to any type of terrorist organization appears to be highest in prison.

VII.   Gang Culture, Membership and Organization

A.   Three R's of gang culture: reputation, respect, and revenge.

1.   Without question, the subcultural value that carries the highest value for all gang members is *respect*.

2.   Disrespect inevitably leads to the third R—revenge.

B.   Gangs are essentially self-operated and self-governed. Some operate by consensus, but most have leaders and a subgoverning structure. Leadership may be single or dual.

C.   Status is generally obtained by joining the gang, but equal status within the gang once joined is not automatically guaranteed.

D.   Symbols

1.   Clothing

2.   Hand signals

3.   Graffiti

4.   Tattoos

E.   Turf and graffiti

1.   Turf: the geographic area of domination that gang members will defend to the death.

2.   Gangs identify their turf through graffiti.

F.   Tattoos: meant to show gang affiliation and indicate rank

VIII.   Gang Activities

A.   In addition to drug dealing, gang members often engage in vandalism, arson, shootings, stabbings, intimidation, swarming, and other forms of violence.

B.   Gangs and drugs

1.   Gangs remain the primary distributors of drugs in the United States.

2.   Use of drugs among gang members is very common.

IX.   Recognizing a Gang Problem

A.   The first step in dealing with a gang problem is to recognize it.

B.   Warning signs of a gang problem: graffiti, obvious colors of clothing, tattoos, initiations, hand signals or handshakes, uncommon terms or phrases and a sudden change in behavior.

X. Identifying Gang Members

 A. Gang members may be identified by their names, symbols (clothing and tattoos), and communication styles, including graffiti and sign language.

 B. Warning signs that a youth may be involved with a gang:

  1. Admits to "hanging out" with kids in gangs

  2. Shows an unusual interest in one or two particular colors of clothing or a particular logo

  3. Has an unusual interest in gangster-influenced music, videos, movies, or Web sites

  4. Uses unusual hand signals to communicate with friends

  5. Has specific drawings of gang symbols on schoolbooks, clothes, walls, or tattoos

  6. Has unexplained physical injuries (fighting-related bruises, injuries to hands/knuckles)

  7. Has unexplained cash or goods, such as clothing or jewelry

  8. Carries a weapon

  9. Has been in trouble with the police

  10. Exhibits negative changes in behavior

 C. Records to keep:

  1. Gang files: type of gangs, ethnic composition, number of active and associate members, territory, hideouts, types of crimes usually committed, method of operation, choice of targets or victims, leadership, and members known to be violent

  2. Moniker files: connects suspected gang members' street names with their legal names

  3. Photographs: great help in conducting photographic identification sessions

  4. Vehicles: includes vehicle make, color, year, body type, license number, distinguishing features, known drivers, and usual parking spots.

  5. Illegal activities: lists the gangs known to engage in the activities

XI. Investigating Illegal Gang Activity

 A. Some disenchanted gang members may become police informants, but obtaining information from gang members is difficult because of the gang's unity.

 B. The immediate area in which a crime occurs may yield much information, such as which gang controls the territory.

 C. Reading and responding to graffiti.

  1. The purpose of marking gang turf:

   a. To disrespect a rival gang or gang member

   b. To memorialize a deceased gang member

      c.   To make a statement

      d.   To send a message

      e.   To conduct business

  2. To document graffiti evidence, take the following steps:

      a.   Photograph it whole and in sections.

      b.   Analyze it while it is intact.

      c.   Remove it.

      d.   Archive the photo.

      e.   Record the colors used.

      f.   Record the gang "Tag" names.

      g.   Record indications of "beef" or violence.

      h.   Create an anti-graffiti program to cover over all graffiti.

D. Challenges in investigating illegal gang activities

  1. Special challenges in investigating the illegal activities of gangs include the multitude of suspects and the unreliability or fear of witnesses.

  2. Evidence may link only a few of the suspects with the crime, and as with organized crime figures, gang members maintain fierce loyalty to each other.

XII.   Approaches to the Gang Problem

A. Four general strategies are being used to deal with gang problems: (1) suppression or law-enforcement efforts, (2) social intervention, (3) opportunities provision, and (4) community organization.

B. Suppression

  1. Law enforcement agencies view the following, in this order, as most effective in preventing and controlling gang crime: suppression tactics, crime prevention activities, and community collaboration.

  2. "Pulling levers": police cracking down on all gang member infractions until violence stops.

  3. Federal agents are using immigration violations to arrest and deport scores of gang members across the country

C. Gang units

  1. Use a combination of prevention, suppression, and intervention.

  2. The suppression component involves collaboration among police, probation, and prosecution, targeting the most active gang members and leaders.

D. Civil gang injunctions and ordinances

  1. Legal tools used with urban gangs that focus on individuals and the locations of their routine activities.

      2. Target specific individuals who intimidate residents and cause other public nuisance issues and restricts these gang members' activities within a specific geographic area.

      3. However, injunctions and ordinances may be challenged as unconstitutional violations of the freedom of speech, the right of association, and due process rights if they do not clearly delineate how officers may apply such orders.

      4. Tougher legislation is also being used as a gang control approach.

XIII.   Collaborative Efforts: Gang Task Forces

    A. Collaboration among law enforcement agencies can greatly enhance efforts to cope with the gang problem.

    B. Multiagency task forces bring together differing perspectives and focus human labor efforts and resources on a common goal, providing a more effective response to the issue of gangs.

    C. Partnerships with the community, parents, and schools significantly increase the likelihood of a successful response.

XIV.   Prosecuting Gang-Related Crimes

    A. The two most often used defense strategies are pleas of diminished capacity and self-defense.

    B. In both large and small jurisdictions, obtaining cooperation of victims and witnesses and intimidation of victims and witnesses present the most problems.

XV.   Federal Efforts to Combat the Gang Problem

    A. The Department of Homeland Security's Immigration and Customs Enforcement (ICE) bureau has established a federal program that trains officers to enforce immigration laws and allows them to tap into an immigration database.

    B. National Youth Gang Center (NYGC) analyzes state and local gang legislation and local antigang ordinances, reviews the literature on gangs, compiles, and analyzes data about gangs and identifies effective gang program strategies.

XVI.   Bias and Hate Crime: An Overview

    A. A bias crime or a hate crime is a criminal act committed because of someone's actual or perceived membership in a particular group.

    B. The number of hate groups operating in America rose to 888 in 2007, up 5 percent from 844 groups in 2006.

    C. There were 7,722 hate crime incidents in 2006, which involved 9,076 offenses, 9,642 victims and 7,324 offenders.

XVII.   Motivation for Hate Crime

A. Bias or hate crimes are motivated by bigotry and hatred against a specific group of people. Race is usually the primary motivation for hate crimes, and African Americans are most often the victims.

B. Offenses

1. Of the 9,080 hate crimes reported to the FBI for 2006, 5,449 (60 percent) were crimes against persons: 31.9 percent of these were simple assault; 46.0 percent, intimidation; 21.6 percent, aggravated assault; 0.2 percent, murder or rape; and 0.3 percent, other types of offenses.

2. A total of 3,593 hate crimes (39.6 percent) were crimes against property: 81.0 percent, destruction/damage/vandalism; 4.0 percent, robbery; 7.3 percent, larceny-theft; 4.3 percent, burglary; 1.1 percent, arson; 0.7 percent, motor vehicle theft; and 1.6 percent, other.

C. Offenders: FBI data shows that of the 7,330 known offenders involved in hate crimes during 2006, 58.6 percent were White, 20.6 percent were Black, 5.7 percent were groups made up of individuals of various races, 1.1 percent were Asian/Pacific Islander, 1.0 percent were American Indian/Alaskan Native, and 12.9 percent were of unknown race.

XVIII. Hate Groups

A. The main hate groups in the United States include skinheads, Christian Identity groups, the Ku Klux Klan, Black separatists, White supremacists, and neo-Nazis.

B. Several watchdog organizations such as the Southern Poverty Law Center and the Anti-Defamation League track the size and activities of racist groups and are good resources for law enforcement.

XIX. The Police Response

A. Respond promptly to reports of hate crime, attempt to reduce the victims' fears, and determine the exact type of prejudice involved.

B. Always provide follow-up information to the victims.

C. Differentiate between hate crimes and hate incidents.

D. Reporting bias and hate crimes

1. The Hate Crime Statistics Act of 1990 requires the attorney general to collect data "about crimes that manifest evidence of prejudice based on race, religion, sexual orientation, or ethnicity."

2. The responsibility for developing the procedures for implementing, collecting, and managing hate crime data was delegated to the director of the FBI, who in turn assigned the tasks to the Uniform Crime Reporting (UCR) Program.

XX. Efforts to Combat Bias and Hate Crimes

A. Two responses have been taken: legislation to expand the scope of the law and increase the severity of punishment for hate crimes and more police focus on and fully investigating such crimes.

B. Other efforts include community-based programs to increase awareness of and offer solutions to the problem of hate crime.

C. Legislation
1. Enhanced penalties
2. Criminal penalties for vandalism of religious institutions
3. Collection of data

D. Legislation must also keep up with the technology used to spread messages of hate. Despite such legislation, those who propagate messages of bigotry, intolerance, and hatred claim they have a constitutionally protected right to do so, citing free speech, due process, and equal protection challenges.

XXI. Ritualistic Crime: An Overview

A. A cult is a system of religious beliefs and rituals, as well as the group of people that subscribes to those beliefs.

B. A less negative term is new religious movement (NRM)
1. Normally, NRMs have a charismatic leader who develops an idea that attracts people looking for fulfillment.
2. The leader is usually self-appointed and claims the right of rule because of a supernatural power of appointment.
3. NRM membership may include males and females, and there is normally no room for democratic participation.
4. Leadership is most often exerted through fear and mysticism.

XXII. Terminology and Symbols of Cults

A. Terminology
1. Antichrist—the son of Satan
2. Beelzebub—powerful demon, right under Satan
3. Coven—group of witches or Satanists
4. Hand of Glory—the left hand of a person who has died
5. Incantation—verbal spell
6. Magick—the "glue" that binds occult groups, a supernatural act or force that causes a change in the environment
7. Occult—secret knowledge of supernormal powers
8. Ritual—prescribed form of religious or mystical ceremony
9. Sabbat—gathering of witches

B. Symbols
1. The *Circle*, which symbolizes totality and wholeness and within which ceremonies are often performed

2. The *inverted cross,* which mocks the Christian cross
3. The *goat's head,* symbolizing the devil
4. The *heart,* symbolizing the center of life
5. The *hexagram* (six-pointed star), purported to protect and control demons
6. The *pentagram* (five-pointed star), representing the four elements of the earth surmounted by "the Spirit"
7. The *horned hand,* a hand signal of recognition used between members

C. Colors
   1. Black—darkness, night, sorrow, evil, the devil
   2. Blue—water, tears, sadness
   3. Green—vegetation, nature, restfulness
   4. Red—blood, physical life, energy, sexuality
   5. White—cleanliness, purity, innocence, virginity
   6. Yellow—perfection, wealth, glory, power

XXIII. The Nature of Ritualistic Crimes

A. A ritualistic crime is an unlawful act committed with or during a ceremony.
B. Ritualistic crimes include vandalism, destruction or theft of religious artifacts; desecration of cemeteries; the maiming, torturing, or killing of animals and people; and the sexual abuse of children.
C. The "Black Masses" of Satanism often incorporate religious articles stolen from churches.
D. "Stoner" gangs consist of middle-class youths involved in drugs, alcohol, and often Satanism.

XXIV. Who Commits Ritualistic Crime?

A. People involved in the occult tend to be creative, imaginative, curious, and daring, as well as intelligent and well-educated, although frequently underachievers.
B. A number of factors may lead an individual to occult involvement, including family alienation, insecurity and a quest for personal power, unfulfilled ambitions, a spiritual search for answers, idealism, nonconformity, adolescent rebellion, a desire for adventure and excitement, a need for attention and recognition and a need to escape reality or the circumstances of his or her own birth.
C. Types of perpetrators:
   1. Dabblers: intermittently involved in the occult and have a strong, curious interest in supernatural belief systems.
   2. True believers: committed to their religion and commit ritualistic crimes because the acts are required by their belief system.

3. True criminals: use the occult as an excuse to justify or rationalize their crimes.

XXV. Investigating Ritualistic Crimes

A. One challenge in investigating ritualistic crime is determining that an act is, in fact, motivated by a religious belief system, rather than by hate or bias.

B. Signs of cult-related activity.

C. Indicators of ritualistic crimes: symbols, candles, makeshift altars, bones, cult-related books, swords, daggers, and chalices.

D. Investigating animal deaths: Unusual circumstances surrounding animal deaths may be important indicators of satanic or cult activity.

E. Investigating homicides

1. Occult murders are usually stabbings or cuttings—seldom are they gunshot wounds—and many victims are cult members or former members.

2. The murderer is typically a White male from a middle- to upper-class family with above-average intelligence and using some form of drug.

3. During postmortem examination, the stomach contents can be of great importance in determining what occurred just before death.

4. Most juries disbelieve seemingly outlandish charges of Satanism and human sacrifice, and most judges do not regard Satanism as a real problem. Hence, most cases are dismissed.

F. Investigating satanic serial killings: Serial killings may be linked to satanic-like rituals in the murder act itself as well as in the killer's behavior following the murder.

G. Investigating youth suicides

1. Increasingly, law enforcement has been faced with satanic "overtones" to suicides committed by young people.

2. Investigators dealing with youth suicides they suspect may be occult related should inquire into the kind of music the youths listened to, the kinds of games they played, whether they had Ouija boards or tarot cards and whether they dabbled in astrology or séances.

XXVI. Special Challenges in Ritualistic Crime Investigations

A. Separating the belief system from the illegal acts.

B. Sensationalism, which frequently accompanies such crimes.

C. "Abnormal" personalities of some victims and suspects.

XXVII. Summary

Chapter Questions

1. The text mentions six reasons why an individual would join a gang. Which of the following is not one of them?
   a. material reasons
   b. recreation
   c. boredom
   d. physical protection

2. All but one of the following is a sign that a youth may be in a gang. Which one is not an indicator?
   a. admits to "hanging out" with kids in gangs
   b. uses unusual hand signals to communicate with friends
   c. has been in trouble with the police
   d. wears baggy jeans with underwear showing

3. The Southern Poverty Law Center is
   a. a watchdog organization for bias and hate crimes.
   b. a group of individuals who try strictly to eliminate poverty.
   c. a law group that lobbies for new laws.
   d. none of these.

4. What 1990 law encouraged police departments to report data on hate crime to the FBI?
   a. Hate Crimes Statistics Act
   b. The Omnibus Crime Act
   c. The Mann Act
   d. The PATRIOT Act

5. With reference to cults, NRM stands for
   a. new rights movement.
   b. new rightist movement.
   c. new religious movement.
   d. none of these.

6. In 2003, the U.S. Supreme Court (*Virginia v. Black et al.*), struck down a Virginia law banning what, saying a state hate crime statute violated the First Amendment:
   a. public praying
   b. cults
   c. cross burning
   d. Nazi regalia

7. Which of the following types of crimes are most often associated with cults or occult groups?
   a. hate crimes
   b. ritualistic crimes
   c. sex offenses
   d. robberies

8. Officers must differentiate between hate crimes and hate incidents: Hate incidents involve behaviors that are motivated by bias, but do not involve which of the following?
   a. criminal acts
   b. slogans or hate speech
   c. slurs or epithets
   d. hateful speech

9. Hate crimes may occur based on a
   a. rumor or innuendo.
   b. perception that the victim is of a certain race, origin, etc.
   c. prior bad act by the victim.
   d. suspects drug use.

10. Which of the following types of gangs are heavily involved in serious crimes (robberies, muggings), the abuse of addictive drugs such as crack cocaine, and may engage in selling drugs but not in organized fashion?
    a. predatory
    b. mercenary
    c. lone wolves
    d. drug cartels

11. High-ranking gang members are often able to exert their influence on the street from within prison. True or False

12. The first step in dealing with a gang problem is to recognize it. True or False

13. The second step of dealing with gangs is to recognize the gang members. True or False

14. Law enforcement agencies do not need to be concerned about records of the monikers for gang members. True or False

15. Gang investigations are completely different from other investigations. True or False

16. The Internet is a source of gang information. True or False

17. Gang members often refuse to use pleas of diminished capacity and self-defense because these would diminish their masculinity, which helps the prosecutor. True or False

18. Gang numbers are rapidly increasing year by year. True or False

19. Street gangs have existed in the United States for most of the country's history and have been studied since the 1920s. True or False

20. Belonging to a gang is now illegal in this country because of federal anti-gang legislation. True or False

21. The number of gangs and gang member has _____ over the last few years.

22. In a cult, the color _____ may signify darkness, night, sorrow, evil, and the devil.

23. _____ means the son of Satan.

24. A(n) _____ is a verbal spell.

25. Research has found _____ public support for harsher penalties for offenders who commit hate crimes than for offenders who commit identical crimes with no biased motivation.

26. Gang graffiti is used to mark the gang's turf (territory) or to _____ a rival gang or gang member.

27. Gang _____ are not only meant to intimidate, show gang affiliation, and indicate rank, they are also a gang member's permanent record, telling who he is, what he believes, what he's done, where he's been, where he did time and for how many years, and how many people he's killed.

28. A Youth Violence Strike Force (YVSF) tells gang members: "We're here because of the shooting. We're not going to leave until it stops. And until it does, nobody is going to so much as jaywalk, nor make any money, nor have any fun." This is referred to as: " _____ levers."

29. Federal agents are using _____ violations to arrest and deport scores of gang members across the country.

30. Civil gang _____ (CGIs) and ordinances are legal tools used with urban gangs that focus on individuals and the locations of their routine activities.

31. Name and define at least five types of gangs.

32. Compare hate crimes with hate incidents. What's the difference?

33. What are two responses to how hate crimes are targeted by law or the police?

34. Why have some civil actions against gangs been challenged as unconstitutional?

35. Discuss how gang members may try to use either diminished capacity or self-defense as a defense strategy? What role can the arresting officer have in this decision?

Case Study

36. There have been a series of burglaries and you have been called in to investigate. Some informants are telling you that the crimes have been committed by a gang, or collection of youths in middle school on the north side of town. The youths are a collection of students with mixed ethnicity, but all male. The items being taken are cash, small valuable items that could be sold, alcohol, and you suspect some drugs, but no one will admit that happening. The burglary rate is being reported on the front page of the newspaper and community pressure to resolve the case is growing. What steps would you take to investigate this case?

Answer Key

1. c
2. d
3. a
4. a
5. c
6. c
7. b
8. a
9. b
10. a

11. True
12. True
13. True
14. False
15. False
16. True
17. False
18. False
19. True
20. False

21. decreased
22. black
23. Antichrist
24. incantation
25. minimal
26. disrespect
27. tattoos
28. pulling
29. immigration
30. injunctions

31. Hedonistic/social gangs—only moderate drug use and offending, involved mainly in using drugs and having a good time; little involvement in crime, especially violent crime.

Party gangs—commonly called "party crews"; relatively high use and sale of drugs, but only one major form of delinquency—vandalism; may contain both genders or may be one gender; many have no specific dress style, but some dress in stylized clothing worn by street gang members, such as baseball caps and oversize clothing; some have tattoos and use hand signs; their flexible turf is called the "party scene"; crews compete over who throws the biggest party, with alcohol, marijuana, nitrous oxide, sex, and music critical party elements.

Predatory gangs—heavily involved in serious crimes (robberies, muggings) and the abuse of addictive drugs such as crack cocaine; may engage in selling drugs but not in organized fashion.

Scavenger gangs—loosely organized groups described as "urban survivors"; prey on the weak in inner cities; engage in rather petty crimes but sometimes violence, often just for fun; members have no greater bond than their impulsiveness and need to belong; lack goals and are low achievers; often illiterate with poor school performance.

Serious delinquent gangs—heavy involvement in both serious and minor crimes, but much lower involvement in drug use and drug sales than party gangs.

Territorial gangs—associated with a specific area or turf and, as a result, get involved in conflicts with other gangs over their respective turfs.

Organized/corporate gangs—heavy involvement in all kinds of crime, heavy use and sale of drugs; may resemble major corporations, with separate divisions handling sales, marketing, discipline, and so on; discipline is strict, and promotion is based on merit.

Drug gangs—smaller than other gangs; much more cohesive; focused on the drug business; strong, centralized leadership with market-defined roles.

32. Hate crime is a criminal act committed because of someone's actual or perceived membership in a particular group. The International Association of Chiefs of Police (IACP) says, "A hate crime is a criminal offense committed against persons, property or society that is motivated, in whole or in part, by an offender's bias against an individual's or a group's race, religion, ethnic/ national origin, gender, age, disability or sexual orientation" (Turner, 1999, p.3). Crimes range from verbal intimidation and harassment to destruction of property, physical violence, and murder. "Hate incidents involve behaviors that, though motivated by bias against a victim's race, religion, ethnic/national origin, gender, age, disability or sexual orientation, are not criminal acts. Hostile or hateful speech or other disrespectful/discriminatory behavior may be motivated by bias but is not illegal" (Turner, 1999, p.4).

33. Regardless of how an agency or individual officer views hate crime, it remains a criminal offense that requires a law enforcement response. Two responses have been taken: legislation to expand the scope of the law and increase the severity of punishment for hate crimes, and more police focus on and fully investigating such crimes. Other efforts include community-based programs to increase awareness of and offer solutions to the problem of hate crime.

34. Injunctions and ordinances may be challenged as unconstitutional violations of the freedom of speech, the right of association, and due process rights if they do not clearly delineate how officers may apply such orders. For example, Chicago passed a gang congregation ordinance to combat the problems created by the city's street gangs. During the 3 years following passage of the ordinance, Chicago police officers issued more than 89,000 dispersal orders and arrested more than 42,000 people. But in *City of Chicago v. Morales* (1999), the Supreme Court struck down the ordinance as unconstitutional because its vague wording failed to provide adequate standards to guide police discretion. The lesson here is that any civil injunctions a city passes must be clear in what officers can and cannot do when they observe what they believe to be gang members congregating in public places.

35. The two most often used defense strategies are pleas of diminished capacity and self-defense. Although some states have eliminated "diminished capacity" as a defense, many have not. Therefore, *document* whether the suspect was under the influence of alcohol or other drugs at the time of the crime. Likewise, *document* whether the suspect was threatened by the victim and could possibly have been acting in self-defense.

Case Study Answer

36. The opportunity to find out about this group is important. The use of the term *gang* has some meaning, but you may in fact be dealing with a collection of youth that appear to be a gang. You will need to gather as much information and evidence as possible so that when an arrest is finally made you have the evidence to break the group and to prosecute. Patterns would be important; the youths will probably follow a method that seems to work. Most likely the burglaries are happening after school and before the people return from work. This means that you probably have a narrow window of time to do stakeouts that help with the case. The school may be able to provide you with some ideas, and attendance records may assist you in determining if there are any days where burglaries occurred that the students were not in class. The school yearbook may assist you. Possibly involving an active Neighborhood Watch program would help you get the needed information to make an arrest. This one will get solved, but it will take a lot of work and assistance from the crime analyst to pull together a strong case.

TERRORISM AND HOMELAND SECURITY

OUTLINE

- Terrorism: An Overview
- Classification of Terrorist Acts
- Terrorist Groups in the United States
- Terrorists as Criminals
- Methods Used by Terrorists
- Funding Terrorism
- The Federal Response to Terrorism
- Hometown Security and Homeland Security
- Investigating Possible Terrorist Activities
- Information Gathering and Intelligence Sharing
- Crucial Collaborations and Partnerships
- Initiatives to Assist in the Fight against Terrorism
- The Role of the Media in the War on Terrorism
- Concerns Related to the War on Terrorism
- Community Policing and Homeland Security

Chapter 20
Terrorism and Homeland Security

By the end of this chapter, you should know how to define the terms and understand the application of the following concepts. Test your understanding of the chapter by verifying that you know this information. If you do not know it, review the chapter.

Can You Define?

asymmetric warfare bioterrorism contagion effect cyberterrorism deconfliction	ecoterrorism fusion center hawala intifada	jihad sleeper cell technological terrorism terrorism

Do you know?

- What most definitions of terrorism have in common?
- What motivates most terrorist attacks?
- How the FBI classifies terrorist acts?
- What groups are commonly identified as Islamic terrorist organizations?
- What domestic terrorist groups exist in the United States?
- What methods terrorists may use?
- What federal office was established as a result of 9/11?
- What the two lead agencies in combating terrorism are?

- How the USA PATRIOT Act enhances counterterrorism efforts by the United States?
- What the first line of defense against terrorism in the United States is?
- What the three-tiered model of al-Qaeda terrorist attacks consists of?
- What a key to successfully combating terrorism is?
- What the Community Protection Act authorizes?
- What two concerns related to the war on terrorism are?
- What balance must be maintained in investigating terrorism?

Chapter Outline

I.   Terrorism: An Overview

    A. Terrorism defined:

        1. The Terrorism Research Center defines terrorism as "the use of force or violence against persons or property in violation of the criminal laws of the United States for purposes of intimidation, coercion or ransom."

        2. The FBI's definition: "Terrorism is the unlawful use of force or violence against persons or property to intimidate or coerce a government, the civilian population, or any segment thereof, in furtherance of political or social objectives."

        3. The U.S. Code Title 22 defines terrorism as the "premeditated, politically motivated violence perpetrated against noncombatant targets by subnational groups or clandestine agents, usually intended to influence an audience."

    B. Terrorism is the systematic use of physical violence, either actual or threatened, against noncombatants to create a climate of fear and exert pressure to bring about some religious, political, or social change.

    C. Motivations for Terrorism

        1. Most terrorist acts result from dissatisfaction with a religious, political, or social system or policy and frustration resulting from an inability to change it through acceptable, nonviolent means.

        2. Religious motives are seen in Islamic extremism.

        3. Political motives are seen in such elements as the Red Army Faction.

        4. Social motives are seen in single-issue groups such as those against abortion or active in animal-rights or environmentalist movements.

II.   Classification of Terrorist Acts

    A. Domestic terrorism: The FBI defines *domestic terrorism* as "the unlawful use, or threatened use, of force or violence by a group or individual based and operating entirely within the United States or its territories without foreign direction committed against persons or property to intimidate or coerce a government, the civilian population or any segment thereof, in furtherance of political or social objectives."

    B. International terrorism

        1. International terrorism is foreign based or directed by countries or groups outside the United States against the United States.

        2. The FBI divides international terrorism into three categories:

            a. Foreign state sponsors using terrorism as a tool of foreign policy, such as Iraq, Libya, and Afghanistan

            b. Formalized terrorist groups such as the Lebanese Hezbollah, the Egyptian al-Gamm'a al-Islamiyya, the Palestinian Harakat al-Muqawamah al-Islamiyyah (HAMAS), and Osama bin Laden's al-Qaeda

    c.   Loosely affiliated international radical extremists who have a variety of identities and travel freely in the United States, unknown to law enforcement or the government.

  3. Asymmetric warfare: a weaker group attacks a superior group not head-on but by targeting areas where the adversary least expects to be hit, causing great psychological shock, along with loss of life among random victims.

  4. Islamic terrorist groups

    a.   Hezbollah

    b.   HAMAS

    c.   Palestinian Islamic Jihad

    d.   Al-Aqsa Martyrs' Brigade

    e.   Al-Qaeda

C.   The threat and reality of terrorism: Conclusions of researchers:

  1. The U.S. will be attacked again.

  2. Residents or citizens of the U.S. will carry out these attacks.

  3. Car bombings will become a tool of choice.

  4. Threat groups will achieve a greater level of organization and sophistication in technologies and weapons.

D.   The dual threat: external and internal terrorists

III.   Terrorist Groups in the United States

A.   White supremacists

  1. Ku Klux Klan

  2. Neo-Nazi groups

B.   Black supremacists: Black Panther Party

C.   The militia movement:

  1. Most are heavily armed.

  2. Members are commonly frustrated, overwhelmed, and socially unable to cope with the modern world.

D.   Other right-wing extremists

E.   Left-wing extremists

F.   Pro-life extremists

G.   Animal rights extremists: Animal Liberation Front

H.   Environmental extremists

  1. Ecoterrorism used to inflict economic damage

  2. Earth Liberation Front

  3. Arson is a favorite weapon

IV. Terrorists as Criminals

    A. Terrorism has caused a blurring of war and crime.

    B. Typical criminals: uncommitted, self-centered, have no cause, untrained, escape/elude oriented.

    C. Terrorists: fight for political objective, motivated by ideology or religion, group focused (even berserkers or lone wolves), consumed with purpose, trained and motivated for the mission, or the attack.

V. Methods Used by Terrorists

    A. Explosives and bombs

        1. Suspicious packages

        2. Suicide bombers

        3. Prevention strategies: authorities commonly use simple tools, such as restricting parking and traffic and putting up concrete median barriers and bollards, security checkpoints, static physical security, active detection methods, vehicle registration, background checks.

    B. Weapons of mass destruction

        1. Biological agents

            a. Bioterrorism involves dissemination of anthrax, botulism, and smallpox as WMDs.

            b. The nation's food and water supplies are especially susceptible to bioterrorism.

        2. Chemical agents

            a. Nerve agents

            b. Blood agents

            c. Choking agents

            d. Blistering agents

        3. Nuclear terrorism

        4. Detecting radiation and other bioterrorism agents

            a. Dosimeters

            b. Electronic nose technology

            c. Robotic detection and identification technology

            d. Global positions systems (GPS)

        5. WMD Team

    C. Technological terrorism

        1. Technological terrorism includes attacks *on* our technology as well as *by* technology.

        2. Cyberterrorism is defined by the FBI as "terrorism that initiates, or threatens to initiate, the exploitation of or attack on information systems."

VI.   Funding Terrorism

  A.   Terrorist groups commonly collaborate with organized criminal groups to deal drugs, arms and, in some instances, people.

  B.   Narcoterrorism refers to the use of terrorist tactics to support drug operations or the use of drug trade profits to finance terrorism.

  C.   Many terrorist operations are financed by charitable groups and wealthy Arabs sympathetic to the group's cause.

  D.   Money laundering: Hawala is an informal banking system based on trust and often bartering, common throughout the Middle East and used to transfer billions of dollars every year. No tax records or paper trails exist.

VII. The Federal Response to Terrorism

  A.   The Department of Homeland Security

    1.   Established as a result of 9/11, reorganizing the departments of the federal government.

    2.   The FBI is the lead agency for responding to acts of domestic terrorism.

    3.   The Federal Emergency Management Agency (FEMA) is the lead agency for consequence management (after an attack).

    4.   Goals of the DHS:

      a.   Increase our ability to keep bad people out of the country.

      b.   Keep bad things out of the country, increasing port security.

      c.   Protect our infrastructure better.

      d.   Continue to build a response capability with modern computer tools.

      e.   Promote intelligence sharing, not only horizontally across the federal government but vertically with the local government as well.

  B.   The USA PATRIOT Act

    1.   The USA PATRIOT Act significantly improves the nation's counterterrorism efforts by

      a.   Allowing investigators to use the tools already available to investigate organized crime and drug trafficking.

      b.   Facilitating information sharing and cooperation among government agencies so they can better "connect the dots."

      c.   Updating the law to reflect new technologies and new threats.

      d.   Increasing the penalties for those who commit or support terrorist crimes.

    2.   Using tools already in use in the war on drugs,

    3.   Facilitating information sharing.

    4.   Controversy over the USA Patriot Act: Some members of Congress and civil liberties groups say the act has given federal agents too

much power to pursue suspected terrorists, threatening the civil rights and privacy of Americans.

   C.   The National Infrastructure Protection Plan (NIPP)

       1.   Comprehensive risk management framework defining critical infrastructure protection roles and responsibilities of federal, state, local, tribal, and private security partners.

       2.   Goal is to "Build a safer, more secure and more resilient America by enhancing protection of the nation's critical infrastructure and key resources (CI/KR) to prevent, deter, neutralize or mitigate the effects of deliberate efforts by terrorists to destroy, incapacitate or exploit them; and to strengthen national preparedness, timely response and rapid recovery in the event of an attack, natural disaster or other emergency."

   D.   Fusion centers:

       1.   An initiative aimed at promoting and facilitating information and intelligence sharing among federal and local law enforcement agencies is the development of fusion centers throughout the country.

       2.   Forty-two fusion centers have been established in 37 states and have begun making some important connections. However, general assessment of the centers is that they are a costly but largely ineffective weapon against terrorism.

VIII.   Hometown Security and Homeland Security

   A.   The IACP has identified five key principles that should form the basis for a national homeland security strategy:

       1.   All terrorism is local.

       2.   Prevention is paramount.

       3.   Hometown security is homeland security.

       4.   Homeland security strategies must be coordinated nationally, not federally.

       5.   Bottom-up engineering is important, involving the diversity of the state, tribal, and local public safety communities in noncompetitive collaboration.

   B.   The first line of defense against terrorism is the patrol officer in the field.

IX.   Investigating Possible Terrorist Activities

   A.   A major challenge in the war on terrorism is ensuring that individual officers remain vigilant.

   B.   Investigators should also be knowledgeable of vulnerable, valuable targets for a terrorist attack.

       1.   Critical infrastructures: agriculture and food, water, public health, emergency services, defense industrial base, telecommunications,

energy, transportation, banking and finance, chemical industry and hazardous materials, and postal and shipping facilities.

2. Key assets: national monuments and icons, nuclear power plants, dams, government facilities, and commercial key assets.

C. Link between terrorism and white-collar crime:

1. Terrorist activities require funding for weaponry, training, travel, and living expenses.

2. Terrorists create and use false identifications to enter the country, gain employment, acquire equipment, and accumulate money.

3. Cases involving money laundering should be looked at as not only a white-collar crime but also as potentially linked to terrorism.

D. The typical stages of a terrorist attack.

1. Research, including surveillance, stakeouts, and local inquiries.

2. Planning, usually conducted behind closed doors.

3. Execution, the actual attack and possible escape, often carried out by a sleeper cell.

   a. The three-tiered model of al-Qaeda terrorist attacks consists of sleeper cells attacking in conjunction with the group's leaders in Afghanistan, sleeper cells attacking on their own apart from centralized command, and individuals attacking with support from small cells.

   b. It is crucial that investigators identify members of sleeper cells within their community.

E. Surveillance cameras as investigative tools

X. Information Gathering and Intelligence Sharing

A. An important distinction differentiates information and intelligence, with intelligence broadening to become organized information.

B. The intelligence cycle:

1. Knowing the intelligence requirements

2. Planning and direction, a function of the FBI

3. Collecting raw information from local, state and federal investigations

4. Processing and exploiting the raw information, that is, converting the collected information into a form usable for analysis

5. Analysis and production, converting the raw information into intelligence

6. Dissemination, which leads back to refinement of intelligence requirements

C. Local networking modules developed among local, state and federal law enforcement agencies are the most effective way to discuss and share investigative and enforcement endeavors to combat terrorism.

D. Deconfliction protocols

E. The National Criminal Intelligence Sharing Plan (NCISP)

1. Unites law enforcement agencies of all sizes and geographic locations in a national effort to prevent terrorism and criminal activity

2. Raises cooperation and communication among local, state, and federal partners to an unprecedented level to strengthen the abilities of the justice community to detect threats and protect American lives and liberties

XI. Crucial Collaborations and Partnerships

A. A key to combating terrorism lies with the local police and the intelligence they can provide to federal authorities.

B. Communication should be the number-one priority in any terrorist-preparedness plan and is number one in collaboration among local, state, and federal law enforcement agencies.

C. Regional Information Sharing Systems (RISS) program: assists state and local agencies by sharing information and intelligence regarding terrorism.

D. Limitations on information sharing have caused tensions in the past, as often information received by the FBI is classified. Rules of federal procedure and grand jury classified material are two other limitations to how much information can be shared.

XII. Initiatives to Assist in the Fight against Terrorism

A. The Community Protection Act

B. Increased border security

C. Community vulnerability assessment methodology

D. The National Memorial Institute for the Prevention of Terrorism

E. The National Center for Food Protection and Defense

F. The National Incident Management System

G. Joint terrorism task forces

XIII. The Role of the Media in the War on Terrorism

A. Contagion effect: coverage of terrorism inspires more terrorism, thus making terrorism, in effect, contagious.

B. Issues of censorship.

XIV. Concerns Related to the War on Terrorism

A. Concerns for civil rights

1. Civil libertarians are concerned that valued American freedoms will be sacrificed in the interest of national safety.

2. A difficult challenge facing law enforcement is balancing the need to enhance security with the need to maintain freedom.

B. Retaliation or discrimination against people of Middle Eastern descent

1. Another concern is that some Americans may retaliate against innocent people of Middle Eastern descent, many of whom were either born in the United States or are naturalized citizens.

2. Four obstacles to improved relations between police and Arab American communities:

   a. Distrust between Arab-American communities and law enforcement

   b. Lack of cultural awareness among law enforcement officers

   c. Language barriers

   d. Concerns about immigration status and fear of deportation

XV. Community Policing and Homeland Security

   A. Community policing is an important concept to adopt in efforts to prepare for and respond to acts of terrorism

   B. Being proactive: sources of information in the community include Neighborhood Watches, hotels, real estate agents, storage facilities, religious groups, social and civic clubs, colleges and universities, print shops, business managers, transportation centers and tourist attractions major industrial enterprises, schools, office building custodians, health care providers, bar and liquor stores, and inspectors and code enforcers.

XVI. Summary

Chapter Questions

1. HAMAS is
   a. literally, the Party of God, a militia group and political party that first emerged as a faction in Lebanon following the Israeli invasion in 1982.
   b. a militant Palestinian Islamic movement in the West Bank and Gaza Strip dedicated to destroying Israel and creating an Islamic state in Palestine.
   c. a broad-based Islamic militant organization founded by Osama bin Laden in the late 1980s.
   d. a group formed in the mean streets of New Jersey

2. Left-wing extremists believe in a pro-Marxist stance that the rich must be brought down and the poor elevated. Presently, the largest groups of supporters for this cause are
   a. anarchists.
   b. monarchists.
   c. royalists.
   d. provocateurs.

3. This group participated in the al-Aqsa intifada and its international branch "is believed to be the most effective terrorist network in the world."
   a. the Covenant, the Sword, and the Arm of the Lord
   b. the PLO
   c. Hezbollah
   d. Earth First!

4. ALF stands for
   a. Al-Qaeda Liberation Front.
   b. Animal Liberation Front.
   c. Anti-Liberation Front.
   d. Allied Liberation Front.

5. Hawala is
   a. a method of terrorism.
   b. a method of informal banking.
   c. a way of creating bombs.
   d. a method of gathering intelligence.

6. The USA PATRIOT Act significantly improved the nation's counterterrorism efforts by all but which of the following measures?
   a. allowing investigators to use the tools available to investigate organized crime and drug trafficking
   b. facilitating information sharing and cooperation among government agencies so they can better "connect the dots"
   c. updating the law to reflect new technologies and new threats, as well as increase the penalties for those who commit or support terrorist crimes
   d. allowing for kidnap and assassination of suspected terrorist leaders

7. A group of terrorists who blend into a community awaiting instructions is known as a
    a. sleeper cell.
    b. shortcut cell.
    c. delayed action group.
    d. temporary action group.

8. The NIMS stands for
    a. National Information Management System.
    b. National Incident Management System.
    c. National Identification Management System.
    d. National Intelligence Matrix System.

9. Which is NOT one of the four common types of chemical weapons?
    a. nerve agents
    b. blood agents
    c. gastrointestinal agents
    d. choking agents

10. Law enforcement agencies use the term *CBR* to include all potential terrorist threats that can have consequences for the health of large numbers of people. These threats include all but which of the following?
    a. chemical agents
    b. biological agents
    c. radiation exposure
    d. petrochemical agents

11. Domestic terrorist groups within the United States include White supremacists and Black separatists. **True or False**

12. Abortion clinics and their staffs are common Army of God targets, with zealots committing crimes ranging from arson to assault to assassination. **True or False**

13. Al-Qaeda terrorists using ordinary box cutters to overpower flight personnel and convert airplanes into weapons of mass destruction, costing billions of dollars of losses to the U.S. economy and tremendous loss of life, is an example of asymmetric warfare. **True or False**

14. Today, a newly reconstituted Black Panther Party for Self-Defense has been organized. However, it does not qualify as a hate group. **True or False**

15. Most researchers believe that the experiences from the war on drugs do not apply to the war in terrorism. **True or False**

16. Most terrorist acts result from dissatisfaction with a religious, political, or social system or policy and frustration resulting from an inability to change it through acceptable, nonviolent means.   True or False

17. A key to combating terrorism lies with the local police and the intelligence they can provide to local and state rather than federal officials.   True or False

18. After 9/11, we have had to give up our Fourth Amendment rights to habeas corpus and all civil liberties.   True or False

19. Community policing is similar to homeland security in that both are proactive.   True or False

20. Hawala is a method of informal banking.   True or False

21. Reports that the prevalence of _____ explosives in terrorist improvised explosive devices is increasing.

22. Today, much concern centers around potential use of nuclear, biological, and chemical agents, also referred to as _____ agents.

23. "If properly released in a well-populated area, _____ gas has the potential to cause tens of thousands of casualties."

24. One agent, _____ toxin, is both a biological and a chemical weapon.

25. _____ is more than 1,000 times more poisonous than cyanide.

26. The concept of _____ refers to the use of terrorist tactics to support drug operations or the use of drug trade profits to finance terrorism.

27. On October 8, 2001, President Bush signed Executive Order 13228 establishing the Department of _____ _____ .

28. _____ (initials) is the lead agency for consequence management (after an attack).

29. The act signed into law, titled "The Uniting and Strengthening America by Providing Appropriate Tools Required to Intercept and Obstruct Terrorism," is known also as the _____ Act.

30. An initiative aimed at promoting and facilitating information and intelligence sharing among federal and local law enforcement agencies is the development of _____ centers throughout the country.

31. Why is homeland security known as the "monster that ate criminal justice?"

32. What are some of the motivations for terrorism?   .

33. What is "domestic terrorism"?

34. What is asymmetric warfare? Give a relevant example.

35. What three issues rejuvenated the right-wing militia movement in the United States?

Case Study

36. A group of five Middle Eastern males, all between 20 and 30 years of age, has moved into an apartment in a middle-class neighborhood in your community. The neighbors have called to inform the department of this group. Based on their national origin and the fact that the members of this group are different from the other people who live in the neighborhood, some of the citizens are very upset and have demanded that the department "do something" to keep them safe. What actions would you take as the individual assigned to the case?

_____

_____

_____

_____

_____

_____

_____

_____

_____

Answer Key

1. b		11. True
2. a		12. True
3. c		13. True
4. b		14. False
5. b		15. False
6. d		16. True
7. a		17. True
8. b		18. False
9. c		19. True
10. d		20. True

21. homemade

22. NBC

23. chlorine

24. ricin

25. Ricin

26. narcoterrorism

27. Homeland Security

28. FEMA

29. USA PATRIOT

30. fusion

31. "The Department of Homeland Security announced $1.9 billion in anti-terrorism grants yesterday, stirring a growing debate among state and local officials nationwide over whether such funds are coming at the expense of other law enforcement priorities that some say are more urgent, such as fighting drugs, gangs, and violent crime" (Hsu, 2008, p.A02). The increase in violent crime in recent years has led some to dub homeland security "the

monster that ate criminal justice" and resulted in louder warnings that local police departments cannot be effective homeland security partners if they are overwhelmed by the responsibilities of their core mission.

32. Most terrorist acts result from dissatisfaction with a religious, political, or social system or policy and frustration resulting from an inability to change it through acceptable, nonviolent means.

33. The FBI defines domestic terrorism as "the unlawful use, or threatened use, of force or violence by a group or individual based and operating entirely within the United States or its territories without foreign direction committed against persons or property to intimidate or coerce a government, the civilian population or any segment thereof, in furtherance of political or social objectives."

34. Asymmetric warfare is combat in which a weaker group attacks a superior group not head-on but by targeting areas where the adversary least expects to be hit, causing great psychological shock, along with loss of life among random victims. Asymmetric warfare aims to empower the powerless and nullify the stronger adversary's ability to use its conventional weapons. A prime example was the use by the 9/11 al-Qaeda terrorists of ordinary box cutters to overpower flight personnel and convert airplanes into weapons of mass destruction, costing billions of dollars of losses to the U.S. economy and tremendous loss of life (at a total estimated cost to the terrorists of $500,000).

35. The passage of the Brady Bill and the Ruby Ridge and Waco incidents. The Brady Bill caused militia groups to fear federal gun control legislation. The Ruby Ridge incident involved an attempt to arrest Randy Weaver, a White supremacist charged with selling illegal firearms to undercover agents of the Bureau of Alcohol, Tobacco and Firearms (ATF). A shootout ensued, resulting in the death of a U.S. marshal and Weaver's young son. The FBI laid siege to Weaver's Ruby Ridge cabin and killed his pregnant wife before Weaver surrendered. The third galvanizing incident occurred with the federal siege of the Branch Davidian compound near Waco, Texas.

Case Study Answer:

36. This case is sensitive, but probably not unusual. Because of recent events, people are wary of people who are from the Middle East. The fact that there are five young males living in one apartment adds to the neighbors' concern. The group may be a "sleeper cell," or it may be completely harmless; you must try to determine which it is to the best of your abilities. The best initial course of action is to learn as much as you possibly can about the individuals, without contacting them directly. Something as simple as looking at the mailbox may give you some names. Running license plates on cars in the area, or talking with the patrol officers assigned to it, may provide additional information. The neighbors who have lodged the complaint may

also have information if they have had any prior contact with the individuals, and they will likely be very willing to cooperate and update you with any new observations about activity in the apartment. Until you have grounds for further action, the investigation should be quick and simple, aimed at excluding the possibility that you have a terrorist cell in your community to reassure the other citizens. Some might argue that unless you have clear grounds for suspicion, you should not do anything. However, talking to the area officers and determining what is known by the people making the complaint is appropriate.

PREPARING FOR AND PRESENTING CASES IN COURT

OUTLINE

- The Final Report
- The Role of the Prosecutor
- Preparing a Case for Prosecution
- The Trial
- Sequence of a Criminal Trial
- While Waiting to Testify
- Testifying under Direct Examination
- Testifying under Cross-Examination
- Concluding Your Testimony
- Advice on Testifying from a Seasoned, "Officer of the Year" Investigator

Chapter 21
Preparing for and Presenting Cases in Court

By the end of this chapter, you should know how to define the terms and understand the application of the following concepts. Test your understanding of the chapter by verifying that you know this information. If you do not know it, review the chapter.

Can You Define?

adversary system	direct examination	rule on witnesses
bench trial	discovery process	subpoena
brackets	exceptionally cleared	surrebuttal
Brady rule	expert witness	the well
cross-examination	impeach	witness sequestration
de minimus	motion in limine	rule
communication	rebuttal	

Do you know?

- What the most important rule to eradicate fear of testifying in court is?
- What to include in the final report?
- The relative importance of the prosecutor in the court system?
- Why some cases are not prosecuted?
- How to prepare a case for court?
- How to review a case?
- What occurs during the pretrial conference?
- What the usual sequence in a criminal trial is?
- What the "win" is for an investigator who testifies in court?

- What kinds of statements are inadmissible in court?
- How to testify most effectively?
- When to use notes while testifying?
- What nonverbal elements can influence courtroom testimony positively and negatively?
- What strategies can make testifying in court more effective?
- What defense attorney tactics to anticipate?
- What a key to testifying during cross-examination is?
- How to avoid objections to your testimony?

Chapter Outline

I.   The Final Report

    A.   The complaint

    B.   The preliminary investigation report

    C.   Follow-up report

    D.   Statements, admissions, and confessions

    E.   Laboratory reports

    F.   Photographs, sketches, and drawings

    G.   Summary of negative evidence

II.   The Role of the Prosecutor

    A.   The prosecutor is the gatekeeper of the court system, determining which cases are prosecuted and which are not.

    B.   On a daily basis, the prosecutor is the only official who works with all actors of the criminal justice system.

    C.   At the county level, the prosecutor, or district attorney (DA), is the chief law enforcement official.

    D.   At the federal level, the prosecutor is called the U.S. attorney, a position appointed by the president, approved by Congress, and confirmed by the Senate.

        1.   Commonly staff investigators are in frequent contact with other federal investigative agencies, such as the Federal Bureau of Investigation (FBI), Drug Enforcement Administration (DEA), Bureau of Alcohol, Tobacco, Firearms and Explosives (ATF), and U.S. Secret Service.

        2.   Unlike local prosecutors, federal prosecutors are typically those who initiate a federal criminal investigation.

    E.   Nonprosecution

        1.   Tensions and conflicts sometimes exist between investigators and prosecutors if a case isn't prosecuted.

        2.   Cases are not prosecuted if

            a.   The complaint is invalid.

            b.   The prosecutor declines after reviewing the case.

            c.   The complainant refuses to prosecute.

            d.   The offender dies.

            e.   The offender is in prison or out of the country and cannot be returned.

            f.   No evidence or leads exist.

        3.   Administrative policy sometimes closes cases to further investigation.

4. In other cases, the report is valid but investigation reveals that witnesses have left the area or that no physical evidence remains at the crime scene.

5. Motion hearings

    a. A motion can lead to a hearing, an appearance before the court to resolve the issue raised in the motion.

    b. If the defense files a motion to suppress, claiming that evidence was illegally obtained or a confession unconstitutionally extracted, and an evidentiary hearing is granted by the court, the possibility exists for the case to fold before ever going to trial, effectively resulting in nonprosecution.

III. Preparing a Case for Prosecution

    A. Review and evaluate all evidence, positive and negative, and the chain of custody.

        1. Concentrate on proving the elements of the crime and establishing the offender's identity.

        2. The pretrial discovery process requires the prosecution and defense to disclose to each other certain evidence they intend to use at trial, thus avoiding surprises: the Brady rule.

        3. Review and evaluate witnesses' statements for credibility.

        4. Assess the witness's relationship to the suspect and the victim.

        5. Establish the suspect's identity by eyewitness testimony, transfer evidence, and supporting evidence such as motive, prior knowledge, opportunity, and known modus operandi.

        6. Depositions: In many states, officers must provide a deposition before trial as part of the discovery.

    B. Review all reports on the case.

    C. Prepare witnesses.

    D. Hold a pretrial conference with the prosecutor:

        1. Review all the evidence.

        2. Discuss the strengths and weaknesses of the case.

        3. Discuss the probable line of questioning by the prosecutor and the defense.

    E. Final preparations:

        1. Know what is expected and the rules of the court.

        2. Dress appropriately.

        3. Be on time.

IV. The Trial

    A. Adversary system:

        1. Judge, or magistrate, presides over the trial.

    2. Jurors hear and evaluate the testimony of all witnesses.

    3. Legal counsel presents the prosecution and defense evidence before the court and jury.

    4. Defendants may or may not take the witness stand.

    5. Witnesses present the facts as they know them.

V.   Sequence of a Criminal Trial

    A. Jury selection

    B. Opening statements by the prosecution and the defense

    C. Presentation of the prosecution's case, cross-examination by the defense

    D. Presentation of the defense's case, cross-examination by the prosecution

    E. Rebuttal and surrebuttal testimony

    F. Closing statements by the prosecution and the defense

    G. Instructions to the jury

    H. Jury deliberations to reach a verdict

    I. Reading the verdict

    J. Acquittal or passing of sentence

VI.   While Waiting to Testify

    A. Do not discuss the case while waiting in the hallway to testify.

    B. De minimus communication—a simple hello or giving of directions—is allowed.

VII.   Testifying under Direct Examination

    A. The best outcome for an investigator who testifies is to have established credibility.

    B. Inadmissible statements:

        1. Opinions and conclusions

        2. Hearsay

        3. Privilege communication

        4. Statements about character and reputation, including the defendant's criminal record

    C. Guidelines for effective testimony are

        1. Speak clearly, firmly, and with expression.

        2. Answer questions directly. Do not volunteer information.

        3. Pause briefly before answering.

        4. Refer to your notes if you do not recall exact details, but do not rely on them excessively.

        5. Admit calmly when you do not know an answer.

        6. Admit any mistakes you make in testifying.

        7. Avoid police jargon, sarcasm, and humor.

8. Tell the complete truth as you know it.

D. Nonverbal factors.

1. Several components:

   a. What is said: the actual words spoken

   b. How it is said: tone of voice, pitch, modulation, and the like

   c. Nonverbal factors: body language, gestures, demeanor

2. Important nonverbal elements include dress, eye contact, posture, gestures, mannerisms, rate of speech, tone of voice, and facial expressions.

E. Strategies for excelling as a witness:

1. Set yourself up.

2. Provoke the defense into giving you a chance to explain.

3. Be unconditional.

4. Do not stall.

F. Expert testimony.

1. An expert witness is a person who has had special training, education, or experience.

2. To testify as an expert, an individual must possess the following:

   a. Present or prior employment in the specific field

   b. Active membership in a professional group in the field

   c. Research work in the field

   d. An educational degree directly related to the field

   e. Direct experience with the subject, if not employed in the field

   f. Papers, treatises, or books published on the subject or teaching experience in it

VIII. Testifying under Cross-Examination

A. Actions that weaken credibility:

1. Using a defensive or evasive tone of voice

2. Appearing ill at ease or nervous

3. Avoiding eye contact

4. Crossing arms defensively across chest

5. Quibbling over common terms

6. Sitting stiffly

7. Looking to attorney for assistance during cross-examination

8. Cracking jokes inappropriately

9. Using lots of "ah's" or "uh's"

B. Actions that add credibility:

1. Displaying an even temperament on direct and cross

2. Not becoming angry or defensive when pressed

   3. Appearing relaxed and at ease
   4. Being likeable and polite
   5. Maintaining eye contact with attorney and jury
   6. Not being affected by interruptions or objections
C. During cross-examination, the defense attorney may
   1. Be disarmingly friendly or intimidatingly rude.
   2. Attack your credibility and impartiality.
   3. Attack your investigative skill.
   4. Attempt to force contradictions or inconsistencies.
   5. Ask leading questions or deliberately misquote you.
   6. Ask for a simple answer to a complex question.
   7. Use rapid-fire questioning.
   8. Use the silent treatment.
D. Handling objections
   1. Three general types of objections are common:
      a. To the form of the question
      b. To the substance of the question
      c. To the answer
   2. To avoid objections to your testimony, avoid conclusions and nonresponsive answers. Answer yes-or-no questions with "yes" or "no."

IX.   Concluding Your Testimony

   A. Do not leave the stand until instructed to do so by counsel or the court.
   B. If you have been a credible witness and told the truth, win or lose in court, you have done your job and should not take the outcome personally.

X.   Advice on Testifying from a Seasoned, "Officer of the Year" Investigator

   A. Preparation
   B. Communication
   C. Credibility

XI.   Summary

Chapter Questions

1. The most important rule to eradicate fear of testifying in court is to
   a. always assist with the conviction of the suspect.
   b. always inform the prosecutor of your plans during testimony.
   c. always understand what the problems are with the case.
   d. always tell the truth.

2. The prosecutor is described by the text as
   a. the leader of the system.
   b. the gatekeeper of the court system.
   c. the final decision-maker in the case.
   d. the hatchet man of the court system.

3. Which of the following is *not* a valid reason for not prosecuting a case?
   a. The complaint is invalid.
   b. The defendant is in prison or out of the country and cannot be returned.
   c. The complainant refuses to assist with the prosecution.
   d. The offender dies.

4. At the pretrial conference with the prosecutor, an officer should do all but which one of the following?
   a. Review all the evidence.
   b. Discuss the strengths and weaknesses of the case.
   c. Discuss the probable line of questioning by the prosecutor and the defense.
   d. Ask for advice from the defense.

5. The adversary system establishes
   a. clearly defined roles for both the prosecution and the defense.
   b. the rules for the prosecutor.
   c. the rules for the defense.
   d. the activities that must occur in the trial.

6. Nonverbal factors include all but which one of the following?
   a. body language
   b. gestures
   c. demeanor
   d. sign language

7. In some instances, a judge may have issued a motion requesting the judge to issue a protective order against prejudicial questions or statements. This is referred to as a
   a. motion to suppress.
   b. motion to squash.
   c. motion in limine.
   d. ex post facto motion.

8. You should not discuss the case while waiting in the hallway to testify. If a juror or another witness hears your statements, you may have created grounds for a
   a. acquittal.
   b. mistrial.
   c. appeal.
   d. directed verdict.

9. In checking a final report, the officer should check for all but which one of the following?
   a. Does the report meet the criteria for an effective report?
   b. Is all relevant information included?
   c. Has the report been proofread?
   d. Has a copy been sent to the Public Information Officer?

10. In many states, officers must provide written responses to questions before trial as part of the discovery process. Testifying at which of the following types of hearing can be particularly stressful for the unprepared officer and, consequently, quite damaging to the prosecution?
    a. administrative hearings
    b. depositions
    c. sentencing hearings
    d. preliminary hearings

11. It is fine to discuss the case with other witnesses scheduled for the trial, unless the judge has ordered that this not occur.   True or False

12. It is fine for trained law enforcement officers to offer opinions and conclusions when testifying.   True or False

13. Nonverbal factors are important when a person testifies in court.   True or False

14. Making eye contact with the jury is unimportant when testifying, but it is critical that you look at the prosecutor whenever possible.   True or False

15. An expert witness is a person who has special training, education, or experience in an area.   True or False

16. While testifying, an investigator should always refer to his or her report as a script.   True or False

17. Do not discuss the case while waiting in the hallway to testify. If a juror or another witness hears your statements, you may have created grounds for a mistrial.   True or False

18. Credibility is the degree to which the jury believes a witness.   True or False

19. Investigators should include a summary of all negative or exculpatory evidence developed during the investigation in a report to the prosecuting attorney.　　　　True or False

20. Cross-examination is questioning by the opposing side to assess the validity of the testimony.　　　　True or False

21. According to Neubauer: "A key characteristic of the American prosecutor is broad _____."

22. Cases are _____ cleared when circumstances outside the investigation result in no charges being filed—for example, the suspect dies.

23. The court acknowledges that it is not possible to avoid all contact with jurors and that chance contacts—passing in the hall or crowded in an elevator—may not be avoidable. In such instances, conversations such as saying "Hello," are ok. These are referred to as _____ communications.

24. Evidence that can prove the innocence of a suspect is also known as negative or _____ evidence.

25. The pretrial _____ process requires the prosecution and defense to disclose to each other certain evidence they intend to use at trial, thus avoiding surprises.

26. There is no general _____ right to discovery in criminal trials (*Weatherford v. Bursey*, 1977).

27. The landmark Supreme Court case in the discovery process is _____ v. *Maryland* (1963).

28. Defense attorneys will try to _____ the testimony of prosecution witnesses; that is, they will try to discredit the testimony, to challenge the truth or accuracy of what a prosecution witness testified to under direct examination.

29. Witnesses usually are _____ from the courtroom during a trial to prevent one witness from hearing another witness's testimony. This is known as the rule on witnesses or witness _____ rule.

30. The prosecution can call _____ witnesses to contradict the testimony (or evidence) presented by the defense. The defense, in turn, can call _____ witnesses to contradict the testimony (or evidence) presented by the prosecution.

31. Why is the prosecutor the single most powerful official in the court system?

32. Give some examples of why complaints are not prosecuted.

33. How are cases "exceptionally cleared"?

34. Explain the landmark Supreme Court case of *Brady v. Maryland* (1963) and its relevance today to the police, now referred to as the Brady Rule.

35. Explain what "de minimus communications" are.

Case Study

36. You are the primary investigator for a burglary case. You learn, just two days before the trial, when you are reviewing the reports, that two important reports have not been completed by officers involved with the case. One report invalidates a suspect's alibi. You have checked with the officers and they simply failed to complete the reports because they were overwhelmed with other work. What action should you take? What do you tell the prosecutor?

_____

_____

_____

_____

_____

_____

_____

_____

_____

_____

Answer Key

1.	d	11.	False
2.	b	12.	False
3.	b	13.	True
4.	d	14.	False
5.	a	15.	True
6.	d	16.	False
7.	c	17.	True
8.	b	18.	True
9.	d	19.	True
10.	b	20.	True

21. discretion
22. exceptionally
23. de minimus
24. exculpatory
25. discovery
26. constitutional
27. Brady
28. impeach
29. excluded, sequestration
30. rebuttal, surrebuttal
31. They alone have the total discretionary power to decide whether or not to charge someone with a crime or not.
32. Cases are not prosecuted if
    - The complaint is invalid.
    - The prosecutor declines after reviewing the case.
    - The complainant refuses to prosecute.

- The offender dies.
- The offender is in prison or out of the country and cannot be returned.
- No evidence or leads exist.

33. When circumstances outside the investigation result in no charges being filed—for example, the suspect dies.

34. This case clarified the need to include exculpatory evidence during the discovery process by the police and prosecution. In *Brady v. Maryland* (1963), the Court held, "The suppression by the prosecution of evidence favorable to the accused upon request violates due process where the evidence is material either to guilt or to punishment, irrespective of the good faith or bad faith of the prosecution." As noted by Gardner and Anderson (2004, p.28), "Although an accused does not have a right to all information available to the prosecutor, he does have the right to information as provided by the statutes of the state and to information required under the Brady rule."

35. Do not discuss the case while waiting in the hallway to testify. If a juror or another witness hears your statements, you may have created grounds for a mistrial. According to Rutledge (2004, p.72), "Perhaps the thing that's most likely to torpedo your case in the middle of trial is unauthorized communication with members of the jury." He acknowledges that it is not possible to avoid all contact with jurors and that chance contacts—passing in the hall or crowded in an elevator—may not be avoidable. A simple hello, greetings, or giving of directions is allowable.

Case Study Answer

36. This error should and would have been discovered much earlier if your investigation had been appropriately thorough. As primary investigator, unfortunately, the responsibility to review all of the reports at the beginning of the case was yours, and the failure to produce finished reports to aid the prosecution reflects as much on you as on the two officers who did not complete them. There will be issues of disclosure, and the defense will likely attempt to have the information excluded. The best action is to contact the prosecuting attorney, to inform him or her of the problem, and to follow the prosecuting attorney's instructions. The issue of the alibi is paramount and may exclude the suspect altogether. What happens after the completion of the case is up to your supervisor. The issue here is that you need to stay on top of the case throughout the investigation and you need to stay in close contact with the prosecuting attorney.

Study Notes

Study Notes

Study Notes

Study Notes

Study Notes

Study Notes

Study Notes

Study Notes

Study Notes

Study Notes

Study Notes

Study Notes

Study Notes

Study Notes

Study Notes

Study Notes